*The Playground of
Psychoanalytic
Therapy*

The Playground of Psychoanalytic Therapy

Jean Sanville

THE ANALYTIC PRESS

1991   Hillsdale, NJ   London

Published by The Analytic Press, Inc.
365 Broadway, Hillsdale, NJ 07642

Set in Schneidler by Lind Graphics, Inc., Upper Saddle River, NJ

Library of Congress Cataloging-in-Publication Data

Sanville, Jean.
    The Playground of Psychoanalytic Therapy / Jean Sanville.
        p.   cm.
    Includes bibliographical references.
    ISBN 0-88163-091-8
    1. Psychotherapy. 2. Play–Psychological aspects.   I. Title.
    RC480.5.S255 1991
    616.89′14–dc20   91-13439
                                                                                        CIP

Printed in United States of America
10 9 8 7 6 5 4 3 2 1

To my father, Forest Bovard, a physician, from whom I learned of the dependence of the would-be healer on the inherent self-righting tendencies of the human being; and to my mother, Ruth Bovard, an educator, from whom I learned that, if one would teach, one must rely on and facilitate the student's innate wish to know.

Acknowledgments

I would first express gratitude to the many patients who, over the years, have been my best supervisors. They have shown me the mutative values of playing in psychotherapy and educated me in the prerequisites for liberating the play spirit, in the obstacles to that goal, and possible modes of surmounting the hindrances. Then I would thank those psychoanalysts of the British Independent Tradition who have particularly influenced my thinking about the realm of illusion, and the many researchers of infancy whose findings have let me imagine ways of implementing Winnicott's notion that psychotherapy ideally takes place in the area of play.

Students in my workshops and seminars and audiences for my lectures have responded with comments and questions that helped me to shape my concepts. And colleagues in the several institutes, universities, and colleges where I have taught have, through both appreciation and cogent criticism, enabled me to hone often tentative formulations further.

Joel Shor has been a constant source of inspiration and support. We have discussed, debated, argued, disputed, and yes, even contended at times. The result has been, to paraphrase a line from a book we did together, that we have reached for the love in work and in play, have enjoyed the work in love and in play, and most deeply have explored the play in working and loving.

I am grateful to many friends who encouraged my writing of this book. Rosalee Shaw, who died shortly after I had sent the first copy to the publisher, had read the entire manuscript and, although she was manifestly prejudiced to favor whatever I did, yet managed to offer some gentle suggestions. Ruth Optner read parts of it, and, as always, her comments were practical and useful. I would thank, too, the friends who could hang on to the knowledge that I loved them, even if, during much of the writing, I did not find the usual leisure to be with them.

Finally I want to thank the people at The Analytic Press: Paul Stepansky, without whose faith in me I might never have done this project; Lenni Kobrin, who wisely questioned some of my language at times but generally conceded when I could persuade her of my reasons; and Carol Lucas, whom I never came to know, but who copy edited the manuscript, curing me, I hope, of an unconscious resort to "which-craft."

Contents

Prelude   xi

1   Meaning Making and Playing in Infancy   1

2   A Child Who Cannot Play   23

3   A Child Who Can Play: A Contemporary Little Hans   47

4   The Scene: Space and Time
of the Therapeutic Playground   67

5   Playgrounds for Transference and Countertransference   83

6   The Work: Building a Playground
with an Unplayful Adult   101

7   Re-railing the Dialogue   125

8   Primary Trauma: Work, Love, and Play Toward Repair   149

9   Dreams as Private Playthings   167

10 The Psychomythology of Everyday Life   189

11 Playing and Interpretation   203

12 Endings and New Beginnings   221

13 The Play of Psychotherapy   243

    References   263

    Index   281

Prelude

When a friend of mine heard that I was writing a book on playing in psychotherapy, he reacted with surprise and shock. "What do you mean, playing?" he demanded. "In all my eight years of analysis, there was nothing that I experienced as playing. Within the first few interviews, I realized I was in for some hard and painful work!" He went on at length about the arduous and agonizing sessions. He reflected that maybe toward the end there may have been a few lighter moments, possibly even a bit of shared laughter, but he was quite skeptical about the playful elements in this process.

Even therapists themselves speak mainly of the work of therapy. I was once in a seminar with a famous analyst who reported that he often gave interpretations preceded by the words "as if," and I told him, "Oh, Dr. K, I like that; it has a playful note." He pulled himself up straight and sternly admonished me, "I'll have you know that psychoanalysis is a serious undertaking!" I replied, "I'll have you know – and all of those in this room who have treated children will have you know – that play is serious business."

Parents who bring their small children for treatment often worry about all the playing that they hear. When, they wonder, are we going to get down to work on the problems? Clearly, if the child and I are having such a good time, then nothing is being accomplished.

Perhaps surprisingly, even the many volumes of *The Psychoanalytic Study of the Child* contained relatively few articles specifically on play in its first 41 issues. It seemed to me highly significant that the 1987 volume at last carried a whole section entitled "Psychoanalytic Views of Play," with 13 articles. Appropriately for that publication, most of them dealt with childhood play. One article, "Play and Playfulness in Holocaust Survivors" (Auerhahn and Laub, 1987), highlighted the centrality of play if healing in these traumatized adults were to begin. Reading it, we reflect how much we take for granted in our ordinary lives that others will react to us with at least a modicum of empathy, and this confidence has much to do with establishing and maintaining a basic link between ourselves and the rest of the human world. The authors write that "when people prove unresponsive or actively malignant on a massive scale, the internal representation of the need-mediating context is destroyed and the individual loses the capacity for wish-organized symbolic functioning" (p. 46). Since play and symbolic functioning are closely related, the survivors of the death camps lost, to some extent, the capacity for play and playfulness. As Moran (1987), in the same issue, affirms, "The pleasure gain associated with playfulness is necessarily linked to the experience of mutuality, whether the interaction occurs with the external object or between internal representations of self and object" (p. 28). To construct the necessary safety of the outer playground or the "potential space" (Winnicott, 1971a) of the internal world requires a "facilitating environment" (Winnicott, 1965).

The patients treated by Auerhahn and Laub did not lose the desire for the sense of safety that could restore the ability to play. The search for lost maternal responsiveness and protection was evident in dreams and in the patients' determination that their children should play. They focused their wish for a benign other on the analyst but had to test her again and again to ascertain whether "the rules of the death camps or the rules of childhood play apply" (p. 57). Only when the latter rules could be experienced as the relevant ones could these patients allow the return of memory, imagination, and playing.

There is an evident and powerful self-righting tendency in the human psyche. Just as the body has a sense of its own wholeness and, when ill or injured, has a built-in inclination to restore that integrity, so the psyche must have a model of health or perfection that guides growth and repair. Shor and I (1978) have seen the origins of the reparative intent to reside in the newborn's experience of primary illusion. We liked the word "illusion," deriving as it does from Latin, *ludere,* to play. We liked too Freud's (1927) affirming, "Illusions need not necessarily be false – that is to say, unrealizable or in contradiction to reality" and his adding that "illusion itself sets no store by verification" (p. 31). We wanted to get away from the old notion of primary narcissism and not to swing to its opposite, primary love (Balint, 1953) but rather to designate the infant's experience of the coexistence of the two from the beginning. This experience, we hypothesized, would consist of an evanescent sense of self and an evanescent sense of other, these two senses gently oscillating, with no conflict between them. In observing infants or a film such as *The Amazing Newborn* (Hack, 1975), one is impressed with the infant's gazing into the eyes of the mother and her return of the raptured look and with the baby's alternating this gaze with averting the eyes and turning away briefly. We imagine that the newborn is beginning a process leading to forging the imago of mother and an image of connectedness and is simultaneously developing a sense of emergent self.

In the special state of "quiet alert" (Wolff, 1959) enjoyed by the neonate whose mother was not overly medicated during birthing and in the special context of a situation that renders boundaries unnecessary, the infant can enjoy both the illusion of fusion and the illusion of self-sufficiency. This "harmonious mix up," as Michael Balint (1953) has called it, is very different from the "seething chaos" that we analysts imagined when we had to infer from very troubled adults the primary state of the human being.

Of course, this blissful experience cannot last. There will be inevitable deprivations, suppressions, and frustrations, and the child will have to develop an array of defenses to deal with these. But the nonverbal memory of serene delight will lay down a model of psychic well-being toward which the person will ever afterward strive. Over the course of development each person etches and carves a unique pattern of spiraling unfolding while engaging in that ongoing dialectic between concern with self and concern with relationships. There do not seem to be two separate lines of development, as Kohut (1971, 1977) thought, but rather two intertwining ones. Some persons will manifest a predominance of the line of connectedness, or what Balint (1959) called "ocnophilia," a love of clinging. Others will mainly prefer autonomy, or what Balint playfully called "philobatism," a love of "doing one's own thing." The two lines alternate as to which is foreground and which is background. When one clings to people and ideas to which one has become attached, there are hovering fantasies of moving apart, exploring new relationships and new concepts. When one is "out there," boldly exploring the stretches of space, it is with a fantasy of a home base somewhere, a symbol of security. One seeks a context in which one can draw on the inherent ability to self-measure, to attend to one's inner promptings, but without sacrificing implicit connections to meaningful others. We all yearn for situations in which we can actualize our own best versions of ourselves, yet not be in conflict with the needs and wishes of those who are important to us.

We seek new versions of the primary illusion most poignantly when we feel the need for self-repair, when relationships seem to fail us, and when both situations occur. Since it is usually not realistic to expect to find someone like the good-enough mother with her "primary maternal preoccupation" (Winnicott, 1960b), manifesting no needs and wishes of her own and attending only to ours, we may seek professional help. If we are fortunate enough to find a therapist who comprehends the importance of play and illusion in human life, we may with that person create the necessary context and make a "new beginning" (M. Balint, 1953).

The purpose of this book is to explore the thesis put forth by Winnicott (1971a): "Psychotherapy takes place in the overlap of two areas of playing, that of the patient and that of the therapist. Psychotherapy has to do with two people playing together. The corollary of this is that where playing is not possible then the work done by the therapist is directed toward bringing the patient from a state of not being able to play into a state of being able to play" (p. 38). The idea is, I propose, also related to one put forth but not developed by Freud (1914a), that of the "transference as a playground."

Perhaps such notions have always been congenial to those of us who have done extensive play therapy with children; we know that play can be serious, and we have witnessed its reparative potential. Colleagues who have limited their practices to adults may be less convinced; neither their theories nor their techniques emphasize playfulness. Part of my thesis is that the current scene may be more open for such ideas, which Freud mentioned almost in passing and which Winnicott, who came to psychoanalysis from pediatrics, developed more fully. Even Winnicott, however, with all his years of work with children, as physician and as psychotherapist, did not yet have at hand the methods of infant observation that researchers of the last several decades have been able to use. Winnicott straddled the old and the new; he hung onto some traditional language, although he gave much of it new meanings. Recent research may let us be even more "philobatic," departing more radically from outworn concepts that no longer adequately serve us.

At meetings of psychoanalysts everywhere we hear these days of a veritable revolution in theories of human development and of the probable need to rethink the basic metapsychology of our field. The effects of that revolution on practice are not yet clear, but we can say there will be effects since our concepts about the persons who seek our help will, to some extent, shape our perceptions of them and of the roles we should take to be maximally useful. In this book, I am interested in the potential of current changes in theory to render more therapeutic the countertransferences we experience with patients.

Already there are shifts in how we view people, as the effects of the thinking of Kohut have infiltrated the theories and practice of psychodynamic therapists. Kohut, like Winnicott, however, was not equipped with new data about infants and the earliest stages of development. His successors will probably find of enormous benefit the information published by people such as Stern (1985), as it provides a much better foundation for their approach than did traditional developmental views.

What most interests me here is what the new research tells us about the role of play and playfulness in the earliest years of life, how it unfolds, what it takes of both participants to engage in the first social play, and what it gives to them. I am assuming that persons who enter psychotherapy are seeking new editions of the primary illusion and are aiming to find or to restore a sense of rich meaning to their lives and that the pleasurable affects connected to playfulness will foster the most benign imaginary regressions. In such a state, the person can best relinquish old fixities and begin to constitute new patterns.

Persons who seek psychotherapy do so with a seemingly contradictory motive: to remain securely themselves while also engaging in a process of wanted transformation. These two apparently opposite intentions, inclinations toward change and toward continuity, are found in all of us. Long ago Friedrich Schiller (1803), German poet, dramatist, and philosopher, pondering these two "impulsions," observed that there was a third in which the two act in concert–the "instinct of play," which "would suppress time in time, to conciliate the state of *transition* or becoming with the absolute being, change with identity" (italics added, p. 51). He believed that each of us carries within "a purely ideal man" (p. 11) and that we approximate this only when we play.

Between Schiller and Winnicott (1971a) there have been psychoanalysts who paid tribute to play and its role in human life. Often, as for Hartmann (1958), it was but instrumental to the "real" goal: "It is possible and even probable that the relationship to reality is learned by way of detours. There are reality adaptations which at first certainly lead away from the real situation. The function of play is an example" (p. 18). Waelder (1932) described children's play as the process of assimilation through repetition, and Róheim (1943) observed that many practical inventions developed from playful activities. Alexander (1958) came up with ideas in some ways closer to those of Winnicott when he observed that culture itself was due less to the sweat of men's brows than to the product of leisures. He even proposed that mutation itself was the playful experimentation of nature with new combinations, not necessarily adaptive but productive of individual variations, some of which would have survival value. Ontogenetically, the relationship between adaptive behavior and play was analogous to the relation between natural selection and mutation in biology. Erikson too had been impressed with the relationship between the ontogeny and the phylogeny of human playfulness, and he based his 1972 book on his Godkin lectures at Harvard on "Play, Vision, and Deception."

Winnicott (1971a) and others of the British Independent Tradition have most highly developed the ideas of psychotherapy and psychoanalysis as forms of playing and of play and illusion as essential to "creative apperception [which] more than anything else makes the individual feel that life is worth living" (p. 65). They have most emphasized the context, the environmental preconditions, that are necessary for the liberation of the spirit of playfulness.

We hope, by providing reliable space and time and by offering ourselves for a special kind of dialogic encounter, one that is analogous to the social play of infancy (Stern, 1985), to enable the patient to elude old fixities, to engage in a process that involves the constructing and reconstructing of ever new versions of the patient's life narrative.

Whatever stories the patient may make, they are not the stories I am interested in telling. Instead, the clinical tale is ideally one that lets the reader sense the process by which the past, present, and future are invented and the roles of the two persons: the patient as major author, the therapist as occasional coauthor.

I initially used the word "collaborator" here but wanted to connote not only working, but playing, together. Struggling to find another word, I thought of "collude," to play together, but realized to my dismay that somewhere along the line it had been contaminated with the notion of deceiving. Moreover, my dictionary (*American Heritage*) says that to collude is also to connive, "to feign ignorance of a wrong, thus implying tacit encouragement or consent," or "to cooperate secretly or conspire." "Connive" comes from Latin *conivere,* to close the eyes. Then I realized that "collaborate," too, had come to have pejorative meanings, such as to cooperate treasonably, as with the enemy occupying one's country. So I stayed with the idea of coauthoring, which at least retains the idea of cocreating, with the patient as the prime originator.

In any event, as all authors know, there will inevitably be both work and play in any creative project. When working is infused with playfulness, however, it may not be easy to distinguish working and playing as separate forms of action.

In this volume I begin with a review of some of the recent findings of psychoanalytically oriented infant observers and researchers, and I especially emphasize the role of playing and meaning making in the first years of life. Then, because it is so easy to take for granted a child's capacity for play and hence to miss its significance for development, I present in chapter 2 the case of an autistic child who, with her mother, was treated for some 10 years. One can see in such cases that the achievement of some playfulness is itself a major goal, after which other gains can take place. By contrast, the third chapter describes the very brief treatment of a playful child with a good-enough family.

Chapter 4 deals with the scene that is necessary for the act of playing, the space and time considerations that go into building a therapeutic playground for the two adults. Included will be my own experiences in a variety of literal settings and their emotional meanings both to patients and to me. Because patients tend to become attached to the place as well as to the person of the therapist, readers will find a description of the home-as-office in which the psychotherapy or psychoanalysis of the adults later to be described occurred.

Freud (1914b) wrote of the "transference as a playground," which I take to be the psychic space between the two participants in the dialogue of psychotherapy. In chapter 5 I will develop the idea he adumbrated long ago and look for the new conditions under which the person can permit former patterns to "expand in almost complete freedom," as Freud prescribed. Drawing some analogies between the therapeutic relationship and the original mother-child relationship, we have to find a playground also for countertransferences. Only then may the choreography that Stern (1977) described for playfulness be at its dialogic best.

Chapter 6 illustrates some of the preceding considerations by describing the work that is the prerequisite for playfulness in a patient as yet unable to avail herself of the potential freedoms of psychoanalytic psychotherapy. This woman manifested some of the obstacles I had encountered in treating autistic children, the main emotion being anger that was not felt as owned but as sweeping over her. One may see in the gradually developing therapeutic relationship the interplay of transferences and countertransferences as the patient struggles to balance her needs for autonomy and her needs for human connectedness in order to reach a new version of the primary illusion.

Chapter 7 plays with the dialogical principle, as articulated by Bakhtin, a literary philosopher, and by René Spitz (1963a,b, 1964), who declared that life begins with the dialogue and that all pathology may be understood as derailment of dialogue. Some vignettes from the analysis of a woman who came requesting analysis but declaring her disbelief in it allow some speculation both about the origins of her lack of trust and about the work necessary for some playfulness to permeate our dialogue. A complication was her recurrently assigning me to alterity, which for her meant the role of one who could not possibly understand, particularly in such crucial matters as sexual orientation.

By contrast, the course of therapy with the analysand described in chapter 8 moved along almost from the beginning, largely because this woman found it possible to "regress to dependence" in the playful way that both Winnicott and Balint thought so necessary for deep repair. Although I have posited a primary trauma, I have posited equally a powerful reparative intent. This, in combination with a fortuitous matching of analyst and analysand, permitted a re-creative experience for this person.

Chapter 9 plays with new data on the dreaming brain, data that suggest that dreams can no longer be seen primarily in the service of disguise and defense. Instead, the new findings promote our thinking of dreaming as a form of playing, potentially in the service not only of healing but of creativity and pleasure, and of dreams as private playthings.

The next chapter explores the relationship between personalized myth and depersonalized dream (Campbell, 1949), narrative fiction as the "veiled autobiography of man" (Fischer, 1987), and the development of tales through dream narrative, fairy tales, legends, and myth (Langer, 1942). As readers will have come to expect by now, the wish that propels this development is seen as originating in occasions of relatively nonconflictual relationship between infant and mother in earlier life, the model for later strivings toward intrapsychic and interpersonal harmony.

Continuing to consider the play ingredient in the therapeutic relationship, chapter 11 offers a philosophical look at the interpretive mode that might best actualize the creativity of the patient. Attending to Freud's idea that every symptom is already an attempt at self-cure, we are led to value comments on the patient's reparative wishes and intents as an aspect of each interpretation. Taking a meaning reorganization view rather than one emphasizing the revelation of "hidden reality," we aim to strengthen patients' sense of emergent self and of core self (Stern, 1985) by drawing on their own interpretive and reinterpretive capacities. To be able to discern meanings and offer explanations may afford therapists a narcissistic high, but patients' self-esteem will be more effectively enhanced when those pleasures are shared with them.

Chapter 12 looks at what have been called terminations and calls attention to reactions beyond those of grief and mourning, which have been traditionally emphasized. Particularly when the analysis or psychoanalytic psychotherapy has been infused with a certain playfulness, the ending phase is likely to manifest this mode as well. Some short vignettes and a longer one are offered to illustrate these possibilities.

The final chapter summarizes the resemblances between psychotherapy of the sort I have been describing and the characteristics of play (Huizinga, 1944). It draws upon Burke's (1945) pentad of terms, *act, scene, agent, agency,* and *purpose,* to generate an abstraction about the type of psychotherapy that might best maximize the play element.

The course of treatment could then be seen as a drama, with the patient as the main character, now reaching for connection and now attempting autonomy, always with the intent to enhance senses of self and capacities for meaningful connectedness, the therapist content with an auxiliary role. When there have been rich experiences with playing in this context, the person goes forth better equipped to live life as play, as both Plato and Winnicott advocated.

The Playground of
Psychoanalytic
Therapy

CHAPTER 1

Meaning Making and Playing in Infancy

The principle of psychic determinism, often associated with psychoanalysis, has been disturbing to some of us because of its being in drastic contrast to the high value we place on psychic freedom. Readers of Freud often comment on the differences between his theoretical metapsychology and his clinical approach. Freud himself seems to have suffered recurrent indecision about whether to conceive of his ideas as natural science, objective, detached, and intellectual or as "an intuitive, receptive mode of relating to others" (Rycroft, 1985, p. 87). Rycroft observed the paradox in traditional thinking. Freud saw the unconscious as "a chaos, a cauldron of seething excitement . . . which was a slave to the pleasure principle and neglected the reality of the external world," and yet the effect of analysis was to create personalities that "embrace just those emotional, imaginative elements that its theoretical conception of a rational ego excludes" (p. 122).

It is central to the thesis of this book that not only psychoanalysis but all of the psychodynamically oriented therapies aim at facilitating the unfolding and integration of the imaginative and creative capacities that are potential in every human being. These therapies concern themselves not so much with causes of psychosocial pathology, with unearthing the repressed and hence hidden events, but rather with discovering with patients how they constructed the particular meaning

1

schemes that they did and how they may reorganize these schemes to comprehend more fully both past events and new phenomena. The method of achieving insight is as significant as the outcome; the means are as important as the ends. The approach eschews imposing the therapist's own meaning schemes but fosters the person's ability to generate his own scheme.

There seems to be a drive toward meaning in human life, a drive originating in biology and brought to fruition in language and syntax. Human beings are innately symbolizing animals, and psychoanalytic therapies are concerned with the semantic (Fuller, 1985). Such therapies involve narrative process, with the therapist an "assistant autobiographer," constructing with patients meaningful biopsychosocial stories. Therapist and patient weave the most satisfying tales when together they can establish an atmosphere in which playfulness can occur.

For many years that group of British psychoanalysts known as the Independent group, such as Balint, Milner, and Winnicott, have been awarding an important place to play and illusion in human life, and they have been joined more recently by others, such as Bollas and Casement. It is not coincidental that these professionals have been deeply interested also in literature, music, and the arts and have linked play and creativity. Winnicott, a pediatrician, grounded his theories in his observations of innumerable infants and children and their mothers. Winnicott (1971a) defined psychoanalysis as a subspecies of play, "a highly specialized form of playing in the service of communication with oneself and others" (p. 41). Its aim was to restore a "creative relation to the world" (p. 38), as Milner (1952) had declared.

Much of the work consists of building the playground in which playfulness can occur. In this regard, we therapists have much to learn from infants and their parents, but since most of us cannot combine pediatrics with our main professions, we turn, instead, to the observers and researchers of the earliest periods of life. Steeping ourselves in their writings, we find ourselves provoked to revise some former notions about human nature, about how persons develop over time, and perhaps about our approach to psychotherapy. We seem to be on the threshold of what many analytically oriented clinicians regard as a veritable revolution.

There is, for example, more evidence for ego instincts at the beginning rather than for id instincts, and, rather than dominating at the start, the pleasure principle appears to function dialectically with the reality principle (Stern, 1985, pp. 238–39.) So we cannot think of psychic reality and external reality as opposed; each is to some extent constitutive of the other. This interrelationship is best exemplified in play. When the dialectic breaks down, there is pathology – at one extreme, psychosis, in which there is both great rigidity and excessive fluidity, and at the other, what Bollas (1987) calls "normotic" illness and what McDougall (1980) calls the "normopath," persons "out of touch with the subjective world and with the creative approach to fact" (Winnicott, 1971a, p. 78).

At this time in history there seems a convergence between the leanings of the British Independent Tradition (Kohon, 1986) and the ever fresh and surprising discoveries of the developmentalists. There is new respect for playing in human life, as it can lead to creativity in constructing the self (Sanville, 1987a), interpersonal relationships, and even our own facilitating environments. This book will explore some of this convergence and its possible implications for a psychodynamic therapeutic approach.

Not so long ago it was rather glibly assumed that a main goal of psychotherapy was to render the patient reality-oriented, and it was, of course, the analyst or therapist who would be the judge of that. Now we are beginning to credit that which lies beyond the reality principle, to allow for an "intermediate area of experience" (Winnicott, 1971a) in which we do not constantly feel under constraint to determine what is objective or outside reality but in which we can enjoy the inevitable ambiguities involved in a philosophy that acknowledges that what we deem to be reality will always be determined in some measure by the theories we hold as we contemplate the world (Sanville, 1976). So therapists try to respect the subjective factors that lead their patients to construct reality in ways different from their own, and hence therapists become increasingly aware of the subjective factors that have entered into their own judgments and of the effects on the therapeutic dialogue of these differences.

The realm of play allows negotiation of those differences with a degree of pleasure because the meanings of phenomena will include generous portions of the subjective. As Piaget (1951) would put it, play is close to pure assimilation, which "makes for satisfaction of the ego rather than its subordination to reality" (p. 167), in contrast to accommodation, in which one molds oneself to reality. If we assume a continuum between the two, then we note that people whom we see as creative tend to veer closer to the pole of assimilation; they are not primarily conformists to the consensually "real." In them, imagination is granted considerable free play.

Freud (1908) was most interested in the origins of imagination, and he proposed that the child at play behaves like the creative writer, rearranging the things of his world in a new way and investing his activity with a high degree of emotion. The child takes playing very seriously but also distinguishes it very well from reality. Both the creative writer and the child reap "important consequences" out of this very unreality since "many things which, if they were real, could give no enjoyment, can do so in the play of fantasy, and many excitements which, in themselves, are actually distressing can become a source of pleasure" (p. 144). Although Freud thought that when we grow up we cast aside play, he noted that we may one day find ourselves "in a mental situation which once more undoes the contrast between play and reality"—as when we throw off our sense of heavy burden by humor (pp. 144–145). Moreover, he recognized that we never fully give up pleasures once experienced but form a "substitute or surrogate" (p. 145). Our propensity for constructing fantasies is one of the adult versions. Unlike the play of the child, these, he found, were not easy to observe, especially because adults tend to be ashamed of their day-dreams and hide them from others. The only way we know that people fantasy is that "the victims of nervous illness" tell us about them in order to be cured.

Thus, Freud's speculations about fantasy were gleaned from trou-bled adults. He even wrote that "a happy person never fantasies, only an unsatisfied one" (p. 146). The motive forces of fantasies were wishes, either ambitious or erotic, often a combination of the two. Fantasies "change with every change in [the daydreamer's] situation" (p. 146). They reflect an earlier, usually infantile, experience, and current impressions, and they also create a situation relating to the future. So, although Freud attributed fantasy to the "sick" ones, he nevertheless envisioned its having far-reaching and even constructive possibilities.

Perhaps fortunately, none of us is ever completely happy, and so fantasy flourishes, both consciously and unconsciously. Over time, we have redefined the wishes that motivate fantasy. What Freud called ambitious we would say has to do with wanting to develop the potentials of self, and what he called erotic we would say has to do with wanting to connect meaningfully with others in such a way that we minimally sacrifice aspects of our being that we feel to be authentic. From his vantage point, Freud called some behaviors infantile, often with a pejorative note. Today we hear that word as anything but depreciatory. We even find in studying the first years of life why Winnicott (1959–1964) saw the patient's capacity to regress as an attempt to bring about self-cure (p. 128).

Data from current infant observation and research let us imagine the meaning making that goes on in the so-called preoedipal period of life, with an especial focus on the qualities of those meanings that are generated in play and playfulness. Some of those imaginings seem most relevant to changing ideas about the psychoanalytic enterprise and about those psychotherapies that are based on psychodynamic principles.

MEANING MAKING AND PLAYING AT THE
START OF LIFE

During the many decades in which we contented ourselves with hypotheses about growth and development that were constructed – we sometimes said "reconstructed" – from the treatment of adult patients, we affirmed a number of things that have subsequently proven questionable or even false. The infant, far from being buffeted by drives so powerful that they make for violent internal excitement, appears instead to arrive equipped with budding ego capacities. The main characteristic of the human mind, we are told, is its tendency to create order (Bruner, 1977), to categorize experiences into conforming and contrasting patterns, to generate "theories." The infant immediately becomes a researcher, avidly reaching out for stimulation with all the peremptoriness once attributed to the drives (Stern, 1985, p. 41). Taking an ecological approach (Gibson, 1979), the newborn begins at once an active evaluation of his perceptions and asks, "Is this the same as that? If it's not, how discrepant is it from what I previously encountered?" (Kegan, Kearsley, and Zelazo, 1978). We observe, in passing, that in later life these questions are crucial for any reparative emotional experience.

Once upon a time we were taught that the infant arrived in a state of "primary narcissism" or "autism," unconnected with the rest of the human world. The baby was assumed to possess a "stimulus barrier" so strong that whatever was outside self was virtually nonexistent (Spitz, 1965b). Of course, when one thinks about it, that kind of narcissism was odd, a narcissism without a self, for the psychological self was not thought to be born with the biological self (Mahler and Furer, 1968) but had to develop later. Now we are accepting the evidence that at birth there are already a sense of self and a sense of the other. Different authors have used different terms to designate this earliest self. Shor and I (1978) wrote of a nascent or evanescent sense of self; Lewis and Brooks-Gunn (1979), of an existential self; Pine (1982), of an experiential self; Emde (1982), of a prerepresentational (affective) self; and Stern (1985), of a sense of emergent self.

There seems consensus that during the first two months of life the infant is actively generating meanings that constitute a "sense of organization in the process of formation," a sense that will remain active for the rest of life (Stern, 1985, p. 38). Stern conceives of infant experience as global, "sensations, perceptions, actions, cognitions, internal states of motivation and states of consciousness" experienced "directly in terms of intensities, shapes, temporal patterns, vitality affects, categorical affects, and hedonic tones" (p. 67). This "fundamental domain of human subjectivity," operating for the most part out of awareness, is the domain "concerned with the coming-into-being of organization that is at the heart of creating and learning" (p. 67). Stern's calling this process of forming perspectives about self and others a "creative act" is in keeping with Winnicott's (1971a) notion of "primary creativity." The infant and the person-to-be are equipped to experience as meaningful the process of organization as well as the result, which we could think of as "product," but a product that is forever unfinished.

Clinical interests propel us toward a very special attention to this sense of emergent self and to the domain of relatedness in which it can occur, for it is the sense that will be evoked whenever the person is in the process of organizing later senses of self, of assimilating what is felt to be meaningful, and of generating new meanings along the way. The richest meaning making, together with the most satisfactory unfolding senses of self and of others, tends to occur out of a paradox: the illusion that one has created this thing, person, or relationship, which had to have been there in the first place, waiting to be found (Winnicott,

1971a). So, like Winnicott, we set forth to find a place for illusion in human life.

No doubt there are meanings that arise out of the constraints of accommodating, in which there is little room for the "me." We might guess that the patients from whom our previous notions about life's beginnings were constructed may have had too early and too frequent impingements on their senses of being. The meanings that they organized led them later to seek in analysis or in therapy to emend and update the schemas that they used to evaluate themselves and their social world. Out of the data of their experiences we nearly came to think of infancy itself as pathological, the baby feeling beset from within her own self by drives that threatened to become unmanageable and unable as yet to perceive whatever might be outside.

In the days when drive theory reigned, we termed the first period of life the oral stage and thought that the infant was aroused mainly to satisfy appetites and then became somnolent when gratified. In a wonderful little film, *The Amazing Newborn* (Hack, 1975), we observe something very different. Providing that the mother has not been drugged to quell her labor pains, the infant will enjoy a rather pro-longed state of what is called the "quiet alert" (Wolff, 1959). The infant is less interested in eating than in gazing into the eyes of the mother, who, of course, gazes back lovingly. From time to time the infant averts gaze, looks away – we might guess to process the experience – and then once more joins mother in this visual exchange. This would seem to be evidence of beginning bonding, of building the "domain of emergent relatedness" (Stern, 1985), but also of claiming a private and ever forming self by "digesting," assimilating to self the experiences with another (Shor and Sanville, 1978).

In the film, we see that when the baby cries, she can be comforted by being picked up and held to the shoulder, from which position daddy is in view. There can be no doubt that this newborn finds meaning and significance in the human face. The film depicts babies being tested as to visual preferences by being put into a contraption in which they are shown patterns of various sorts; they manifest a marked preference for those that resemble the human face. Hearing, as we now know, is well established in the late months in utero, and the newborn can be seen moving in rhythm to the adult voice, arms and legs stretching and contracting with the cadences of the sound. One can see the roots of attunement and empathy in those movements. Although they seem to have no immediate purpose, they reveal the infant's nascent capacity to resonate with the feelings of other persons.

No wonder, then, that Spitz (1963a), in his later years, came to declare that life begins with dialogue and that "man, when he is deprived of the dialogue from infancy, turns into an empty asocial husk, spiritually dead, a candidate for custodial care" (p. 159).

Realists often inquire how we know what the infant is feeling and thinking. The newborn does arrive already equipped with all the facial expressiveness that we have come to associate with the different affects, and so we may be warranted in assuming the emotions behind the expressiveness. Perhaps, however, reality is not the whole issue. We could posit that the self is born of illusion, that because the mother and father believe that a self is there, they call it into being by their own responsiveness. The parents in the film *The Amazing Newborn* are clearly of the good-enough kind, which I define as possessing a capacity to assume beyond any real evidence that there is a little person in their new baby. Such parents attribute meanings to the baby's behavior and bring the baby into the framework of their own meaning systems. As we know, they entertain fantasies as to who this infant is and will become – fantasies that gradually exert their influences on the growing child. These "ghosts in the nursery" may lead to impaired mother-child relationships (Fraiberg, Adelson, and Shapiro, 1975) or perhaps to great things if those fantasies are congruent with the aptitudes and talents in the infant. In any event, we who watch the film or, better still, have an opportunity to be around a wee one, will find ourselves imagining the sense of emergent self evolving out of each encounter of this infant with the social world.

It is worth reflecting on the qualities in a parent that might best foster this sense of emerging in the offspring. Stern (1985) preoccupies himself with the qualities inherent in the infant in the first two months of life and does not elaborate on those in the mother that promote their unfolding. But Winnicott (1963b) wrote of the importance of primary maternal preoccupation. Loving paradox, which is in many ways at the heart of play, he declared this engrossment to be a sort of "normal illness," which one must be healthy to develop and which one will outgrow in due time.

This primary maternal preoccupation is close to what Michael Balint (1932) calls primary love, in which the mother during this beginning period has, according to the baby's illusion, no needs or wishes of her own but is simply there for her infant so that the latter may enjoy a state of tranquil well-being. In the stage when the baby is absolutely dependent, the mother can identify, make use of "projective identification" to positive ends, and surmise what the baby is feeling and needing and wanting. She meets the baby's "ego needs."

Winnicott, like the current researchers, affirms that the infant's needs are not confined to instinctual tensions. The mother who can thus lend herself to a high degree of adaptation to her baby's needs, who can refrain from impingements stemming from her own, thus protects her infant's "going-on-being" and enables him to act and not just to react. The infant, at first unaware of this maternal provision, can take for granted the "holding environment." Something analogous to this is what many, perhaps most, patients require in the beginning phases of treatment.

As the mother identifies with her infant, so the infant may accomplish feelings of at-one-ness with her. Greenacre (1969) writes that the prolonged postnatal body relationship between infant and mother involves a complexity of communication in which the mother puts her abilities at the infant's disposal and he gradually "absorbs them into his own maturational patterns" (p. 358). Though gross or sudden changes in maternal gestalt may be reacted to by the infant with the stress of withdrawal, lesser changes may "furnish accessory stimulation for responses over and above what is necessary for the maturational stage" (p. 358). Although the "liberating stimuli" come from outside, the operating introjective-projective mechanisms let the baby experience them as his own, so these "mirroring reactions" are not yet imitation. Rather, when the mother holds and cuddles her baby, what goes on in her resonates in him. This includes not only the "impact of her body tensions and visible tensions in her appearance, but some reactions to the rhythms of her respiration and possibly even of her heartbeat, as well as to the larger rhythms of her walkings, speech, singing, etc." (p. 359).

Greenacre deems such responses to be the earliest forerunners of play, in that they are not immediately useful but afford opportunity for variations in activity not necessary for survival. Later these behaviors will no longer be dependent on the presence of the mother but will be elicited by similar stimuli and will gain in uniqueness and spontaneity.

Kestenberg (1978), too, is interested in the psychosomatic interactions between infant and caretaker and sees in the nonnutritive aspects of the nursing situation the psychophysiological base of the body image and the psychosocial base for later play with transitional objects (p. 64). Movements that are stretching rather than flexing are responsible for changes in position, and stretching enhances breathing and circulation. The stretched-out body area "becomes imbued with a feeling of vitality, as if life were flowing through it" (p. 65). As movement becomes smoother and respiration regular, the baby lies happily and cozily, and the hand of the adult can rest on a "trusting" baby belly. Kestenberg uses the term "transsensus" for the experience of "going out of one's boundaries and incorporating others" (p. 66). The trusting stretching-toward is a manifestation of an alert state of being; it need not be visible movement but can be an inner experience of expanding boundaries and seeking out or melting into an object. Something of this illusory fusion probably accounts for those moments of felt merger that Greenacre describes and that Stern (1985), too, thinks of as achievements. For all of these observers, symbiosis thus does not represent an inability to distinguish self from nonself but is a positive accomplishment, attained when a sufficient sense of safety prevails.

Kestenberg (1978) tells us:

> Play on the mother's body releases the grasp reflex, opens the fist and makes out of the active hand the principal tool of doing (being mobile) while the arms are holding (being stable). . . . The doing, playing hand becomes the foremost proponent of creativity: a bearer of communication and a transmitter of culture (p. 70).

PLAYING AND THE ESTABLISHMENT
OF THE CORE SELF

According to Stern (1985), around two or three months of age infants arrive at a new organizing perspective, with a well-integrated sense of self and a sense of others as distinct and separate. The sense of core self results from the experiential integration of four ingredients: the sense of *self agency*, that is, of "authorship of one's own actions," and expecting consequences of those actions; the sense of *self coherence*, of being a nonfragmented whole, a locus of action; the sense of *self affectivity*, experiencing patterned qualities of inner feelings that belong with other experiences of the self; and the sense of *self history,* a continuity with one's own past (p. 71).

The playful contributions of the caregiver during this time are well known to all who have been around babies who are in this very social period of life. Adults tend to talk baby talk to the infant, using raised pitch, simplified syntax, reduced rate, and exaggerated pitch contours (Stern, 1977). To attract the baby's attention, they move in closer and make strangely exaggerated faces as well as sounds.

As Winnicott (1971a) asserts, the potential space available for playing is best established by a mother who, in the beginning, allows her baby some experience of magical control, an illusion of omnipotence. Confidence in the mother creates the intermediate playground in which the baby can experience playing as enormously exciting. The animation and high energy level emerge not because instincts are aroused, but because playing entails recurrent testing of the limits of the illusion of being all-powerful and of the safety of behaving spontaneously. Although at one moment the baby may feel, "Whoever I am and whatever I do is perfectly all right with mother," he senses also that, in the next moment, she may not be so finely attuned and then he will have to curb his exuberant expressiveness to accommodate to her. Winnicott hints at a dialectic here: when mother has provided the baby opportunities to play in her nonintervening presence, he develops the capacity to be alone; internalizing her silent presence, he develops a self-assurance that he can be by himself, so it becomes safer psychologically to reach for connection with her or ask for help when he needs it. The mother who can initially fit in with the baby's predilections will gradually be permitted by him to introduce her own playing. They can play together.

In an earlier work, Stern (1977) describes the earliest play as "moments that are almost purely social in nature" (p. 2), occurring at unlikely times, as in the space between other activities. As an example, he pictures for us a nursing baby of three and a half months. During the first half of the feeding the baby is sucking away, working seriously. From time to time he looks at his mother, but she does not talk or change expression until he lets go of the nipple and smiles faintly at her. She responds by opening her eyes wider and raising her eyebrows a bit. When he does not return to sucking, she says, "Well, hello [pitch rising]. . . . Oooh, ya wanta play, do ya?!" Mother moves closer, frowning, but with a twinkle in her eye, exclaims, "I'm gonna get ya!"

and poses her hand "to begin a finger-tickle march up the baby's belly into the hilarious recesses of his neck and armpits." He smiles and squirms but does not break eye contact. She moves her head back and away, and her eyes wander off as if she were thinking of a new plan; he watches, fascinated. She rushes forward again, and he is momentarily caught off-guard, showing more surprise than pleasure. Noting that she has misgauged the limits of his tolerance for this game, she sits back, talking to herself. When she resumes, she leaves out the tickle march and establishes a more regular and marked cadence. This time he smiles an easy smile, face tilted up. The cycle is repeated several times, and the mounting excitement of both participants contains elements of glee and danger. There is the risk element in all play. The baby finally breaks gaze, and seems to compose himself. He grins, and mother responds with her most suspenseful cycle. It turns out to be too much for him, and he averts his face and frowns. She picks up his cue immediately, stops the game, and says softly, "Oh honey, maybe you're still hungry," and the moment of social interaction is over.

These moments of free play between mother and infant, Stern declares, are the most crucial experiences in the infant's first phase of learning. The infant has, by the end of the first six months,

> developed schemas of the human face, voice, and touch, and within those categories he knows the specific face, voice, and touch and movements of his primary caregiver. He has acquired schemas of the various changes they undergo to form different human emotional expressions and signals. He has "got" the temporal patterning of human behavior and the *meaning* of different changes and variations in tempo and rhythm. He has learned the social cues and conventions that are mutually effective in initiating, maintaining, terminating, and avoiding interactions with his mother. He has learned different discursive or dialogic modes, such as turn-taking. And he now has the foundation of some internal composite picture of his mother so that, a few months after this phase is over, we can speak of his having established object permanence—or an enduring representation of mother that he carries around with him with or without her presence (italics added, pp. 5,6).

He is on the way from interaction to relationship (p. 95).

It must have been his abundant observations of such interchanges between mother and infant that led Winnicott (1971a) to declare "that psychotherapy of a deep-going kind may be done without interpretive work" (p. 50). Of course, we could note that in this playing episode, each of the participants is interpreting the behaviors of the other, and mother is even voicing her inferences about what the baby wants. But the dialogue, although in an affective and bodily mode, flows as long as each accurately reads the other's signals and responds accordingly. Winnicott's principle of not interpreting outside the ripeness of the material holds.

There are clear analogies to the therapeutic situation, which usually also begins with work, when there are urgencies felt by the patient, needs for basic supplies. Both members focus attention on the behaviors of the other and react or respond with behaviors of their own. Stern calls our attention to the two aspects of the scenario: a period of engagement, in which the infant forms and tests hypotheses and shows a major intention, and time-out episodes, "returning units" to reassess, to evaluate affect, to formulate goal-correcting strategies, and maybe to reset a different course and implement a new intention. Clinicians may learn much from mothers about the equal importance of both the periods of connection and the intermissions.

Appropriate timing, as well as safe space, is also a consideration. The described play occurs when the infant is in a most attentive state and is actively conveying to mother a receptivity to outside stimulation. Babies know when they are in a state in which they can control their attention and can build up to excitation but reduce it at will – the latter requiring confidence that one's self-measure will be respected. They know their own levels of tolerance and rapidly turn off when they experience too much stimulation. Mothers who show deference to the measure of the infant and therapists who show deference to the measure of the patient will best nourish the other's capacity for self-determination.

Under the rubric of "proxemics," Stern (1977) posits an entity called interpersonal space (pp. 20–21). Metaphorically, each of us goes around in a psychological "bubble" and defines an optimal distance for others to keep from its perimeter. He proposes that the mother's space-violating behavior serves to prepare the infant later to tolerate greater intimacy; kissing and snuggling may partly depend on the baby's experiences of these early playful encounters. It can matter a great deal whether one's boundaries are bubblelike, with flexible expansion and contraction, or rigid and impenetrable. We might guess that when the mother is unable to read and respond to the baby's cues, the infant would likely have to reinforce his barriers to protect from being overwhelmed.

Not all mothers manage to avoid intrusiveness; some make too many "missteps in the dance." One of the mothers in Stern's (1977) study was so unrelenting in her chase, so ignoring of the infant's dodge that autistic development seemed a likelihood. Such behaviors on the mother's part do interfere with self-regulating capacities, and the child must learn more drastic ways to terminate the interaction. The baby then loses the opportunity to learn that he can successfully regulate the external world as a by-product of his affective state, that is, as a result of true emotional communication.

Like Stern, Winnicott (1960a) views impingements as pathogenic. They endanger the true self. The child may conform but will lose touch with the "spontaneous gesture," which is the route to playing and to creativity. For Winnicott, the diagnosis of false self is more important than any of the psychiatric classifications, for it is associated with the most rigid defenses. He would have therapists stay alert to the possibility that the patient may seemingly conform but that such acquiescing may be the most powerful resistance.

Of course, there can be an opposite error on the part of caretakers – understimulation. There are mothers who themselves cannot play, perhaps because no one played with them when they were children or because they are depressed or obsessed with survival worries. They are not optimally available emotionally, not sending forth signals that the baby can comprehend, and not receiving the latter's signals reliably. Sustained distress, rather than interest and pleasure, then characterizes the relationship, and the child later may tend to turn off affective reactions or become depressed and sad.

The best of mothers, like the best of therapists, will unavoidably make "missteps in the dance" by overshooting or undershooting the person's tolerance limit. The infant can learn to deal with that occurrence when the mother can facilitate some repair of the rift between them. What matters is how she is able to respond the great proportion of the time and how well she can promote remedy when she has failed her baby. The infant is not usually traumatized by occasional moments when the mother misses a beat, provided the infant can generally rely on her as a "self-regulating" other during the period of development of the core self and provided the two of them can discover ways to "re-rail the dialogue" (Spitz, 1964).

An abundance of experiences with a mother associated with pleasure and fun lets the infant include in the mother imago that he is building that of the playing one, in which case the work that they must sometimes do together will be infused with playing. Moreover, in separate experiences the baby will carry over that spirit, distilled from play episodes.

The baby is always generalizing from experiences, making representations out of memories of episodes of interactions with others. Stern (1985) calls these "representations of interactions generalized" or RIGs. They create "expectations of actions, of feelings, of sensations, and so on that can either be met or be violated" (p. 97). RIGs are the basic units for representing the core self, for in them are integrated the senses of agency, coherence, affectivity, and continuity.

When the RIG of being with another is activated, there is a sense of evoked companion, the memory, conscious or unconscious, of the person with whom one had some similar experience. This association permits the comparing of new experiences with former ones and the consequent constant updating of the representations. "They are a record of the past informing the present" (Stern, 1985, p. 116). In a sense one is never alone; the self-regulating other is always present in memory. But the quality of that other clearly will differ depending on what the lived experiences of "being-with" have been. It is the thesis here that when a certain playfulness has infused original relationships, the dialogue between past and present will flow most freely. When playing was impeded, it will take some freeing of the play spirit to rerail that dialogue. Then the delight and exuberance felt in new playful situations will be the result not only of successful mastery but of evoking the presence of the "transformational object" (Bollas, 1987) with whom one enjoyed such feelings. No longer dependent on the original liberating stimuli, the person may set about making the "quasi-borrowed activity patterns" (Greenacre, 1969, p. 359) his own – unique, spontaneous, and individual.

PLAY AND MEANINGS IN THE DOMAIN OF THE INTERSUBJECTIVE

By approximately the seventh to the ninth month of life, the infant discovers that she has a mind and that others do as well. The new organizing perspective brings a sense of subjective self and the momentous realization that inner experiences are potentially shareable. What now acquires meaning is to know and be known, to discover what part of experience is shareable and what is not. The infant seeks to share attention, intention, and affective states (Stern, 1985), all without language being yet available. Call (1980) wrote that language begins from the end of the index finger. Infants of nine months not only follow visually the direction of the mother's pointing but also begin to point themselves, gazing alternately at the target and at mother's face to ascertain if she is attending to their focus. There is now not simply the wish to influence the other; there are also an intention to communicate and an assumption that the other will comprehend–say, that she wants a cookie–and will comply.

From the earliest life, affects are both the primary medium and the primary subject of communication (Tronick, Als, and Adamson, 1979). Even when protolinguistic exchanges involving attention and intention come into being, these are simultaneously affective communications. Whereas the younger infant expresses motivational states through emotion, at the age that we now consider the latter half of the first year, that emotional expression is used in the process of negotiation with the other, providing, of course, that there were plenty of play episodes that built the infant's confidence that such affective communication would be effective.

Emotion sharing begins with sharing of positive emotions, shown by smiling or by interest (Emde, 1988). Negative emotion sharing seems more frequent in populations under stress or at risk. Emde's studies of "social referencing" are by now fairly familiar, and he sees this as behavior that develops the executive sense of "we," of the significant other being present, and hence imparts a sense of increased power and control. There are three interacting pathways of self and shared meaning: the sense of "I," the sense of "other," and the sense of "we." The basic motives of activity, self-regulation, social fittedness, and affective monitoring underlie the formation of "we" discourse. Klein's (1976) idea that psychoanalysis needed a theory of "we-go" to complement its ego is currently receiving new appreciation.

How are affects shared? Strict imitation, Stern (1985) tells us, will not do, although this was a big part of the mother's repertoire in the first six months or so of the infant's life. Mother now engages in a kind of cross-modal matching, using a channel not the same as that of the infant to express the quality of feeling she senses in the infant. Her responses represent the emotional state, not its behavioral manifestations.

Stern differentiates affect attunement from mirroring, which implies temporal synchrony and also that "the mother is helping to create something within the infant that was only dimly or partially there until her reflection acted somehow to solidify its existence" (p. 144). He differentiates it, too, from empathy, which is more conscious and more cognitive. Attunement, also based on emotional resonance (Hoffman, 1978), occurs mainly out of awareness, almost automatically. It must be that the capacity for affect attunement is innate in the human species, a biological given. The newborn manifests it when moving arms and legs in rhythm with the parent's voice and using a motoric channel rather than an auditory one.

One of the criteria for whether the baby senses that mother is correctly attuned is that the baby "simply continues to play without missing a beat" (Stern, 1985, p. 150), while if mother is misattuned, the baby quickly stops playing and looks to her to see what is going on. We could say that her attunement is part of the experience of safe space, or of Winnicott's (1971a) "potential space."

Winnicott (1971a) writes that in the experience of the fortunate baby (and we translate that here as one having a well-attuned mother)

> the question of separation in separating does not arrive, because in the potential space between the baby and the mother there appears the creative playing that arises naturally out of the relaxed state; it is here that there develops a use of symbols that stand at one and the same time for the external world phenomena and for phenomena of the individual person (p. 109).

All this, he says, "eventually adds up to a cultural life," particularly if the parents are "ready to put each child in touch with appropriate elements of the cultural heritage" (p. 110).

Shape, intensity, and time can all be perceived amodally; were this not so, metaphors could not work. Poets, creative writers, and artists assume this underlying capacity for transposition of amodal information and rely on the colors and shapes of hearing and on the sounds and tempo of colors and patterns. The Los Angeles County Museum of Art opened its new wing for modern art with a show called "Synethesia," featuring the match between the visual and the auditory. The works of art seemed to present aspects of felt life, although the feeling presented was illusion, "virtual feeling," imagined rather than coming from a real emotional situation (Langer, 1967). The music matched the paintings in intensity, changes of intensity, rhythms, shape, and duration.

The attunement of the mother to her baby is a precursor to the capacity to experience such art, as well as to use symbols. Mother attunes not only to categorical affects such as joy or sadness but to "vitality affects," which reside in any and all behaviors – in the feeling states involved in the organic processes of being alive. These "forms of feeling" (Langer, 1967) children learn by their own actions and bodily processes and by observing and interacting with people around them. They come to realize that there are transformational means for translating perceptions of the external into internal feelings; they manifest this knowledge through spontaneous social behaviors.

PLAY AND MEANING IN THE REALM OF VERBAL EXCHANGE

As language develops in the second year of life, it renders possible new ways of being with other persons. Complex imitation in children around 15 to 18 months lets them imagine and represent things in their minds and refer to themselves as external, objective. The ability to imitate enables them to compare in their minds the original act and their own execution of it and to adjust one to the other. They can thus transcend immediate experience, engage in symbolic play, and imagine about their interpersonal lives. They can form wishes about how things ought to be and, via language, can hold these wishes even in a context in which they are ungratified.

A prime motive for the infant to learn speech is to establish "being-with" experiences (Dore, 1985) or to reestablish the "personal order" (MacMurray, 1961). We might say that a new game is set up, one in which the risk element for the infant is that he may be tugged away from self-predilections toward accommodation to the social order. Like the transitional object, the word may in fact be given by the parent, but there will be inner thoughts that correspond to it. There will then be pleasurable discoveries by the child; those satisfying words and phrases can be rehearsed and can provide links to the not-there parent. There is an expansion of "intermediate space" (Winnicott, 1971a).

Language also brings with it new problems in the integration of self experience and self-with-other experiences. There is a difference between "experience as lived" and experience "as it is verbally represented," and this makes for a "split in the experience of the self" (Stern, 1985, pp. 162–163). The consequence can be an alienating effect on both self experience and togetherness. Language captures just a part of the global experience of feeling, sensation, perception, and cognition, and it transforms even that part by making it an experience different from the original (Werner and Kaplan, 1963). Although sometimes the language version seems beautifully to encompass the preverbal experience, more often there is a dissonance between the two, with resulting discontinuity of experience. As Stern (1985) observes, "The infant gains entrance into a wider cultural membership, but at the risk of losing the force and wholeness of original experience" (p. 177).

We could guess that when the relationship between parent and child has been good-enough up to this age, then the inevitable misunderstandings simply motivate the infant to learn language better. Frustrations are bound to exist, since language lends itself better to classes of things, generalized episodes rather than specific ones. It is easier to label categorical states than their dimensional features: how happy, how sad (Stern, 1985, p. 179). The gradient features of interpersonal communications affect meaning; it is not just *what* the other says, but *how*.

The infant also has to come to grips with the clashes that can occur between the nonverbal and the verbal, the "double-bind" (Bateson et al., 1956). He can resort to the use of double-binds himself as a way of preserving some possible expression of feelings that can then be denied, the word rather than the gesture being the accountable act. The complications of this defense are that what is deniable to others can be deniable to oneself. Whereas the child was previously reality-oriented, he now has the tools to distort and to transcend reality – either for better or for worse!

It is provoking to think about Stern's proposal that the domain of verbal relatedness can be subdivided into a sense of the *categorical* self that objectifies and labels and a *narrated* self that weaves into a life story elements from the other senses of the self (1985, p. 174). Parents may sometimes label a child in a certain way so that the child takes this label to be what he is; other experiences that do not fit with this may go underground, become unconscious. Clinicians in their eagerness to diagnose may do likewise with patients, at similar cost to the latter's fuller senses of self. When both life and therapy are narrative projects, there is room for ongoing growth and change, for finding space for what may not be in evidence cross-sectionally.

Fortunately, children have ways of protecting themselves from the tyranny of the word, from the prison of categorization, by using symbolic play as a dynamic, individual mode to preserve subjective feelings when collective language proves inadequate (Piaget, 1951). Piaget tells us that in play the child engages in interiorized imitations and in imagery, which is transitional between indices for recognizing objects and verbal signs that are arbitrary. In the image the child preserves individual thought, while the pure sign, language, is always social. A main function of play is its capacity to express conscious and unconscious fantasy and at the same time to harmonize inner images with the external world (Greenacre, 1959a).

In the dialectic between individual truth and collective and impersonal truth, however, both may become more meaningful. In play the child develops a large part of her life narrative, and the less constrained her imagination, the more interesting the story will be. In play, the special quality of fantasy makes it the stuff of which creative products are made (Greenacre, 1959).

Language, which had its origins in the earliest forms of communication between mother and baby and especially in those play episodes that occur throughout the prelinguistic period, will also best be emended by speakers who are able to avail themselves of the necessary intermediate space to play with language itself. They will take it seriously, as they do play and playfulness, but they will be mindful that words are never the precise equivalents of experience. We must have "the words to say it" (Cardinal, 1983), but we can rarely assume that we know anything fully because we have put it into words. Dissatisfied with our expressiveness and our communication, we will give ourselves leeway and scope to improve both.

The current trend toward experience-near concepts rather than the old metapsychology is one possible attempt. Like the child at play, we sometimes have to knock down the tower, this time the tower of Babel, in order to build up a more satisfactory one. But rebuild it we will, in our ongoing efforts to make models of the human mind both to explain meanings and motives and to deal with issues of causation.

Perhaps in psychoanalytic theory, too, there must be that ongoing dialectic between the personal and the impersonal.

MEANING MAKING AND PLAYING IN LIFE AND IN THERAPY

It has often been averred that to focus on play is to focus on the nonutilitarian aspects of human life; however, it is hard to imagine why nature equipped all the mammalian species with an instinct to play if playing is quite useless. It is true, as the 18th-century German poet Schiller (1795) wrote, that we play when we have an abundance of energy over and above what is required for survival and general welfare. In play we are relieved of the immediate tasks of adaptation and can build the world according to our own fantasies (Alexander, 1958). Alexander once compared the relation between adaptive behavior and play with the relation between natural selection and biology and saw mutations as playful experimentations of nature with new combinations, not necessarily adaptive, but sometimes so. Perhaps there is an unconscious intent in playfulness to experiment with ways of being that are departures from our past ways, perhaps to actualize those that are, indeed, felt to be improvements over the past. Erikson (1963) meant something like this when he said that play was the royal road to understanding the ego's effort at synthesis, its purpose being to "hallucinate ego mastery and yet also to practice it in an intermediate reality between fantasy and actuality" (p. 212).

Freud (1908) saw play mainly in the service of the wish to grow up. Erikson (1963) described some of the stages in the development of play as the child did grow up. The infant began with "autocosmic play," centering on the body and involving repetition of sensual perceptions. For this bodily play to move into genital play, the autoerotism that is necessary to the survival of the species, reciprocity with a real mother was necessary. Throughout life, the reciprocity that began in play with the mother was essential to setting in motion the stages in ritualization of experience, deemed by Erikson (1977) to be at the heart of political imagination.

We are dealing here with the reciprocity between infant and caretaker as highlighted by recent infant research and observation. Reciprocity contributes to meaning making in early life and will also contribute to the revisions of meanings that occur in adult psychother-apy. In the therapeutic relationship will be found many analogies to the relationship between the good-enough mother and baby in the beginnings of life. For self-repair to be maximized the patient may be enabled to play at a sort of regression, seemingly opposite to the "wish to grow up," but perhaps necessary to profound self-repair.

If creativity is the "capacity or activity of making something new, original, or inventive, no matter in what field" (Greenacre, 1959a, p. 556), then psychoanalysis and psychoanalytically oriented psycho-therapies at best facilitate creativity in the arena of emending patients' formerly held schemas, no longer felt to be good-enough.

CHAPTER 2

A Child Who Cannot Play

One way of beginning to comprehend the role of play in human development and in psychotherapy is to look at those children who are unable to play. Descriptively, these children do not send forth the usual affective signals that let the other person know what they are intending to do and what they are feeling; they seem unable to take into account the domain of relatedness. Their repetitive behaviors appear to us as minimally pleasurable and, unlike the playfulness of "normal" children, serve more to perpetuate than to violate fixities. They are called autistic, and some therapists even question whether they can learn to play (Solnit, 1987). I believe they can if therapists are willing to invest in very long-term treatment and if the parents are willing and able to participate in an endeavor that, for extended periods, may be more arduous than playful.

The diagnosis of autism connotes to the clinician the most severe label that can be attributed and, in and of itself, may lead to a sort of negative prognostication that can be discouraging to all who are involved. Before proceeding, we might engage in some philosophical reflections about both its linguistic and its psychological meanings.

The term was introduced by Bleuler (1913). We still have something to learn from the ideas he put forth then, for he called attention both to its pathological and to its "normal" manifestations. His definition was simple: "the preponderance of inner life with an active turning away from the external world" (Rapaport, 1951, p. 399). Such thought, he said, aims at a search for pleasure and an avoidance of the painful. Bleuler saw different degrees of deviation, dreams and schizophrenia being completely independent of reality and, indeed, replacing it. On the other hand, he suggested that most of us engage in a few fleeting seconds of autistic thinking quite regularly, and many people spin yarns that they distinguish from the "real." Indeed, he claimed, this normal autism is part of the play of fantasy, which leads to creative new combinations, as in children's play and the productions of poets. Although he said that the relationship between autistic thinking and realistic thinking is, in many ways, that of opposition, when they can be combined, the results can be new insights that can lead to discoveries or inventions. Thus he implicitly recognized the importance of the dialectic between the two if creativity, rather than pathology, is to be the result.

Interestingly, what Bleuler said 75 years ago tallies closely with today's statements by infant researchers such as Stern (1985) that the autistic function is not as primitive as the reality function. He thought it was only after some complicated concepts had been developed and combined with experiences that wishes could be formed and "bliss attained by their fantasied fulfillment" and that environment could be transformed in thought by "self-invented pleasurable ideas" (Rapaport, 1951, p. 429). The "mechanisms" were inborn, for they were to be found in affects and in the tendency of the baby to organize ideas in accord with their pleasurable goals.

Bleuler was thus solidly on the side of a positive value in autism, observing that "anticipated pleasure enforces consideration and preparation prior to an endeavor and enhances the energy of the striving" (p. 434). Thus autism contributes to thinking ability, particularly in the kind of playing in which our abilities to combine fantasy and reality are enhanced. He concludes, "Real enthusiasm is unthinkable without autism" (Rapaport, 1951, p. 435).

Of course, when that writer alluded to the beneficial aspects of autism, he was always referring to its interactions with reality. The word itself derived from *autos*, self, plus *ismos*, a suffix used in Greek to form nouns of action from verbs. Isms are generally used disparagingly to designate distinctive doctrines, systems, or theories, and there is a connotation of fixity and rigidity. These connotations led Kanner

(1944) to apply the term to children suffering a singular stuckness in their inability to engage in interpersonal contact with the human world. Even the *American Heritage Dictionary* defines the word pejoratively: (1) "abnormal subjectivity; acceptance of fantasy rather than reality" and (2) "a form of childhood schizophrenia characterized by acting out and withdrawal."

There is an irony in our use of the term autism for these children, for they do not fantasy, dream, or play like other children; mostly asymbolic, there is little in their "empty fortresses" (Bettleheim, 1967) to which they might retreat. The self cannot develop by itself. Without experiences of interaction with a good-enough mother and others in a facilitating environment, the nascent self is constricted, deformed. We may assume there is some sense of self, for there seem to be intentions, motives of a sort, adroitly to avoid taking in from the outer world. We might coin a term to designate what they are lacking: "heterism" – interpersonal exchange with others, or what psychoanalysis calls "object relationships." Without that dialectic between autism and heterism that enables the child to constitute human experience, a certain stasis ensues, an absence of potential space in which movement can occur.

In what appears to be an attempt to rescue the concept, Ogden (1989) offers the idea of the "autistic-contiguous position." Basing his work on the contributions of some of the writers from the British Independent Tradition, he proposes that the most primitive state of the human infant is associated with a mode of attributing meaning to experience by forming presymbolic connections between sensory impressions that come to constitute bounded surfaces. The experience of surfaces touching one another is the principal medium. Sensory contiguity of skin is basic, as is rhythmicity; experiences are "object related" in this sense. He differentiates this "position" from a phase, in that "position" designates an ongoing mode. There is developmental directionality, in contrast to the pathological form, in which the effort is to maintain a closed system by walling off the body sensations from transforming experiences so that there can be no dialectical interplay of the sensory and the symbolic. Like Tustin (1981, 1984, 1986), he extends these concepts to understand adult neurotic patients.

Tustin (1984) describes these autistic children as "quirky," idiosyncratic; only what they can easily manipulate seems real to them. They make "shapes" from bodily substances or nonbodily equivalents, often by spinning or swinging, and they are preoccupied with the impression of those shapes on their bodily surfaces. They seem to experience their skin surfaces as "adhering" to other surfaces (Bick, 1968). Autistic "objects" serve to assuage a terror of falling apart; the children develop "adhesive equations" with them (Meltzer et al., 1975). Tustin sees the objects differing from the shapes, in that they arise from hard substances and are rigid and static, not changing like the fluid shapes. Both serve purposes for the child; the softness of the shapes is soothing and comforting, and the hardness and surface definition of the objects help the child to feel safe and secure, "all buttoned up" (Tustin, 1984, p. 283).

As for the etiological factors in autism, Mahler (1952) posited an inherent ego deficiency that predisposes these children to become or remain alienated from reality, but she also left room for the possibility that the mother's pathology and lack of empathy might be causative, especially if they led to very early deprivation. Winnicott (1959–1964) declared that in psychosis very primitive defenses are "brought into play and organized *because of environmental abnormalities*" (p. 135). He, too, thought that these same "primitive defenses do not have to be organized if in the earliest stages of near-absolute dependence the good-enough environmental provision does in fact exist" (p. 135). Aware that such drastic opinions were critically greeted, in a separate lecture around the same period (1963), he said that maturational failures could be associated with pathological hereditary factors but that even these were related to failures in the facilitating environment (p. 220).

Tustin (1984) thinks of childhood autism as "the result of an interaction between a temporary state of depression or underconfidence in the mother during the child's early infancy, and the particular nature of the child" (p. 285). The child then retracts his "psychological feelers," and the consequent lack of empathy is a handicap in relating to others. Tustin is one of the few writers on the topic to comment on the role of the father and sees him as "either absent or too malleable for this powerful child" (p. 285).

My main interest in thinking of causation is that the therapist's ideas about it will affect the therapeutic approach. The years of preference for blaming the "schizophrenogenic mother" led clinicians to pejorative attitudes toward mothers that eventuated in grave damage; there were obstacles in the treatment relationship for all participants. In the absence of firmer data about causative factors, I see an advantage in remaining open to possible discoveries about the contributions of neurological or endocrinological factors, in maintaining an agnostic attitude. I am also convinced that if there is severe parental pathology of such magnitude that it leads to drastic privations at the start of life, that could well be manifest in organic ways. If, as recent research has shown, an enriched environment can result in the proliferation of dendritic structures even in old age, while an impoverished one results in their atrophy (Diamond, 1978), that relationship must also be true at the beginnings of life. The human organism needs interaction with the external world to develop its potentials. As clinicians, however, ideally we assume a humility about the unknown. The surround may be ready to provide, but the child may not be able to make use of the provision.

For whatever reasons, autistic children have suffered failures in the form of qualitatively and quantitatively insufficient accumulation of early memories either of gratification or of playfulness. Tustin sees that our therapeutic task is to lead them away from their idiosyncratic madness, while yet preserving their individuality and originality. She hopes that our insight into their uses of shapes and objects may let us "tactfully"[1] enter their worlds. Mahler (1952) tells us to lure them out of their shells with whatever devices we can imagine or invent, such as "music, rhythmic activities and pleasurable stimulation of the sense organs" (p. 302). She also warns, however, that bodily contact, such as touching or cuddling, is of no avail and is even a deterrent, since it can lead to the child's being thrown into a catatonic state.

In work with these children – and it is work at first – we easily find ourselves with "complementary countertransference" (Racker, 1968) as we identify with the mother and her difficulties. Even the cry of the very young child seems singularly uncommunicative; it does not evoke an easy empathy. Since eye contact is generally adroitly avoided, there is not the usual signal that the normal baby sends to indicate the seeking of a playful encounter. It was the mother's fate that when her child attained some representation of her, it did not include the image of the playing mother; hence the work that the two of them have had

---

[1]Tustin clearly enjoys this play on words: the word tact etymologically is derived from *tactus,* the sense of touch. Our appreciation of the meanings autistic children establish from that sense enables us to make empathic and fitting responses.

to do together has taken place without the leavening influence of a certain playfulness. It is easy to feel swamped and fatigued by the child's confusion, and the obsessive perseverations may be hard to endure. The fantasy play that makes therapy with most children so much fun is absent for a long while, since, unable to distinguish fantasy and reality, this child cannot pretend (Gavshon, 1987).

It is often possible, however, to make use of this very sort of countertransference for a playful empathy with the mother, which then may modify her attitudes to the child in such a way that some *spielraum* is created between them. The therapist will also have a much needed ally in the therapeutic process.

ONE AUTISTIC LITTLE GIRL

Katie, age two and one-half, was exquisite in physical appearance: tiny of bone structure, but well nourished, with auburn hair done up in two wee pigtails, tanned face with fine features, brown eyes. There was, however, a disturbing quality about her; she seemed not quite with us. I tried to catch her gaze as I introduced myself, but she was glancing into the air just beyond my right temple. She showed no reluctance to leave her mother and hardly seemed aware that she was doing so. Taking my proffered hand rather mechanically, she walked with me down the hall; she was dragging her weight and moving uncertainly from side to side as we passed the doors to other offices, but she gave no evidence of observing what was around or of wishing to explore, as one might expect of a child of this age.

In the playroom, she let go of my hand, made at once for the sandbox, climbed in, and sat down. Leaning over with her whole torso, she smelled the sand, picked up a handful, and smelled it again. I sat down on the edge and began to talk to her, but she made no response or even a sign that she had heard. I tried clapping my hands behind her head; she did not even turn to look, yet her pediatrician had assured me that her hearing was intact. I felt I might as well not have been in the room with her. She continued just to pick up sand and let it sift through her fingers. When I began to do the same, she vaguely noticed my hand, so I started to let my handfuls fall each time on her hand. This sensation she obviously enjoyed, and she even smiled to herself, and when I ceased this play, she grabbed my hand to make it repeat. That hand, however, seemed a being in its own right; there was still no contact with the owner.

This activity continued until she happened to notice sand covering her dress. She stood, then, and gave that scream which her parents had described to me, harsh and strident, singularly lacking in any identifiable human emotion, or even, I thought, in any quality of emotion such as what I had often imagined in the cries of wild animals. One might have inferred distress over the soiled dress, but when I attempted to help her brush off the sand and I spoke soothingly, she was not comforted, only more agitated. Presently, however, she sat down abruptly. There were no tears, and she began again the same play, smelling the sand, picking it up, letting it sift through her fingers.

When the end of the hour arrived and I told her it was time to go find mommy, she answered with the same raucous yell, after which she left the room with me, as passively as she had entered it. She had spoken no word during the entire session.

Her parents had claimed that she had once begun to speak and that, indeed, that she had been quite normal until about the age of two. Gradually–they could not give any exact date–she had seemed to withdraw into herself. She paid absolutely no attention to mother or father, not even to other children. When her baby sister arrived, Katie was 21 months old but appeared oblivious to the infant's existence. Speech had by then disappeared altogether. When she wanted something, she would take her mother's hand and lead her to the area where it could be obtained, but she would give no other clue. When the mother could not understand, the little girl would emit unearthly howls. Sometimes, too, these occurred when there was no obvious frustration, and nothing anyone could do would give her any solace. Mrs. E described herself as at the end of her rope and ready to scream herself if help could not be found.

This mother impressed me as quiet, intelligent, attractive, but naturally tense and apprehensive about her daughter. She had tried to meet the problem as she had others in her life, by an intellectual approach. She had gone to the library, taken out volumes on child psychology, and read enough to know that there was a strong probability that her child was autistic. Mrs. E was the oldest child in a large family and had taken much responsibility for her younger siblings. She had been considered the brightest, and there had been considerable push for her to achieve. Her husband was a somewhat depressed man, occasionally

plagued by full-blown obsessive symptoms and complaining, for example, of thoughts that he might kill his wife. Compared with his
wife, he was relatively inarticulate and indecisive and was, throughout
the period in which I knew this family, having trouble with his work
life. There were times when she had to go to work to support the
family, and this behavior, combined with the many ways in which
Mrs. E's energies had to be devoted to their first child, aroused in him
resentment of his own felt deprivation and even a certain competitive-
ness toward Katie. Nevertheless, one or the other parent drove the child
many miles twice a week to see me and also presented themselves for
consultations.

Among the problems that tested the patience of both parents and
therapist was the child's resistance to toilet training. During that first
year, Katie and her mother were at war over Katie's propensity for
wetting or soiling wherever and whenever she happened to be so
inclined. Mother would put her on the potty for long periods, to no
avail, but the moment she would lift her into the bathtub, Katie would
do her bowel movements. During her hours with me, she wet quite
regularly, mostly wherever she might be, but occasionally into recep-
tacles such as the Tinker Toy box, on which she liked to sit. (It seemed
one of her hard objects, and the urine running down her legs seemed
one of her soft ones.)

One day the mother and I noticed a particularly bad odor in the
playroom when we went for Katie. (I would sometimes talk with
mother in a room adjacent to the playroom, a room with a one-way
mirror, so that we could see the child.) She had taken off her pants and
buried them in the sand. After mother left, I investigated the source of
the persistent smell, and to my astonishment, I found the mother doll,
selected from the playhouse family, and the mother doll from the hand
puppets covered with feces. Until this time she had paid no attention to
the dolls at all and, indeed, had used only containers, such as the
bathtub or the icebox from the dollhouse, and had mainly filled them
with sand. So, I was encouraged by this development, the soft shapes
used in the unmistakable service of expression, which we could take as
communication.

Mother and I began to work toward a relaxation of her tense
attitudes about training this child. She learned to give Katie crayons
only under supervision; previously Katie had marked up all the walls
each time she got her hands on them. We also gave her soft clay, and

mother used it with her. Shortly, she was toilet trained, and this achievement greatly improved their relationship – and resulted in greater sanitation in the playroom. Most of all, mother experienced herself as a kind of cotherapist with me. We were able to draw on her intellectual defenses – much as therapists with such cases draw on their theoretical constructs – to generate the necessary space, a certain optimal distance that renders one less at the mercy of some otherwise quite natural reactions to children of this sort. The result was that she was not so prone to anguish over events that she inevitably felt to be failures. She joined me in wonderment about what we were dealing with in this little girl and was herself freed for some degree of playfulness in interactions with her.

By the end of a year of our combined work and play, Katie began to notice things more, both in her hours with me and at home. We could no longer keep up the practice of her staying in the playroom while Mrs. E and I talked. She began to wander out, evidently in search of us. Although she would still rarely look directly into a person's eyes, she showed joy at being with me, hugged me around the legs, and touched my hair. She started to use materials other than the sand. Since a favorite activity for a while was to take water into her mouth, spit it out, and watch it trickle over whatever, I obtained a bubble pipe, which she learned to use. Her first word was "bubble," which she applied to a balloon at home.

The mother and I followed the course of using old things in new ways and gradually introducing new materials somewhat related to the old. We tried to stay in the "zone of proximate development," bringing in things for which Katie seemed to be ready. When I presented my little patient with simple puzzles, it was clear that she had an aptitude for them. Although at first she would scream (but a more "readable" scream by now) when she could not immediately put a piece in place, she would persist until she succeeded. Moreover, once having mastered a puzzle inside of its wooden outlines, she would dump the pieces on the floor and do the puzzle without the outlines. Again, I was encouraged that she did not simply perseverate but found new challenges for herself – among them, eluding old "frames," and showing herself that she could do without them.

There were two noticeable setbacks during that first year. One occurred when I went on vacation, and the other occurred when a baby brother was born. The parents reported considerable crying and emotional upheavals during those periods. Katie, however, showed much more interest in this baby than in her younger sister. She would say "baby brobber" and would compare his hands and feet with her own.

Of course, the path is not always upward; in fact, some gains can themselves create new problems. Mrs. E began to report that Katie was much more demanding at home and wanted "me to play with her all the time." For both Katie's and the mother's sake, we planned for a special nursery school experience, with very few children and a teacher trained to work with "atypical" ones. There Katie was "sometimes better and sometimes worse." She had to be supervised closely because of aggression toward the others. She would throw paint, spit in the fountain, and perform other unacceptable acts. But she was responsive to music and would even sing songs together with the other children. Her pronunciation was unclear, but she could carry the tunes, and she found pleasure from this singing. Mrs. E reported what seemed a puzzling new symptom for a while, that Katie would shut her eyes and fumble about, feeling things. When we learned that there was a blind child in the nursery, we felt encouraged that she was now capable of imitating!

With some interruptions I worked and played with this family over a 10-year period. On several occasions they moved far away but kept in touch with me via letters. When Katie and I had reunions, I was generally pleased to see that she had continued to make gains. At seven and one-half, after an absence of almost a year, she greeted me with manifest pleasure, even looking at me directly for a brief moment, and on the second meeting she looked at me for a long while, smiling happily. She eagerly went for the things in the playroom that she remembered. We had shared experiences; there were now shared memories. Language, which depends upon shared meanings, was developing. A new feature was that she accompanied her play with words, for example, saying as she did puzzles, "This goes here." She could ask for and receive some verbal hints from me, as "Let's look for the corner piece." She even manifested a reasonable flexibility: "Turn it around." With unfamiliar puzzles she was less sanguine and manifested rapid mood shifts dependent on whether she was successful with them or not, being joyful if triumphant, near to angry tears when failing.

Perhaps it was her own ability to anticipate such reactions that led her in ensuing sessions to demand, "Want a soft puzzle." "Soft" was her adjective for "easy." She found one representing a children's hospital hard, not just because of its technical difficulties but because of the fact that she did "not want girl in hospital." I knew that a doctor had suggested to the family that she should be hospitalized, so I guessed she had reasons for distress at this idea. She could, however, be calmed when I told her, "She will go home soon."

During this eighth year of her life, she showed increasing capacity for symbolic play. She made greater use of the dolls. One day, observing a mark on the neck of a baby doll that she was dressing, she exclaimed, "Poor baby, hurt self, get doctor." When I added (knowing that she had recently hurt herself), "Yes, she got hurt climbing a fence," Katie agreed, telling me, "She has to get the splinters out." She pretended to cry for the doll. Along with this capacity for play came the greater ability to express her own wishes directly. At the end of an hour she would say, "Don't want to get mommie. Want to stay here." Although her language was pretty much confined to matters here and now, she showed some sense of the future when she could leave without furor because of my assuring her that she would come the following week.

During a period in which her parents were having some accelerated marital problems, Katie could express some of her reactions in doll play. "Don't want daddy," she said, casting aside the father doll. Moreover, she added, "Don't want boys; don't like boys." She proceeded to turn all the boy dolls into girls by plastering clay on their heads to make long hair. At the end of hours, she would declare, "Not want mommie; want new mommie."

This bad time passed, and there ensued some of the most promising developments to date. She began to inform me about events in her world outside of therapy, saying, for example, "Saw a clown at the circus." She connected better with neighborhood children, her mother reported. Once, accused by them of taking a hose nozzle, she defended herself verbally, "Tatie [her pronunciation of her own name] didn't take it!" She surprised me one day by bringing me a gift, a paper doll that she had drawn and colored. She asked for my scissors and used them rather deftly to cut it out. She then dashed to my desk, deposited it in the drawer, and declared, "Not your [still her pronoun for herself] doll — Jean's doll!" I thanked her and spontaneously hugged her, and she awkwardly but pleasurably accepted my gesture. She tried the puzzles once felt to be difficult and pronounced, "Hard puzzles changed to soft!" as she easily assembled them. For the first time she answered a direct question from me and said, "We have puzzles at school."

At seven years and eight months of age, Katie developed something of a transitional object, albeit a hard rather than a soft one. Mrs. E (now working and so unable to keep regular appointments) wrote me that Katie had been playing with a doll's head, long ago removed from the body and now given a name, Annabella. Katie would put her fingers through the neck aperture and allow two fingers to stick out for "hands." Changing her voice to a shrill falsetto, she would say, "Hello, my name is Annabella!" On her other hand she would have another doll's head, this one named Charley. In a deep voice, she would announce, "Hello, my name is Charley."[2] There were various other puppets so constructed, but Annabella was her favorite. If Annabella was misplaced, she had to be found immediately, or Katie would become anxious and panicky. In the middle of other activities, Katie would suddenly demand, "Where's Annabella?" If mother could tell her, she would smile and relax, but if not, "pandemonium would break loose." Mrs. E wrote, "If Annabella were ever permanently lost, that would be the end for us all!"

Then it seemed that the worst had happened. Mrs. E one night noticed the doll's head outside and meant to take it in before morning but was distracted and forgot. When the children had gone off to school, she remembered and dashed out to the yard, only to find no Annabella. She recalled that some neighbor children had been in the yard that morning, so she went to their homes and checked with their mothers, to no avail. She held the "slim hope" that maybe Katie had gone out early and moved the head to some special spot. She feared to say anything to the child, lest that not be so. "I decided to play a waiting game," she said. The next morning Katie darted out to the backyard and came in with Charley and Annabella, and she told mother, in answer to her question, that they had "slept outside at the forest in the mountains." Mrs. E took this report to be an aspect of a memory of their experiences as a family in a summer camp.

Later Mrs. E wrote that Katie had been "putting Annabella in a position of peril" by leaving her, for example, in the middle of the

---

[2]The remarkable thing about this play was the first evidence of experimentation with the personal pronoun "my." True, the dolls were speaking, not Katie, but it seemed to me that transitions were occurring.

driveway or sidewalk and then having her rescued, saying, "If someone takes Annabella, Katie will cry." We saw this child as engaging in some high-risk play at this time, perhaps testing how much matters would be under her own control as well as whether others could be trusted not to harm or make off with the doll's head.

In one play session, something of the theme was reenacted. For there, too, she had a favorite, called Margaret, one of the two baby dolls. On this occasion she could not find it, and she burst at once into hysterical tears and threw her whole body around. She did not let me console her. Although we both searched, Margaret was not to be found. She kept moaning, "Want the baby!" Then she snatched the scissors and said that she would cut the other baby so as to make two. I took the scissors from her and said that then we would have no baby. She did not persist then, although later she returned to the idea. I offered to make one out of clay, but that would not do. Finally at the end of the hour she had another idea: "Go in Jean's car and get a new baby." I promised that next time, if the baby had not turned up, we would get another. She left, eyes swollen, a child apart at the seams.

As she approached the age of eight, mother reported her own ups and downs, coinciding with those of this daughter. On the positive side, she wrote that Katie had seen *The Wizard of Oz* and that her play had been dominated by "transforming herself into Glinda," the good and beautiful witch. Mother clearly enjoyed this drama herself and hauled out an old formal that Katie donned, making herself a crown to complete the costume. One of the encouraging aspects of this development was that Katie would now sing herself to sleep with "Over the Rainbow."

This play had been preceded by a spate of bedtime behavior that mother found "dismaying." After prayers were said and Katie was tucked in, she would begin to giggle and laugh in a silly and uncontrollable way. Mrs. E had tried to quiet her by saying that it was time to sleep and that she was keeping the younger children awake. Since this approach was ineffective, she had increasingly found herself losing her temper and "resorting to the switch to control her." As her guilt was huge over this behavior, which she felt was "handling it all wrong," she would try to control her feelings and ignore the noisy and annoying laughter. One night, after an especially trying day, Katie was laughing again, and this time mother first tried to comfort and embrace her, again futilely. Mother was suffused with hopeless despair, and the tears started uncontrollably. Katie was startled, quickly stopped her giggling, threw herself against mother, pulled the latter's arms around her, put her own arms around mother's neck, and said, "I love you, Katie."[3] She seems to have been impelled to repair mother to salvage the affection she recognized as important for herself. For the mother, Katie's behavior was a rare example of this child's affect attunement with her. Interestingly enough, that night was the end of the "inane bedtime laughter."

At the age of eight, Katie became intrigued with proteins, and both with me and at home she was constantly drawing elongated, tear-shaped items, which she would usually color red, and she would tell us, "A protein go down in the body." This preoccupation had begun when Katie observed her mother reading in *Life* magazine an article about the human digestive system and asked about it, especially what had happened to the ham sandwich the boy in the photo had eaten, since one could not see it in the body. Mother had explained that the sandwich had been changed into proteins, carbohydrates, and fats, which were depicted in the photos as shapes of yellow, blue, green, and red (the latter elongated proteins), so that the body could use these good things. Katie may also have been aware that a doctor recently consulted had advised the mother to give this child a diet high in proteins— not easy to do, since Katie had obvious preferences for carbohydrates.

One day Katie asked mother for the "protein book," and Mrs. E told her that the old issue of *Life* had been thrown out or misplaced. The child interrupted, saying, "No, want to find Katie's new protein book that she made in school." Mother was happy over that response and saw it as the first example of her ability to understand and correct verbally a misconception of what she wanted. Now, instead of a tantrum, Katie could participate in a "re-railing of the dialogue." There were other evidences of a growing use of "I" and of "mine." Whereas formerly she showed no reaction when her little sister would scribble in her books, she became indignant when Susie drew in her "protein book." "Don't want Susie to color in Katie's new schoolbook!" she told her.

Shortly the new interests in physiology led to curiosity about reproductive systems. One day in her session she was making proteins

---

[3]Here again, Katie is experimenting with the personal pronoun and is now throwing it out as a line she wishes to hear from mother, as in her behavior she elicits the reassuring hug.

with clay and became sillier and sillier. I reacted by restructuring our play; I made a little figure, invited her to "feed" it the proteins, and then made it grow big and strong by making muscles and letting it grow taller. To grow bigger was a clearly valued accomplishment for this girl. Katie then said something about a baby in a mommie, so I made a woman with a big belly and said she was carrying a baby inside. Katie became calm, absorbed. She made a "belly button" on the woman and a "cover" that appeared to be a sanitary napkin. She said the baby was going to come out. I agreed, said it grows and grows until it is big enough to do that. Katie said, "But not in daddies," and I agreed. We gave the mommie breasts "so she can feed her baby." Katie then went over all this information and said, "Daddy came out a boy, and Katie came out a girl." She instructed me to make a baby, make the mother's tummy smaller, and put the baby in mother's arms. I made a wee cord and told her that when the baby is inside the mommie, she is connected by that so she can eat (I was thus making a link with the protein theme), and I added that she had been attached to her mother by such a cord where her belly button is. Throughout this play Katie was in a state of "quiet alert," calm and connected with me and looking directly into my eyes. She asked to take the figures home with her. Mrs. E reported such conversations at home, too, and described Katie's making many anatomical drawings "to help reinforce her understanding."

The next preoccupation was with death and spiritual life. This seems to have been stimulated by her daily examination of the family Bible, with its many illustrations of the life of Jesus Christ. Katie was extremely puzzled by the halo above the infant's head and the head of the grown Jesus and by his having long hair and wearing gowns, both previously associated with femaleness. She was troubled by the pictures of Christ on the cross and asked many questions that Mrs. E found difficult to explain since her own understanding was, as she wrote, "liberally punctuated with question marks." Whether because of this breakdown in the dialogue or because of some other reason, Katie's concerns became focused on the spelling of Jesus. She demanded to know why the name should be spelled with a *J* when it was pronounced "Gee-sus." We could not become sure whether there was a wish to dissociate me, with my name beginning with "J," from a person whose fate had been death, but, in any event, Katie was most emotional about the issue and said, "Katie cries, Katie is unhappy. Katie wants Jesus to start with a *G,* not a *J."* This protest was carried over to school as well and was only checked somewhat when the teacher told her that when she would become a big girl, she would know that Jesus must start with a *J*!

At about this time, Mrs. E reported that Katie had become intensely reactive to the emotions of others. She was watching much television, and when one of the cartoon characters was unhappy and crying, Katie would become distressed, even hitting the TV screen and saying, "Don't want the girl to be unhappy!" She would have even more intense reactions when she observed distress in her mother. Probably there was much of that to be observed then because mother and father were having considerable difficulty with each other. Her mother found this behavior less of a problem than other behaviors, because Katie was communicating and could be reassured.

The father had enrolled in night school, with the aim of bettering his economic opportunities. He was absorbed in that, and Mrs. E was feeling "left alone with the children." She had, she told me, begun to feel sorry for herself, but then, impatient with this "self-pity," she decided she had to do something "just for me." She did much self-examination, asked herself what would be of real interest to her, and recalled an old envy of those who could make beautiful music with a piano. She managed to rent an old piano cheaply and asked for some money for her birthday so that she could pay a neighborhood teacher two dollars an hour for lessons for several months. She also borrowed some language records to teach herself French. Then an unexpected opportunity came along; she had made friends with a singer who, on hearing Mrs. E sing, invited her to join a group of young vocalists. She reported stage fright at first, but then she thoroughly enjoyed the applause that she received. I think that these gratifications enabled her to stand the strain of parenting this complicated child for several more years.

My last contact with this family was when Katie was 12. Although it was clear that the child had made gains, there were persisting emotional problems. Katie had developed a panic about saying her own name. She told us, "I'll be dead if I say that word. Put me to sleep and give me a new head that won't be afraid!" I recalled that her first use of "I" and "me" had been to attribute them to Charley and Arabella, the puppets she had constructed by removing the heads from two dolls, and by using her own hands to move them, and her own voice to let them speak. With Charley and Arabella she had created that "intermediate area of experience" in which "me" and "not me" do not have to be clearly differentiated (Winnicott, 1971); in that space she felt safe to experiment with personal pronouns referring to the self. Now, however, her very increasing reality sense was forcing her to recognize that her own head was not comparable to those of other children; it did not work as well as theirs. She expressed some longing not to be so different from her age mates. It was a time of distrusting her own subjectivity, so she suffered a temporary loss of the sense of agency that once enabled her to create transitional objects. The solution she imagined was to acquire a more satisfactory head, one that would not contain the terrors of annihilation that seemed to accompany her own. In her still somewhat concrete way, she was expressing a wish quite like that of many less disturbed patients whose fantasies of cure entail others doing something to them.

For a number of reasons the family decided that the time had come to consider a residential treatment program. Katie was on the threshold of adolescence, and new problems could be anticipated. Mrs. E had separated from her husband and she was again working, this time as a teacher's aide, using some of the skills she had learned with her own child. Katie had been tested by psychologists in the public school. She was found to be at a third- or fourth-grade level in spelling and reading and at fifth-grade level in math. Language was thus still lagging, but in the more impersonal arena of numbers Katie was almost up to others her age. Both her mother and I felt that she would do well in the school they had selected, for she was motivated to learn now and the therapeutic ambiance that would be provided seemed close to an ideal context for further development.

DISCUSSION

In my initial interview with Katie, I met with a two and a-half year old who did not manifest the facial, vocal, or gestural signs of feelings that Darwin (1872, 1877) long ago described in the newborn. She was not the first autistic child I had seen, but each time I felt confronted anew with a mystery. Although the mother had claimed that this little girl had been "normal" at first, she later told of her pain as she compared her baby's development with that of others in her neighborhood. Did she just not realize that her firstborn was somehow different? Or was there a time when Katie did manifest emotions, and later, because of "underconfidence in the mother," did she turn away from the human world and concentrate on "me-centered manipulations and auto-sensuousness," as Tustin (1984, p. 285) has suggested?

Did she too easily leave mother to come with me? Many children of that age would insist on mother's accompanying them. At the least, the child usually would size up this new person and make a determination whether to come to the playroom alone. Katie's hold on my hand was loose and did not convey the trusting that one sometimes feels in a child's grip. As I think of this beginning, I think of Trevarthen's (1984) thesis that "early development of behavior appropriate to exploration and use of objects is to a high degree separate from development of mental engagement with persons" (p. 131). The comprehension of emotions in others and the use of one's own feelings to regulate interactions with others are highly elaborated before an infant masters nonhuman objects. Yet here was Katie, bypassing the human relationship and absorbed with the sand. Like other such "atypical" children I had seen, she resorted first to smell.

If we play with analogies from the course of development, then we might reflect that the olfactory sense is the most primitive of all, this system first appearing at about 30 days of gestation (Tuchmann-Duplessis, Auroux, and Haegel, 1975). Even infants born prematurely as early as 28 weeks can detect odor (Sarnat, 1978), and neonates are known to be able to discern their mother's breast pads from those of other women (MacFarlane, 1975). We might say that among the means by which Katie makes her diagnosis of this situation is her nose. Whether that includes information about the therapist we may never know for sure!

Katie first leaned down with her whole body to smell the sand. In contrast to her somewhat uncertain navigation down the hall with me, while she manifested what Kestenberg (1975) might call *free flow of tension,* she now became purposeful, in a *bound flow of tension* (p. 196). Her ability thus to regulate tension coincided with changes in body shape. *"Growing* and *shrinking of body shape* are the basic elements of *shape flow,"* Kestenberg says (p. 196), and when there is coordination of tension flow and shape flow, "the groundwork is laid not only for harmony between feelings and self-expression, but also for conflict-free learning of new skills" (pp. 197–198). Such learning could include playing, for playing is initially doing, involving the body (Winnicott, 1971a).

After that first global body movement toward the sand, Katie refined her approach and used her hands. As I began similarly to use mine and to let the grains sift down on her hand, I was rewarded by seeing a smile–not at me yet, but clearly an expression of her own pleasure. Whether sand is to be considered hard or soft may be debatable, but that I was now clearly invited to share this substance with her encouraged me greatly. We could note that she "transferred" to me her use of the "talking hand" as a medium for communication.

How to understand the seeming distress about the sand on her dress? My best guess is that the spill was not intended; something had happened that was not experienced as under her control. The disruption was brief, although I did not feel that my attempt at soothing had particularly contributed to her restoration of equanimity. The disruption was similarly of short duration when I told her that it was time to go find mommie. I noted that there was at least some comprehension of spoken language, and she did not employ bodily resistance to leaving the playroom.

She did, however, use bodily resistance to her mother's attempts to toilet train her. In this period, I think Mrs. E and I had a chance to "diagnose" our relationship with each other as a most workable and playable one. She easily grasped the advantages of the model I had followed in that first hour and joined the child in her activity. Katie then rewarded her by becoming toilet trained, able to endure that her feces, once having left her body, were not hers any more but could be a bridge to her mother. This achievement rendered the child infinitely more acceptable to this mother–and indeed to us all. The climate in their domain of relatedness became fairly favorable for the further evolving of playfulness, in which all objects could have the potential of becoming transitional objects.

The most dramatic changes we witnessed were in the realm of emotional expressiveness; both joy and anguish and all their intermediate variations became easier to read in Katie. In addition, the greater felt safety allowed her to explore other materials, other activities. I think she was now able to experience both mother and me as "transformational objects," and we "cotherapists" were elated when that first word, "bubbles," was uttered.

If, as Schafer (1982a) declared, "Analysts need stamina like they need oxygen" (p. 48) and if such endurance is a feature of the "second self" of the professional, what may we posit about the need of the mother of the autistic child for such capacity for "empathizing sturdily, steadfastly, and patiently"? The therapist, after all, sees the patient for a 50-minute hour at a time; the mother must carry on all the rest of the hours. If analysts need from time to time to take stock and slow down the pace or achieve some greater distance from the clinical situation to "recreate the experience of self-cohesiveness and self-consistency" (p. 48), must not that recess be even more necessary for the mother? Perhaps for any mother, some access to a "second self" while performing her motherly functions is highly desirable; she might then play that role without letting it constitute her whole sense of self. Even more than the therapist, mothers of "atypical" children need some time-out from the rather one-sided empathizing that for a long while must characterize their relationships with these children.

The very effectiveness of therapy creates at some point a problem opposite to the one with which it began. Katie, who originally ignored the members of her family, began to demand constant attention. As though to make up for lost time and missed play space, she wanted constant attention and play with mother. So it was thought desirable that she begin to have some experiences with people and situations different both from those at home and from those in my office. In the condensed story of the treatment, I have not included the details of my contacts with the nursery school and its staff, but they included some of the same measures as with the mother – enabling them to survive and transcend the problems Katie brought with her, to facilitate her participation, and to feel pleasure when she was able to make manifest gains.

One manifestation of her progress was the ability to engage in deferred imitation, which requires the capacity to act on the basis of an internal representation of the original (Piaget, 1954). Katie had to have had two versions available to her: the observed behaviors of the blind child and her own execution of the imitation (Stern, 1985, p. 164). Moreover, she must have perceived some relationship between herself and that child to have a way of representing herself as similar. So the act could be seen as evidence for a creative split: self as objective category and self as experience (Lewis and Brooks-Gunn, 1979). Katie was thus able to transcend immediate experience, to imagine interpersonal life (Lichtenberg, 1983), to share knowledge and experience, and to play in the symbolic realm.

I hoped that this newfound ability would enable her to hold onto some images of me during the year's interruption of treatment that subsequently occurred. If we can measure her object constancy by the manifest pleasure she showed in our reunion, then it seems clear she did remember our relationship and the play space we had made together. I was happy with her increased use of speech and increased flexibility. In the sessions that followed, Katie was able to use play to depict her tensions with the marital discord at home and her dissatisfactions with both parents – much as any of our child patients. She could increasingly talk of situations in her world outside.

Her play themes became ever more elaborate. Then, sometime after age seven, she created Annabella and subsequently Charley. Why did she remove the bodies and use these dolls' heads in the manner of hand puppets? She had seen and used hand puppets in my playroom, but not extensively; they had never been her favorite toys. We could imagine that there was importance to her of making them herself, of the use of the head where thinking and talking go on, of her own hands, which had been her original mode of communicating, and of her own voice, which at one time had not been used to make words. Annabella and Charley, once inanimate and silent, were animated by her – perhaps as she sensed that she herself had been via interactions with mother and me. In any event, this considerably delayed arrival of what might be seen as a sort of cross between transitional objects and imaginary companions led to improvisation of scripts of great intricacy. Katie seemed to play out themes of separation and reunion, of adventure, of danger and rescue.

As Winnicott (1967, 1971a) would have predicted, Katie's ability to fill in the potential space involved in separation with creative playing and the use of symbols began to add up to partaking of cultural life. Having concocted her own plays, she became intrigued with those of other authors, and in partaking of their imaginations, she extended her own. She now began to be an actress in the plays and to sing the songs she learned from some musicals to soothe herself into sleep – making of the musical version of speech an even better transitional phenomenon, one that could nevermore be lost.

Somewhere in the midst of this progress there also occurred regressions in the form of silliness, which Katie's mother found quite unbearable. How might we view this? The synonyms for "silly" are words like "foolish, fatuous, preposterous, ridiculous, ludicrous." "Silly" suggests, according to the dictionary, what lacks point, purpose, or semblance of intellectual content. As we are psychologists and not the writers of dictionaries, we note that all such attributions would be in the judgment of the observer, and we are interested in the impulse within the child that might set off such behavior. Perhaps it could be some wish to break away from conformity or some impatience with too much attending to the "real" or the "objective." In Winnicott's (1958) terms, maybe it could be some initially playful return to the unstructured, "to become unintegrated, to flounder, to be in a state in which there is no orientation, to be able to exist for a time without being either a reactor to an external impingement or an active person with a direction of interest or movement" (p. 34). The aim is to restore a sense of feeling real.

Winnicott did suggest, however, that such states are best manifested in aloneness; although Katie chose to be silly at bedtime, which might ordinarily be her private moments, her mother could hear her silliness. Two factors contributed to her mother's extreme agitation about it. We had worked long and hard to enable this girl to transcend her autistic ways, and mother feared that this regression to the inane was a sign we were losing the battle. Then, she herself was having marital problems that depleted her ability to hold onto that "second self" she had so often managed. She tried both anger and attempts to comfort. Katie continued to giggle and laugh, probably feeling both of mother's reactions to be misattunements at the moment. Then mother experienced her daughter's continuing with the frivolous behaviors as a threat that could obliterate her own sense of self.

When the mother's misattunement escalated to anguish and tears, the episode came to a surprising ending as the child stopped the silliness and became for the moment the self-regulating one for the mother. Indeed, the incident seemed to presage a period of intense attunement on Katie's part to the emotions of others and hence to the re-railing of the dialogue with them.

In the later situation in the playroom with me, we could say that Katie was absorbed with issues psychoanalysis has attributed to "instincts," issues to do with the body and with reproduction. When for a few minutes she attempted to deal with her tensions about it all by resorting to silliness, my calm comments seemed to let her bind that tension so that we could together shape the dialogue about matters of intense concern to her. Winnicott (1958) asked whether there may not be value in considering a difference in the quality as well as the quantity of "id," as when we compare "the game that is satisfactory with the instinct that crudely underlies the game" (p. 35). I would put it that the quality of the strong emotions that Katie was struggling with in that session was rendered less frightening to her precisely because of the context—that is, the presence of a playful other who she could by now trust would not herself "regress" in the face of this new topic. Instead, she let me play the "self-regulating other" and shape with her the dialogue that she needed toward sexual enlightenment. Her rapt attention and active participation in that discussion were more like what Winnicott (1958) had in mind when he wrote of a "climax in ego-relatedness" in contrast to the compulsive excitation of an "instinctual" experience (which, I think, was what she feared and against which the silliness was a defense.)

Thus what could have been seen as devoid of meaning or coherence attained both meaning and coherence. When the role of the other is not one of judgment and is not qualified by a sense of personal failure when momentarily left "out of it," then the frivolous child is enabled to reach toward a state of greater consciousness rather than to dazedness. In this session, I saw Katie in a state of quiet alert, calm and connected with me. Most promising was her subsequent engagement of mother in similar play and similar conversation.

As I said before, the gains often entail a price. Her ever-growing interest in the culture around her led her to invite mother to read to her from the stories in the Bible, and she learned about the crucifixion of Christ. Like many "atypical" children, Katie probably suffered a chronic fear for her life, but now she had a name, "death," for what she feared, and she became obsessed with it. Why was she so perturbed by the fantasies aroused by the Jesus story? Could it be that, having just begun to own her body, she is told that it is time-bound? Having begun to care for others, does she learn that they will someday die? Having learned empathy for others, does she feel for the murdered Jesus? These and other possibilities occur to us. But perhaps her fear of death is the equivalent of Winnicott's (1974) "fear of breakdown." He describes the dread of a psychotic break, which has already occurred, but in a period of life before the person had the emotional and cognitive development actually to experience it. Katie had had something close to a state of nonbeing in her "autism." Whatever its causes, it must have involved some of the "unthinkable anxiety" or "primitive agony" that Winnicott posits as present whenever the infant cannot experience that necessary illusion of omnipotence that a good-enough environment permits. For Winnicott the route to cure may be seen precisely in the person's seeming to court the very situation that is feared, to put it finally into the past.

One of the great frustrations of the therapist is that the book may often have to be put down before the story has sufficiently unfolded. My hope is that, in her residential setting, Katie has found a therapist toward whom she is transferring memories of our working and playing relationship, as well as memories that have gone into the "representations of interactions generalized" (Stern, 1985) from her family of origin. I imagine her in the process of updating those RIGs, creating new meanings and even a new life history.

CHAPTER 3

A Child Who Can Play

A Contemporary Little Hans

PLAY OF CHILDREN

Over the years as psychoanalysis has speculated on the role of play in the lives of children, play has been seen as a sort of practicing for adult life. Motivated by a wish to grow up, the child is pushed from within by maturational unfoldings and pulled from without by observations of the capabilities and privileges of those who are older (Freud, 1908). It has been postulated that in play the child has an opportunity to turn passive into active, to dose herself with amounts of the stimuli that are manageable and hence to achieve a sense of mastery. Wish fulfillment may be involved. The relationship of play to the repetition compulsion has been explored, and hypotheses have been made about the admixture of fantasy and reality that seems to allow some abreaction to take place so that anxiety is reduced (Waelder, 1932). Hence play is often the mode in which the child can deal with experiences felt to be traumatic at the time, situations in which the child has felt a certain helplessness. It has also been thought that children have an instinct to master, that is, to perfect their functioning in various areas (Hendrick, 1942). Others have doubted this basic motivation and whether it would even be apparent were it not for identification and rivalry (Greenacre, 1959a), although they do see play as a species of "function pleasure" (Buhler, 1927).

Greenacre (1959a) has focused on play and creative imagination. Anticipating what we now call "developmental regressions" (Trevarthen, 1982), she declared that oscillations between progression and regression occur regularly during the period of the child's greatest growth. The nature and content of the regressions are dependent upon "the libidinal stage, especially influenced by the impact of untoward external events" (p. 565). When mental imagery and thought develop, there would be the beginning of imagination – and also of anxiety. Only then, she believed, could the child wish, as Freud had suggested, to be grown up, that is, in control.

A number of writers have felt that in playing, the solution of a problem is not imperative. Play comes from surplus energy, combined with a sense of almost unlimited freedom. Play is essentially experimental; to the extent that it is repetitive, it renders useful functions automatic. In creative people, play can lead to the novel and the original (Alexander, 1958).

According to Greenacre (1959a), one of the main functions of play in connection with creative imagination is that it "aids in delivering the unconscious fantasy and harmonizing it with the external world" (p. 571). Although she was writing specifically about creative people, those who are capable of making a product that is original and new, some of us have seen the idea as applicable to all persons, the product being a fresh sense of emerging self and renewal of meaningful relationships with others (Sanville, 1987a).

Children's play has been studied both for the light it might shed on the nature and genesis of thought itself and on the unfoldings of the symbolic and for its role as precursor to sublimation (Galenson, 1969). Greenacre (1969), in her discussion of Galenson's paper, emphasized the sensorimotor responses of the child to the environment, always involved in play, and she noted that these dimensions intermingle with the verbal, even in adult psychotherapy. She summarized the views of Thompson (1927), a biologist:

> Play is partly a safety valve for overflowing energy, partly an expression of imitativeness, partly a correlate of agreeable feelings, but mainly an irresponsible apprenticeship for adult activities and an opportunity for testing new departures, especially in habit. Play is not directly useful, but has a prospective value in educating efficiency (p. 356).

Postulating that thought entails the ability to maintain and use inner images that originated in sensorimotor experiences, experienced at different times and circumstances, she imagined that the long postnatal relationship of the infant with the body of the mother must provide such *"variables* within the framework of the *constancy"* (p. 358). These must be the earliest forerunners of play, those shifts in the mother's bodily behavior furnishing "liberating stimuli which come from outside the infant, but, in accordance with the strength of the introjective-projective mechanism, seem to be experienced also as belonging to the infant himself" (p. 358). These events, she believed, would occur during Mahler's symbiotic stage; later, as individuation proceeded, the mother's activities would be imitated or complemented. These developments depend on an internalized body image. Walking contributes to this, to the sense of relative size and of effectiveness of motor behaviors. Speech itself "develops in stages, each of which is preceded by a period of playfulness" (p. 360), and what starts as play becomes communication. So thought itself is "gestated in play activity"; there is "a kind of somatic foundation for symbolism" (p. 361).

Greenacre's article on thought and childhood play ends with a tribute to the clinical observation, which was under criticism for being only anecdotal, rather than scientific. Although she recognized the need for the clinical report's being complemented by laboratory experiments and controlled observations, she affirmed the special value of data from the treatment situation. What is impressive is the degree to which her views were in accord with those of infant researchers contemporaneous with her, such as Spitz (1963a) with his ideas of dialogues from infancy and the later writings of Stern (1977) on the learning of dialogue in the earliest social play between mother and infant.

If, like Bion (1962b), we regard thinking as a fundamental link between human beings and see its origins in the mother's thinking lovingly about her infant so that the infant's feelings can be transformed into something known and tolerated, then we glimpse the significance of life's first interactions, their potentials, and their problems.

In contrast to therapy with an autistic child, which has to begin with the relative lack of the child's ability to play, therapy with a child who is moving naturally into the "play age and the dramatic" (Erikson, 1977) can be relatively easy and often accomplished in a relatively brief time. I now present a case in which we can guess that a little boy and his mother probably enjoyed those bits of playful routine that, from the start of life, enabled him to develop an essentially "benevolent self image (a certified narcissism, we may say) grounded in the recognition of an all-powerful and mostly benevolent (if sometimes strangely malevolent) Other" (p. 8).

To compare this case and the case of Katie may provoke realization that Winnicott's concept of the good-enough mother has to be supplemented by a concept of the good-enough child, that is, one whose basic equipment permits the interaction with the environment that is essential to development. We would have to affirm that there is such a thing as a baby and that not all babies are created equal. Parents have always known this fact, but it has taken many professionals a long time to discover the ways in which innate qualities of the infant in combination with both innate and acquired qualities of the parents will affect the shape of things to come. Winnicott, of course, was not unaware of possible defects in the baby itself. He alludes to impairments that create difficulties, as when he mentions the anencephalic infant in whom the lack of a normal brain leads to obvious defects in that capacity to organize that we have called ego (1962, p. 56).

We could also reflect that in his very coining of the term "good-enough mother," Winnicott (1960b, 1962) left room for the desirability that she also be a bad-enough mother, perhaps also able to attend to her own needs and wishes even at the risk of sometimes frustrating her child. In an early paper (1947b), he affirmed that the mother "hates her infant from the word go" (p. 201), even when the infant is a boy! He listed a whole page of reasons for this feeling. If the mother cannot tolerate her negative feelings without acting on them, there is a likelihood she will be so anxious to meet her child's every need that it will be as though the two of them were eternally merged, and the offspring will be inhibited in moving toward separateness. Most mothers are able to contain some hateful feelings without expressing them, other than in playful ways such as singing to the infant nursery rhymes such as "Rockabye Baby," the words of which relate to birth symbolism. She may also, as did the mother whom I will describe, cultivate the capacity for the "light touch," closely connected with playfulness, which can help her to transcend holding when her child is ready to be let go.

We might well posit that mothers of children such as Katie may have great difficulty tolerating their hateful feelings, both because these feelings must be greatly increased in a relationship in which there does not develop even the mutuality of recognition by face and by name that the ordinary mother enjoys and because these mothers tend to experience intense guilt in a surround that tends to blame mothers for the defects in their children.

Even mothers of "normal" children, however, tend to be affected by this common assumption, particularly, perhaps, when they are of a certain socioeconomic and educational segment of our culture. They strive to be perfect mothers, and that striving rarely includes being comfortable with occasional feelings that they might prefer to be childless. Moreover, their apprehensions about making errors in their rearing of the child render them something less than playful in their approach to problems. Lacking confidence in their potential spontaneity, they turn readily to professional help, and we can count on their having "both affectionate care and scientific interest," as Freud (1909) did with the father of Little Hans.

THE CASE OF RICKIE

Like that classic case, Rickie had manifested some phobic inclinations, and his presenting symptoms concerned some reactions to the processes of conception and birth. Unlike the parents of Little Hans, however, Rickie's parents had never told him the stork story, but they had some questions about what to tell him, when, and how. In their earnest ways, they wanted to spare him – and themselves – anxieties. Rickie, like Hans, was an inquisitive child, with much sexual curiosity; he had that "spirit of inquiry" that, once liberated, "enabled him to arrive at genuine abstract knowledge" (Freud, 1909, p. 9).

Unlike the treatment approach with Little Hans, in which Freud worked through the father, my approach was directly to involve both parents initially and then to work and play together with mother and child since the father, with his busy professional life, could not accommodate regular sessions. Freud commented that Hans's mother was "excellent and devoted" but that it was "not without some show of justice" that the father accused her of being responsible for the child's neurosis because of her demonstrativeness to him and her too frequently taking him to her bed. Rickie's father made it clear in the initial session that he had little patience with his wife's proclivity to turn for professional help with parenting, and he instructed me that he did not want therapy to be "doing it for Rickie"; I should find a way to help mother do the play therapy herself. Since this view coincided rather closely with my own mode, I readily agreed that we would try for something like that. I respected what I took to be his antiauthoritarian stance and did not want Rickie to have to ask him, "Does the Professor talk to God?" as did Little Hans after Freud told him that before he was born, he had known that he "would be so fond of his mother that he would be bound to feel afraid of his father because of it" (p. 42).

Mr. and Mrs. B consulted me because their three-year-old son was withholding his bowel movements. Mrs. B did most of the talking and began by telling me how the parents had delayed toilet training Rickie until he was about two and one-half years old because he "did not seem to be ready." Then she had consulted a developmental psychologist about how to train him, and training was quite easily accomplished.

When he suffered some slight constipation, he had been for a while somewhat reluctant to have bowel movements, but a mild laxative that the doctor gave him seemed to relieve him. Two months previous to this first interview, Rickie had entered nursery school. Mrs. B explained that she had not wanted to tell him of her pregnancy "until he was safely started there," but about that time a neighbor asked within his earshot whether Rickie was aware about the coming baby. He looked at her directly and asked, "Is there going to be a baby?" She, of course, had to acknowledge that fact, but before going further with any information, she sought professional advice about just how to inform him. She was instructed not to tell him more than he asked and especially not to talk of how the baby would come out. This bright and inquisitive child asked many questions, however, and she had to obtain a picture book to show him about this process. Shortly after, Rickie began to retain his feces and to talk a great deal about the situation: "We are going to have a baby. Mother is going to have a baby. Daddy is going to have a baby." Taking this last statement to be an "intellectual error," mother informed him that only women have babies.

Rickie had begun to complain of pain on defecation, so mother "checked with the doctor to make sure there was no physical problem;" he assured her that the child's stool was soft because of the mild laxative. Mrs. B explained to me that whenever Rickie experienced pain with anything, it was hard to make him go back to that activity again. She gave an example of his being frightened by the sounds that emanated from a house being built next door. She had helped him to overcome some of those fears by playing with him around the theme of building a house. It was clear that she had an appreciation of the value of the child's actively doing what had been only passively experienced.

She described herself as an anxious mother. Rickie was her firstborn; he arrived rather late in her life, when she was 38 years old. She nursed him for 14 months and temporarily suspended her own professional career. When he was around a year old, she began to worry that he was overly clinging, that "something was wrong." She sought therapy and discovered that she had "an unrecognized hostility" to him, since his existence deprived her of accustomed freedoms. Fearful of doing something "which might harm the baby," she said that she had tried to be a perfect mother. Out of her therapy she became convinced that she had not harmed him; he was "simply of an introverted nature, and very bright." Mr. B confirmed all that she was saying, and we agreed that therapy "should help people to help themselves."

We talked of the parents' preference to keep the therapy brief, set a satisfactory fee and method of paying it, and arranged a convenient time. Mrs. B wanted to know what to tell Rickie about seeing me. I said that the parents knew this boy best; what could they be comfortable saying to him? They decided that they would like to tell him that he and mother would be coming to see a friend.

When I opened the door to the waiting room, my first impression was that it would be difficult to say which of its two occupants was the "more pregnant." This beautiful, solemn, manifestly anxious little boy had a stomach that appeared painfully distended. He looked at me but did not take my proffered hand. Mother came into the playroom with him, and he clung to her skirts, glued himself to her on the couch, and from time to time climbed all over her. At first he did not respond to my casual comments but looked to his mother to talk with me.

I sat down on the floor and began to scribble on a large piece of paper. Shortly he began to show interest, slid down, and accepted the box of crayons from me. He took out one color after another; he seemed to choose carefully and whispered under his breath the name of the color. Responding to the "liberating stimulus" of my own scribbling, he began to color and to accompany his activity with some chatting of his own to me. He alternated between drawing things very small, constricted, and then moving to large, sweeping strokes. Then he drew several "bananas" and asked me to draw bananas. Becoming increasingly absorbed, he began making on page after page a small, somewhat circular shape surrounded by a large circular shape, and on these papers he asked me to write his name. At first he found the paper too big; he settled for a smaller pad, then decided to go back to the larger one. I began to comment on these repeated shapes and said that something small seemed to be inside of a big, round shape, maybe growing in there. He shortly responded, "Babies!" and enthusiastically drew more and more of these, and at times he instructed me to write his name in big letters and again in small. I commented that not only was mother having a baby, but Rickie would like to have one too. He agreed and began to talk animatedly of how he was going to take these pictures home and hang them on his wall. His mother was mainly silent during all of this play and observed closely. From time to time, he would turn to look up at her or to touch her, but he ceased to have her speak for him; he was well able to talk for himself.

When the time came to a close, he obviously did not want to go and asked, "Why do I have to go?" I replied that I did not have any more time today, but wondered if perhaps he might want to visit again. He nodded. (Like most small children, he could not quite comprehend the arbitrary ending of the session, but he manifested a confidence that there would be a future time.) Accepting, albeit reluctantly, the end of the session, he began to put the crayons back in the box. When I inquired if he wanted me to help, he said firmly, "No, I can do it myself." (Autonomy was already important to him. I thought of how his father must approve this affirmation of self-sufficiency!) To replace those crayons seemed an important part of his play, for he was intrigued with whether they would all fit back into that box. He commented that there would be seven babies, and he showed me that he could write that number, as well as "three," and that he could write his own name. As he left, his movements were more open; he was carrying his load of drawings and not clinging to mother. He permitted himself a look around my house and yard and said, "I want to look around sometime."

Children like Rickie make a therapist understand what Winnicott (1971b) described as his sense that the initial interview is a sacred occasion when the child quickly develops such a trusting relationship that one has confidence that "deep work" can be done in a relatively brief time (pp. 6–7). This assurance is clearly facilitated by the existence of parental belief in the therapist and in the therapeutic process and by the therapist's sense of being able to count on the parents for that "average expectable environment" that will let the child continue to build on the transformations that may take place.

I saw this boy as using his own body to represent a situation that challenged both his cognitive and his emotional equipment. Already familiar with abdominal distensions and discomforts, he was engaging in a sort of cross-modal transfer of information from within to perceptions of his mother's pregnancy, and vice versa. He had, I guessed, strong identifications with his mother and was well able to engage in imitations of her. Those very identifications were an aspect of his own anxiety at this time. Her own discomforts about discourse with him on the topic of pregnancy and birth, I was speculating, may have momentarily "derailed the dialogue" (Spitz, 1964) and forced him to employ body language rather than images and words. In this first session, however, he manifested an intent to move toward making shapes and using speech to learn what he needed to know.

In the second hour Rickie continued his drawings of these shapes, sometimes including "bananas." He experimented briefly with some plasticine but found it difficult to handle and asked for "water clay." I did not have it immediately available but promised it for next time. Rickie spoke directly of how mother had a baby in her tummy, and he struggled with the issue of how the baby could get out of that place. He kept depicting little doors on his round shapes, but they did not satisfy him. He said determinedly, "I am going to work it out!" I heard this statement as a clear indication that, although I could stand by to be of help if invited, I was not to intrude upon his "primary creative activity" (Winnicott, 1971a, p. 2). He was able to be verbally explicit about wanting to be alone, albeit in my presence, when at times I would make a comment and he was totally absorbed with his own images. He would say to me, "I'm not answering you right now because I am busy!" He became increasingly frustrated, however, by his inability to figure how the baby would get out. When he said in his discouragement, "I guess I'll have to give up; it'll have to just stay in there," I took this comment as a call for assistance, and he was then open to that. I took a rubber band and said, "Do you think there might be an opening that could stretch?" He liked that idea very much and played the rest of the session with placing the rubber band over the little doors that he had drawn.

I was now speculating that the problem of how the fetus could exit from the womb was also Rickie's problem of how to make a separation from the mother without hurting her. Increasingly impressed with his basically strong sense of core self as manifest in his clearly setting himself up as the center of this action, his awareness of his own feelings and dilemmas, and his purposefulness in his play and having no doubts about his "going-on being," I had no difficulty following Winnicott's (1971b) prescription to let the interviews be dominated by the child and not by me (p. 10). He was demonstrating that I was allowed to intervene if and when he requested my help.

In the third and, as it turned out, the last session, which I was able to allow to go on an extra half hour, I had prepared the "water clay" that he had suggested. As before, he sat beside me on the floor, while mother watched intently. With the clay Rickie made big, round shapes, placed a tiny baby rubber doll in the middle, and closed it all up in there. "Now, how will he get out?" he asked himself. He took some clay tools, opened up the shape and removed the baby (a cesarean of sorts, I thought). He tried to make the infant stand up, but it could not do so. "He'll have to be born again," Rickie announced, and he wrapped the baby up in clay again and commented, "He should be able to stand up." I noted casually that babies usually cannot stand at first, but Rickie answered, "Pretty soon!" He went through this play several times; he would take the baby out, try to stand him up, and put him back in. Several times he worried that the baby might be hungry, so he gave him some "pizza" to eat while in there and offered mother and me each a piece, which we were to pretend to devour.

He experimented with making little openings and said at one point, "One to go in, and three to come out." Mother and I both took this comment (as I learned in a subsequent hour with her) to indicate some awareness of a third orifice in her body, as the pictures she had shown him indicated, including one he might not possess. That he was not relinquishing absolutely his own possible "openings" as suitable was perhaps indicated in his occasional questioning of me, "Whose baby is it?" When I echoed his question, "Whose?" he declared, "Rickie's!" I said, "Rickie wishes he could make a baby, too." He sighed and said, "It is taking mother a very long time!" (as though to affirm that he might do it more expeditiously).

Now he began to struggle with the time factor and debated leaving the baby enclosed in the clay while he was gone, because it "might not be ready" to come out until he came back. Then he decided that it would be born. He piled the clay on very high and used half the crock, and the clay did look quite like mother's bulging tummy. There was so much clay that he could hardly find the baby, which he had immersed in water in the "womb" (mother and I reminded him of this word, which was in the book she had shown him to designate the "special place" in her body for the baby). He said, "Now it can float out of its room – I mean womb." The baby and the little obstetrician both became very messy in this process. He handed the baby to me to clean, and we both went into the adjacent bathroom to wash.

When we came back into the playroom, Rickie for the first time paid attention to the dollhouse and its contents. Noticing the little toilet, he had the daddy doll stand and urinate, then the boy doll, too. I thought that the penis was about to find its way into this drama. If he had to reconcile himself to the absence of a womb, he would be able to console himself with a piece of equipment daddies and their sons have that mommies do not, and perhaps he was on the way to discovering some of its potential role in the making of babies.

There was a final interview with Mrs. B, who reported that she had found the whole experience fascinating, and to her amazement her son's bowel withholding had ceased. "Sometimes he makes a bit of a fuss when I tell him to go to the toilet, but then he surprises me by doing it on his own!" She had bought him "water clay" and had rather imitated my simply staying by as a potential resource, ready to answer questions or make suggestions if he wanted. Most of all, she was enjoying the process, and her tensions about him and doubts about her mothering were significantly diminished. She was pleased with her son and with herself, and, of course, Mr. B approved her taking over the situation. In view of the imminent birth of the second baby, it was decided that no further appointments would be made. Mrs. B, however, called me several times over the next year to report that "the problem is totally gone," that Rickie had shown a basically loving attitude to the new sibling, and that he was "just terrific."

DISCUSSION

Readers familiar with Freud's (1909) case of Little Hans may be struck by the fact that both Hans and Little Rickie were entertaining fantasies of anal babies, but the therapists viewed their cases differently and conducted treatment very differently.

Freud approached Hans from the standpoint of his drive theory, and he interpreted events in oedipal terms and emphasized the relationship with the father. He knew ahead of time the interpretations that would have to be made to Little Hans, albeit through the father. In his supervision of the father's interventions, however, he did become aware that the latter was asking too many questions and pushing the inquiry along his own lines (p. 64) – an easy thing to do when one starts out with definite preconceptions. The questioning approach was not congruent with Freud's recommendation of "unbiased attention to every point that arises" (p. 65). Yet he was convinced that Hans "had to be told many things that he could not say himself, that he had to be presented with thoughts which he had so far shown no signs of possessing, and that his attention had to be turned in the direction from which his father was expecting something to come" (p. 104). He did not seem to suggest that, in response to questions that Hans might himself directly ask, the father might consider telling the boy the truth as he knew it. Yet he saw Hans tell of a box full of babies as "revenge against the father for the stork story." Freud manifested delight when he could observe that the little patient was taking an active stance in the treatment and, indeed, that the father was finding it hard to catch up.

Rereading that famous case, one could worry lest Hans develop something of a "false self" (Winnicott, 1960a) out of some need to comply with the barrage of insistent interpretations. Certainly the domain of verbal relatedness presented him with more than even the usual dangers that he could be alienated from the "personal, immediate level intrinsic to the other domains of relatedness" (Stern, 1985, p. 163). Although I doubt that his creative spirit could be completely squelched, he did declare to his father (who was at the time pushing his oedipal interpretations), "You know everything; I didn't know any-thing" (Freud, 1909, p. 90). If a main goal of all therapy is to restore and strengthen the sense of agency in the patient, that statement could inform the therapist that something had gone wrong. One might, however, suspect that Hans's comment was made tongue in cheek, a complication of play, perhaps playing along; father had behaved as though he knew it all, and Hans would "admit" to an ignorance that was not real! Freud acknowledged that the child knows "in his uncon-scious" where babies come from (p. 129), for he feels sensations in his "widdler" when he thinks of these things.

With little Rickie, I was less impressed with oedipal problems than with a threatened derailing of dialogue with the mother, whom I saw as a good-enough mother. In her overeagerness to perform her role perfectly, she was behaving as though she might wound him by simply answering his questions as they came. Her constraints around dealing with matters verbally may have been one reason for his resorting to body symbolism to comprehend pregnancy and birth. I suspect that his sensitivity to her body language may have revealed to him her discomfort even about showing him the book with its illustrations and reading to him from it. The nonverbal and the verbal dialogue intermingled and rather canceled out each other.

I also hypothesized some motivations from within Rickie himself. Kestenberg (1975), out of her extensive studies of infants and of preverbal behavior, posited that when boys hold back feces or urine, they sense pressure on the inner genital organs. While immediate release is "experienced as surrender to both bodily demands and mother's commands," holding back can afford the child the experience of making and forming the bowel movement, which otherwise would be rather fluid. So the experience of making can be felt as a practical, creative process, associated with the illusory creativeness of the transitional object (p. 31). Or, as Shor (1954) suggested, the passive yielding of infancy may have to give way to a stage of active holding and containing, so that the inner object can be possessed. Only then can the child enjoy the active experience of giving (p. 16).

Kestenberg saw the inner genital drives as the "primary sources of male 'motherliness' " (p. 52), and she did not imagine that the boy's entertaining the image of a shared baby means that he wants to become a woman. Growing up to be a mother would "rob him of his precious organ," but growing up to be a father would mean that he could never have a baby inside. As Kestenberg put it, "The anal baby is not only a possession but also a product from which the child parts with sorrow before he is able to give it away to his mother as a present" (p. 31). To give up this preoedipal union, this primary identification with mother, is one of the steps in developing a self-representation as separate from that of the mother. Rickie's affirmation of maleness in that final scene of his therapy would seem to be in that direction, and his subsequent "gift" of feces to mother was perhaps possible because he had claimed primary ownership.

I would not rule out that oedipal features may be lurking somewhere in the picture. What seems significant to me, however, is what kind of equipment the child brings to the negotiation of the triangular relationship. It will be, to a large extent, dependent on the qualities of the primary dyadic relationship with the mother. In the very earliest sensorimotor connectedness with the mother, the infant may sense some of her attitudes toward the father, and the infant's impressions then may be reinforced later in the period of heightened "social referencing" (Emde and Sorce, 1983). Although there seemed to be some manifest tensions between Rickie's parents, Mr. B proclaiming the high value of autonomy and Mrs. B declaring for the merits of turning to experts for advice, they did some compromising with each other, out of which both may have gained. Rickie showed identifications with both; he took charge of his own therapy but could also accept my input. So the gains were minimally because of interpretations and maximally because he and I both believed we could rely on "playing it out."

My approach also differs markedly from that of the Kleinians, with their emphasis on interpretation. They imagine that in the earliest stages of life the infant fantasies the mother as containing the father's penis, or even the whole father, and the father as containing the mother's breasts and vagina—all in a state of perpetual gratification (O'Shaughnessy, 1987). The child, ill-equipped to negotiate the oedipal period, tries to keep the conflict invisible by fracturing the combined parents and keeping them widely apart. I suggest that the conflict may be somewhat invisible, too, in those children especially well ready to deal with it, and they may show minimum need to separate the parents. We could note that Rickie did not rule out that the baby was to be the father's; it was more that he ruled in that it was also to be his. One had the impression that these three members of the triangle enjoyed each other; they might play out oedipal conflicts, too.

Rickie gave me reasons from the very first interview to trust in his self-reparative inclinations. He seemed to regard me as a new object in a new context, and, after allowing himself the time he felt necessary to size me up diagnostically, he moved into conjoint play to figure out the mysteries of pregnancy and birth. He was able to dose himself and to instruct me as to when he wanted or did not want my interventions. Although there was certainly a purposefulness about him, it was something less than urgent, and he could enjoy the process without impatience for some final product or result.

Treatment was simultaneous of child and mother. Bion (1962b) tells us that the mother who would transform the infant's unpleasant affects into something tolerable and manageable must be able to engage in reverie – an openness to whatever that baby presents. Mrs. B seemed to emulate my simply attending, with interest and without anxiety, to what Rickie did and said. She had previously tended to be overidentified with him and dared to manifest only empathy, but she had not dared to maintain her own separateness. He was to some extent her product, and she was having difficulty "letting him out." She may have absorbed some of my confidence in his self-righting tendencies, and that could enable her son's trust in her to grow so that their dialogue could become more playful. She could then cease communicating that some topics are unspeakable and hence potentially unthinkable.

When I first read "Little Hans," I remember being sad at Freud's (1909) stating at the end of the treatment that he "learnt nothing new from this analysis" (p. 147). I feel that if I have learned nothing new, perhaps the patient has not either. Children like Rickie have taught me and continue to teach me many things, including how some of Freud's own ideas appear in the clinical situation and how these intermesh with more current writings. The idea that "the ego is first and foremost a body ego" (Freud, 1923, p. 26) comes to life with the child who is at the junction of psychosomatic representation with that of the verbal. Winnicott (1960a) takes the matter further with his emphasis on pleasure and spontaneity in human life and his affirmation that the true self is "the summation of sensory motor aliveness" (p. 149). In the beginning, he writes, psyche and soma are not distinguished; the psyche develops by "imaginative elaboration of somatic parts, feelings, and functions" (1949, p. 244). In time the body, with its inside and outside, is *"felt by the individual"* to form the core of the imaginative self (p. 244). The first imagery will be based on body sensations, and as significant persons respond empathically to this "symbolism of the body," it will be gradually transformed into images that are "motivated signs" (Piaget, 1951), that is, still close to the sense of body self. To ring true, something outside must be congruent with the inside sense. To stay close to the ideas that the patient portrays may enable the child – or the adult – to arrive at concepts that are intermediate between inner and outer and hence to enjoy her primary creativity (Winnicott, 1971a, p. 2).

Both Little Hans and Rickie were looking for words to express the mysteries they sought to understand, for only with words could they hope to transcend both body language and imagery. When children feel that the words that adults offer are suitable containers for their "unthought knowns" (Bollas, 1987), they can maintain their sense of having, in some measure, created the thought themselves. Their trust in the other will be enhanced, and they will not be stuck in authoritarian constructs but will move on playfully to emend whatever theories they have evolved to date.

LEARNING FROM CHILDREN ABOUT PLAY IN THERAPY

Each child entering a therapist's playroom first tests the safety of the literal and emotional space to ascertain its relative freedom from potential dangers, among them whether she could dare to express herself without unwanted impingements from this new adult and whether the other would be there to help if and when called on. Then the little patient uses the resources provided to make her own images and stories. In the course of that activity, the child will sometimes want experiences of being "alone together" (Winnicott, 1971) and of plumbing her own depths for "news from within" (Bollas, 1987). At other times, she reaches to be "together together" and to share meanings in ways that feel as though they expand the sense of individual space and of what might be accomplished within it. Then she may move back to her separate realm, meanings enhanced by the shared moments, the "capacity to be alone" strengthened (Winnicott, 1958). Throughout the therapy, one can observe this dialectic process.

Children generally take charge of their own therapy. They assign the roles and admit us to their space voluntarily or not at all. They are skilled protectors of their own privacy, often in ways that "polite" adults would abjure. Adults are more likely either to conform to imagined expectations or to manifest subtle defenses against compliance. They are also more inclined to award the therapist the role of expert and to elicit advice. Children keep themselves in the role of engineers of the oscillating distancing and drawing closer; they insist on being designers of the dialectic.

Child therapists differ in their opinions about the centrality of the role of interpretation. Melanie Klein (1955) tends to make it central and sees her task as making the unconscious conscious. Others of us feel it possible that an overemphasis on a verbal interpretive approach may itself become repressive and thwart the child's spontaneous development of self-knowledge. We feel that it may be unnecessary to aim too directly at the undoing of defenses when we could rely on the health-promoting aspects of playing itself and on the "power of the unfolding, relatively undefended transitional play process" (Downey, 1987, p. 109).

While Klein sees the language of play as an essential part of the child's mode of expression, she is mainly interested in it to decipher its symbolism, which she sees as similar to that of the language of dreams, requiring interpretation. Certainly children like Rickie, with highly developed psycholinguistic capacities, create highly imaginative play and can use language to report on the past, project into the future, and explore beyond the realities with which they are familiar. In a state of play they can in some measure arrive at their own interpretations or ask for assistance when they feel stuck. Such children manifest great flexibility of themes if they are in a longer therapy than was Rickie, and the same play may at different times manifest different concerns. The oedipal child can suspend disbelief and at the same time perceive the inconsistencies between his feelings – say, of wanting to make a baby himself – and actuality.

Klein often reports her child patients teaching her that they do know the difference between make-believe and "for real." A little boy to whom she had interpreted that his damaging a toy represented attacks on his brother assured her that he would attack only the toy brother.

For some of us, Klein (1955) does not attend enough to the actual world of the child outside therapy. As I recently reread her interpretation to one child that, when he smashed toys, his behavior "stood in his unconscious for smashing his father's genital" (p. 12), I thought of an adult patient of mine who recurrently reported that when he and his brother had fought over a toy, the father had become enraged and stamped the contested item to smithereens. If this story had been related to Klein, would she have found a way to weave it into her interpretation? As I view her, she overemphasizes the role of fantasy and does not sufficiently conceptualize its interplay with events in the child's real world. As it happened, Klein's little patient, then three years and nine months old, had just rejected an earlier interpretation, then seemingly accepted it, but then went on to vent anger at a toy! It is possible that his rage may have been at his analyst's insistent interpretation.

However critical I may sound about Klein's overzealous interpreting, I am grateful to her for her rich contributions. Many of her conclusions about child development have been validated by infant observation and research. Object relations do start almost at first, and all aspects of mental life are tied up with object relations. Whereas previous psychoanalysts emphasized the father, Klein enables us to see in both boy and girl babies an early identification with the mother. Current researchers confirm the importance of the mother, not only for identification but for experiences of "primary intersubjectivity" (Trevarthen, 1979). They do not, however, find evidence for a paranoid schizoid stage, except maybe in the case of high-risk babies.

Today, many of us posit more interactive play with the mother than Klein knew was possible, and we observe that eyes are as important as breasts in early human connectedness. While we agree with Klein that the superego has roots in life far earlier than the oedipal period, we do not see the early conscience as therefore cruel and sadistic. Rather, if there has been good-enough mothering, there is likely a "capacity for concern" (Winnicott, 1963a).

Klein, like a number of analysts who have treated children, feels that her contributions to psychoanalytic theory derived from the play technique she evolved with young children. Like her, I have found it a great advantage to have treated both children and adults. One learns from children how they process present experiences of various kinds, and one learns from adults about memories of analogous experiences, now reprocessed with the relatively mature emotional and mental equipment acquired in later years. Not only are genetic reconstructions facilitated, but the therapist is better equipped to enable the patient to experience empathy for her own earlier versions of the self and the others who were significant during the growing-up years. As Klein foresaw, the insights psychoanalysis has gained have thus made it possible for us to attempt treatment with patients once considered unsuitable for our method.

The therapist who can keep the play spirit alive in herself as she ventures to treat those previously thought to be untreatable has a great advantage, for she will have enhanced ways to cope with the potentially troublesome countertransferences that can otherwise impede therapy. Playfulness can do for her what I have cited Greenacre (1959a) declaring it can do for the child; it can aid "in delivering the unconscious fantasy and harmonizing it with the external world" (p. 571).

I find myself thinking of Jekels, who, with Bergler (1934), more than a half century ago, was already speculating about the preoedipal period as its effects were manifest in adult analysands. In one of Jekels's papers (1932), he ends up musing that "the gods turn to pleasure the work of the man they love," and he explains the hidden meaning of that statement: "He who works is loved by the gods, loved by his super-ego – and has no sense of guilt" (p. 87). Although Jekels makes no mention of playing, he seems to have imagined a situation in which a certain playfulness would pervade work, and eros would "not only tame aggression but put it to use for its own purposes" (p. 85).

CHAPTER 4

The Scene: Space and Time of the Therapeutic Playground

The scene, says Burke (1945), a philosopher of language and human conduct, "must constitute a fit container for the act." Since the action that I want to facilitate is infused with playfulness, I concern myself with a setting that the patient may experience as safe, out of which he may construct both "intermediate space" (Winnicott, 1971a) and, inextricably related to it, "intermediate time." If we see psychotherapy and psychoanalysis as possible modes of creating fresh versions of the self, then, just as in the making of a work of art, there needs to be room for "the unique psycho-physical rhythms of the person making it. Otherwise it will have no life in it whatever, for there is no other source of life" (Milner, 1957, p. 230). Both space and time ideally will allow for the externalization of these subjective aspects and their intermingling with the objective, so that the patient may experience a sense of his own creativity, rather than his accommodating to conditions imposed from outside. It is, says Winnicott (1971a), "creative apperception more than anything else that makes the individual feel that life is worth living" (p. 65).

Huizinga (1944), whose work on play has been very important for me, writes that "all play has its being within a playground marked off beforehand, either materially or ideally, deliberately or as a matter of course" (p. 10). Echoing both Burke and Huizinga, Milner (1957) observes that "frames can be thought of both in time and space. . . . An acted play is usually, nowadays, framed by the stage, in space, and by the raising and lowering of the curtain in time" (p. 225). She (1952) would have the analytic frame allow for "contemplative action" as distinguished from the expedient, for "the capacity to achieve mind-lessness" (p. 81), which she elsewhere equates with reverie. In other words, there must be, as in childhood, room for becoming lost in play.

Here I attend to some aspects of the material playground as they facilitate such actions between the two participants, but since Burke's schema includes each person as part of the scene for the other, I occasionally include some aspects of myself and my own philosophy.

Therapists are not always in charge of constructing the material playground. My first professional experience was in a hospital where I both lived and worked. Interviews with patients were, for the most part, on the ward, with minimal privacy. When I saw them on leave or discharge from the hospital, I visited them in their homes, where other members of the family often hovered and claimed their time and space. In neither locale was it easy to keep to any clear and predictable schedule, and the place was dubiously safe. Yet, often the patient and I could seemingly transcend the literal scene and constitute a psychic scene for one another. I have often been grateful for having had those experiences, since many circumstances can come along that make such rising above the situation necessary.

When I first began to work with children, I was employed in a large family service agency, which provided no playroom at all. Had I not had the encouragement and supervision of Margaret Mahler, I should never have dared to do play therapy as I did—with Central Park for the literal playground. Safe time and space were not easy to achieve. I had to pick up my little patients in their apartment dwellings, and we took buses or subways to the park. These children were, for the most part, "atypical," and I could not easily relax as I had to hold tightly to their hands to prevent their impulsive darting away, as they, at times, seemed oblivious to traffic or to losing me. In the park we trudged to their favorite spots, which we often did not have to ourselves. Again, I found that in spite of obstacles, outside and inside, over time we could develop something of a working-playing relationship, which—supple-mented by collaboration with mothers and, occasionally, fathers—could bring about changes. Interviews with the parents often had to be conducted in the family's home, usually because the mother could not leave her several children to come to the office but sometimes because no office was available when she or the father could come. It was a kind of musical chairs situation, with therapists' scheduling office space for given hours. So even if we were fortunate enough to land a room, we had to bear in mind that we had to be out by such and such a time; we had a sense of borrowed space.

When, at last, I was employed in a psychiatric clinic, I enjoyed an office of my own. It was, of course, somewhat barren, furnished by some agency of government, but I rendered it more "mine" by endowing it with a few personal belongings. Then, in the private clinic where I worked, I had not only an office for my adult patients but a playroom that I could design for children, complete with sandbox, water, and a supply of toys and creative materials such as easels, papers, paints, and clay. I daubed the white walls with splashes of color, so that the occasional daubing of children would be of little consequence. For many years I felt professionally at home in that setting, and my patients were attached to the place, too.

Then, for various reasons, I decided to go into private practice, but not without some wrenching feelings. I discovered both in myself and in many of my patients the love of place that Bachelard (1958) calls "topophilia." We had loved the previous space; it had seemed to hold our togetherness, almost to represent it. Particularly those children who had in their personal lives experienced unwanted moving found this change of scene difficult. Some were able to be angry with me about it and were resentful and scolding. Others acted it out in overt hostility to the new offices. Adults took the change more politely, but both they and I sometimes dreamed or daydreamed of the former setting, and we clearly held onto this piece of the meaningful past. As Bachelard writes, "In its countless alveoli space contains compressed time. That is what space is for" (p. 8).

The new space was ultimately accepted by us all. I had an opportunity, purely according to my tastes, to furnish both the office for seeing adults and the playroom for children. By now that space, too, has been relegated to memory, as have the subsequent office and the resistances of its tenant and clients to the further moves. There was at least a decade in each; although few clients were around that long, for many who worked and played deeply in those scenes, those "domains of intimacy" probably exerted ongoing powers of attraction, since the clients created that space in their imaginations – or in some instances several of those spaces if they, at times, interrupted and then resumed therapy.

"It is better," says Bachelard (1958) "to live in a state of impermanence than in one of finality" (p. 61). It was not for that reason that I moved my office once again–this time to home, and I do hope to "house" that desirable impermanence somewhere other than in this material place, for I very much like this being "at home with patients."

As with other moves, there were patients who vehemently chastised me for departing from that last office. Some were not comfortable with driving the hill or worried about parking their cars on a slope, lest brakes give way. For those so concerned, there were blocks to put behind their wheels, and soon they discovered that putting the gear in park and setting their own brakes were sufficient. Others took to the new place quickly. They loved the quiet of the neighborhood and the view, and they appreciated not having to pay for parking as they had to do in a business building. Some of the young and energetic athletes among them elected to park at the bottom of the hill and to walk, run, or bicycle up the 1.8 miles to my house, and they occasionally stopped to enjoy an ocean view. So the meanings were different for different persons, but, in time, all came to create their own images of this new scene.

New patients who do not have to deal with their own reluctances to move from old scenes tend to discover many features that lend themselves to their twofold imaginations: their projections and their introjections about time and space. To begin with, there is the waiting room. Unlike those waiting rooms in most professional office buildings, this one is not hermetically sealed but is quite open, with a skylight above and large floor-to-ceiling windows revealing the garden five steps below, and in the distance are the city, the ocean, and–on those days when the smog permits–the island of Catalina. When I take on new patients, I explain that they are to ring the doorbell so that I know they are here and that they may wait in this room. There is, of course, a table with magazines and newspapers. I also inform them of the nearby location of the lavatory.

Most patients come a few minutes early, relax, and often sit quietly. They report a contemplative mood and sometimes reflect that it feels "healing" just to be there. Some are attentive to the plants and watch for signs of blooming or of the close of the flowering season, and we find that these observations may be congruent with internal rhythms.

Others watch the birds, including the hummingbirds that sip from red sugar water in the feeders hanging from the roof outside, and are alert to those species that are regular dwellers here and those that come and go with the seasons. Still others never comment on such matters but preoccupy themselves with the morning newspaper or the journals.

There are a few who never wait at all. They arrive at the precise moment when their appointments are scheduled and stand by the door until I come for them. Neither open spaces nor open times seem to be experienced by them as "friendly expanses" (Balint, 1959) as they begin their therapies. Their felt urgencies are obstacles to reverie and to playfulness. Of course, there are those who rather consistently arrive late, in which case I am forced to be the waiting one, and how I deal with that issue is a function both of my personal relationships with open time and of my professional philosophy about the time dimensions of psychotherapy.

For all human beings affect has been the element responsible over the course of development for the sense of time as duration (Spitz, 1972). Writing of the earliest experiences of time, Spitz sees the

> bond between affect and percept as a bridge, made of duration, antici-
> pation, and *meaning:* a bridge to span the void across the chasm in front
> of the soma, a bridge reaching toward the shore of an as yet nonexistent
> psychic system – toward a shore which anticipation and meaning are in
> the act of creating and fashioning; and on which duration uses predictive
> hypotheses to mix the cement for the engrams of the first landing stage,
> (italics added), [p. 316].

In this rather poetic style, Spitz suggests what E. Balint (1953) puts in another way. She says that waiting will be easier or harder depending on how well the person has "overcome at an early age the difficulty caused by the time-lag between one satisfaction and the next by transferring enjoyment and love from the satisfactory moment itself to the ability to pass through the time between two satisfactions" (p. 127). Perhaps that ability means that the person had some sense of "creating and fashioning" and hence could even enjoy some empty time.

When we experience inefficiencies of the self as tension or unpleasure that cannot be mastered promptly, we want relief from a "good" object. If, in our early lives, we experienced our caretakers as providing that relief before we became distraught, we came actively to feel a positive expectation, for the most part. For Freud (1925b) this capacity to anticipate need fulfillment was the beginning of the thinking process. For Erikson (1956) it contributed "temporal elements to the formation of basic trust" (p. 97). So the ability to wait depended in the beginning on the quality of object relationships, and the repair of the inability to wait depends on some re-creation of the original situation, but with different outcomes.

There is a quality in the infant that persists throughout life, a preference for contour and movement, which "is clearly adaptive, for the focus of change is likely to contain the most information about the presence of his mother or of danger" (Kagan, 1970, p. 828). As James (1890) wrote long ago, "Awareness of change is the condition on which our perception of time's flow depends" (p. 620). Hartocollis (1983) proposed that "time is the experience of change with reference to a personal self. To the extent that attention is on the self, the perception of change around it is accentuated," and "to the extent that attention is away from the self, change is perceived but little; the time sense merges into the essence of one's self–time ceases to exist" (p. 5). This experience is quite familiar to people during a creative process.

Probably in most office buildings the passage from the waiting room is directly into the consulting room. In my home office, there is not such an instantaneous move. Instead, there are a few seconds of transitional space and time. The patient glimpses parts of the living area of the house before entering the hallway leading to the office. To the right is an indoor garden, with a sunken hot tub and a pool with goldfish. I recognized when I first made my office at home that patients would know more about me by this location. I quickly learned that no two of them would 'know' the same things and that what they would make of what they perceived would be significant for our dialogue.

For instance, an attorney, referred by his wife, reluctantly accepted an exploratory session because she was alarmed about their deteriorating relationship. He arrived late, with no time for waiting, and his brisk walk with me to the office seemed to have allowed little time to take in much. He sat down, looked at me sternly, and accused me, "You are breaking the law!" I had no idea to what he referred, but he went on, "You have a policeman's club!" Now, he was right, I did have one, a gift to me by the police of Guyana, where I had done some extensive mental health consultation. Interestingly enough, the police themselves in that country had felt initially forced to attend my seminars for them but then had ended up enthusiastic and had expressed their gratitude by giving me a ceremonial club made of gorgeous Guayanese hardwood. I had never displayed it prominently; in fact, for some years it had lain on top of some bookcases above the eye level of most guests in the house and had never even been commented on before. Certainly I did not know that in possessing it I was breaking the law. It was easy to interpret this man's indictment of me as a collusion with his wife's authoritarian demand that he seek some therapy "or else." Since I would not continue with any person who felt he was here only under duress, I rather quickly dispelled his sense of coercion, and we subsequently engaged in several years of treatment, out of which he overcame his habit of arriving at trials so late that several judges had threatened to ban him from their courts.

Often the dreams of patients will take as their "day residue" some aspect of my house but will turn it into a symbol for something with which they are struggling. Thus, one patient who worried from the beginning whether he could make anything of his analysis and who indeed had a chronic self-complaint about superficiality, reported what he called "a piece of a dream": "I am in the backyard of a house. There is a pond in which the water has dropped drastically. A man says to me, 'Now the water is good for drinking.' I am surprised, since it would seem to be the opposite, but I do not argue the matter since I know I am not going to drink it." Now, in fact, the water had dropped in my fish pond in response to both the summer heat and a small leak. The analysand associated to water and how he was always drawn to it. He had, he said, noticed my pool but it had "no deep significance" for him. His father had once built a pond; he and a friend had once been looking for a snake that they thought crawled into it, and they had punctured the bottom with a pitchfork. On a nearby stream they had loved to explore the "deeper" pools because they contained curious things. "We were always trying to find out what was on the bottom." Like many dreams with their associations, this one was pregnant with possible meanings, but the one that was then closest to our concerns was that he was creating a metaphor for his analysis as well as his modus operandi in life—that he was curious (sometimes he declared little curiosity) and that he wanted to look both for snakes (bad, possibly dangerous) and for treasures (good, surprising). There was some voice within that would settle for drinking shallowly, but the main feeling, on which he intended to act, was that he would not partake of such shallowness. He would plumb the depths.

Bachelard (1958), in his ponderings on the dialectics of inside and outside, observes that "the door is an entire cosmos of the Half-open. In fact, it is one of its primal images, the very origin of a daydream that accumulates desires and temptations: the temptation to open up the ultimate depths of being, and the desire to conquer all reticent beings" (p. 222). It may be closed or open, and we may cross the threshold hesitantly or eagerly.

One enters my office itself through a sliding door. Most patients close it behind them. Others regularly leave it open. Recently an analysand lay on the couch and reflected on the many ways I must have seen her entering that door: in the beginning, when she wore only the most casual of clothing, baggy slacks and big shirts that concealed her feminine attributes; other periods when she arrived dripping with sweat, clad in form-fitting jogging shorts and tops, after she had run up the hill; then, in embarrassment, when she dressed in the first garments she ever bought for herself and was uncertain of her tastes and half-wishing not to be seen; and more recently, when she wore lovely dresses, nice jewelry, perfume. Over all that time, we were looking at what was going on under those surface appearances and attempting to render the sartorial realm one in which playful experimentation was possible. Here this young woman was imagining her entrances and the effect on her audience of one and reflecting not only on content but on processes as the door itself provoked the memories of her changing images of her self. She was, in her way, answering the question posed by Bachelard (1958) as to whether the one who opens the door is the same being who closed it. He writes, "If one were to give an account of all the doors one has closed and opened, of all the doors one would like to re-open, one would have to tell the story of one's entire life" (p. 224).

There are also those who make ritual entrances. One woman casts a brief glance at me and greets me peremptorily as she enters, places her coat carefully on a nearby chair, then busies her eyes with a look out the window as she seats herself on the couch. She places her handbag on the coffee table, takes off her dark glasses and places them into their case, and, in turn, places this into her handbag. From it she removes the regular glasses in their case, takes them out, dons them. Then she leans over, removes her shoes, and lies down. (She is my only patient who takes off shoes; there is a small rug on the foot of the couch that clearly announces that removing shoes is not necessary.) Quite frequently some change then falls from the pocket of her slacks, and she collects it and places it on the coffee table. Then she looks around a bit, even at me. (I sit off to the patient's right side, only slightly behind the area of the pillow, so the person can easily see me.) This woman may ask questions such as "How do you feel to have your trees trimmed?" or "Why do you sometimes pull the drapes?" These questions are interconnected, since having the trees trimmed means that the morning sun comes in more strongly, and on very sunny days the room can become too warm unless the drapes are shut. I answer all such direct questions directly but look for ways in which they may be metaphors for other themes of the patient. This patient does not yet show much of the "quiet alert"; rather, she shows a predominance of an "anxious alert" to everything outside herself that accompanies a reticence to focus very much on what is inside. This anxious state includes a hyperalertness about time. She teases me about the bird's-eye maple clock that I keep on the high wall above the alcove to the room and claims that it is never precisely accurate. There are no numbers on its face, but one can generally know about where we are in the 50-minute hour. Nevertheless, she often inquires toward the end, "How many more minutes have we?" She may decide to leave a minute or two early when she feels she has come to the end of what she wants to say just then. Neither space nor time feels quite safe to her as yet, and certainly she has not let herself experience the sense of timelessness that might accompany a benign regression.

Some of my analytic colleagues question the wisdom of having a clock visible to the analysand; they fear that it will discourage the development of a transference neurosis. Indeed, Doolittle (1956) reports that Freud chided her for even looking at her watch and told her, "I keep an eye on the time. I will tell you when the session is over" (p. 17). I have not found that the presence of the clock impedes desirable regression. What has been called the "repetition compulsion" I think of as a manifestation of the reparative urge and an unconscious sense that something must be relived in a new context if deep changes are to occur. Ideally, I see the patient in charge of the timing and duration of regressive experiences in therapy and of the rebounds from such immersions into past versions of self and of relationships. When the patient can feel that the therapist does not force a variety of play for which he does not feel ready, the playground will have gained in safety. The regression, when it comes, is much more likely to be benign. Otherwise, there is danger of an iatrogenic transference neurosis.

To have a clock in view does permit patients to utilize some old defenses until they have ascertained that there is no need for them. Thus, one woman who was particularly apprehensive about being rejected chose for some while to leave her session before I announced the end of the time. She was thus able to maintain the initiative; she left me before I dismissed her. This behavior required no interpretation; we both understood it without words. She dropped it when she was secure that I really wanted her as a patient.

Some patients seem quite unaware that there is a clock. They never seem to look at it, and they are content to wait for me to signal the end of the session. They allow themselves perhaps an illusion of timelessness.

In fact, many persons seem relatively oblivious of the contents of the room much of the time. Then, at some moment, they may suddenly notice something that has been there all along and will ask if it is a new acquisition. Recently I became aware of a smile breaking out on the face of a patient who had allowed herself some moments of silence. Out of her state of quiet alert she had been surprised to note the small statue of Freud on an end table by the couch. She said, "I never noticed him before! He's looking at my feet!" It was a period in which her work and play were aimed at achieving some integration of a long enduring "split" between body and mind. So Freud's attention to her feet, her "under-standing," amused us both.

I do not prescribe the position a patient should assume, not even for analysis, since I believe that, given a freedom to experiment, each will discover whether lying down or sitting up is best conducive to changing states and aims. This leeway may diminish the likelihood that therapy itself becomes ritualistic. As Greenacre (1959a) writes, "It is likely . . . that the original, the new (whether in form or content) will be derived from fantasy or play which is less rather than more bound by the repetition compulsion" (p. 568). She adds, "Play by definition involves motion or action and usually spontaneity and pleasure" (p. 354). The couch and speaking all thoughts whatsoever can delimit active movement, but, as Greenacre notes, not altogether; we still depend in some measure on elements of the nonverbal.

Some persons always prefer to sit up; others sometimes do so. The positions they assume afford both them and me additional data, from alternative "points of view."

For patients who choose to sit up, the space is different. My chair is placed diagonally in the corner of the room, and there are floor-to-ceiling windows on either side of me. The patient's chair is directly opposite mine, and there is a footstool between us that we may both share. Here again, not all patients use it. Some never do; some always do; and others occasionally do. Patients can see out both windows; the main view is of a canyon, so that birds in flight appear at eye level. There may be hawks and ravens in addition to the many species of smaller birds. If a person comes long enough, he may well see a deer. One day a man, his eyes widening, exclaimed, "Well, a deer is eavesdropping!" The event provides a momentary distraction, perhaps less harshly intrusive than the sounds of jackhammers and shouting workmen, which can interrupt the process in many office quarters.

Depending on the time of day, I may or may not be sharply visible to the seated patient. If the person is bothered by the backlighting, the drapes can be adjusted to compensate, and there are some who regularly request this adjustment. After some initial sessions most patients tend to gaze a lot at the scene, which they do not particularly see but which invokes a kind of reverie, perhaps analogous to what analysts hope the couch will provide. This abstracted musing seems to happen when they have looked at me enough to be able to see in their inner minds the likely expressions on my face. When they have this internal image sufficiently, they are then freer to oscillate between visually connecting with me and plumbing their inside worlds.

I, of course, have an opportunity to see the faces of my seated patients as I can never fully see those of patients on the couch, even from my somewhat modified analytic position. I am aware that there is an optimal attention that each patient somehow finds comfortable that may shift depending on the issues of the moment. At base the degree of comfort or discomfort may depend on the sort of mirroring that characterized early relationships with the caregivers. If my patients received abundant good mirroring, then to be looked at is not an adverse experience. But if they saw in the eyes of parents negative reflections of themselves, they can suffer some paranoid reactions when they feel the eyes of others too steadily on them. As therapists, we pick up subtle clues from patients as to whether they are at any moment willing to be seen, and probably without conscious decision, we adjust our looking accordingly. As Balint (1968) says, it is important that the therapist be present, but at an optimal distance – "neither so far that the patient might feel lost or abandoned, nor so close that the patient might feel encumbered and unfree" (p. 179).

In some ways the face-to-face position presents additional complications, and no doubt Freud's design of the method of the couch was, in part, to avoid these. Indeed, there are patients who find the couch much easier than the sitting-up position. Perhaps they have but little hope for positive mirroring, such as glimpsing the "gleam in the mother's eye," which Kohut (1971, 1977) thought so essential for self-esteem, or for being able to elicit playful interactions with others by their own eye signals. Clearly if, in the course of analysis, such patients come to want periods of sitting up, these should not be thought of as resistances but as evidence of diminished apprehension about face-to-face encounters.

Does the change of scene change the act? Is there a difference in the rules of discourse depending on whether the patient elects the couch or a sitting position? In all conversations there are certain rules of the game. At least two players are involved. While there is conventional social pressure that decrees that one has a certain obligation to speak when spoken to, that convention is somewhat suspended when one of the two is reclining and the other is somewhere behind. Perhaps the analyst most disengages from this rule and arrogates to herself silences but often regards those of the patient as resistances. Unsophisticated patients are frequently at a loss at first, for, even if the analyst does not explicitly request free association, the absence of the usual regulations of discourse can be distressing. It can take some time before persons can do anything like free-associating or having faith in the value of the muddle it can get them into. To be invited to free-associate is to be invited to break the rules, and that freedom initially feels dangerous to many persons.

NOTES ON THE NONVISUAL PLAY
SPACE FOR DIALOGUE

In his "metalogical" discourse with his daughter, Bateson (1953) uses her questions about why he calls conversations a sort of game to ponder exactly the question that concerns us as therapists interested in the play element in psychotherapy. She thinks that if it is a game, it cannot be serious. Bateson takes on his daughter with her doubts, and they get into a "muddle." This distresses her somewhat, but he shows her that muddles make a sort of sense, that "in order to think new thoughts or say new things, we have to break up all our ready-made ideas and shuffle the pieces" (p. 16). The only alternative is ready-made phrases and ideas, clichés, the same old stuff. She wonders whether, nevertheless, they may somehow have to keep the pieces of thoughts in some order to prevent going mad; he agrees but is not sure just what order. (Perhaps Bateson had an intuition about that "inner organizing pattern-making force" to which Milner (1957) referred and which infant researchers claim to be the basic tendency of the human mind. A confidence in that force could render one less fearful of "going mad.")

Father and daughter go on talking of the rules of talking. He tells her that talking follows some of the same rules as does playing. He draws analogies to the child building with blocks, the latter themselves making some of the rules, since in certain positions they will balance and in others, they will fall; ideas, too, can support each other, but if wrongly put together, the whole structure will collapse. Logic makes them cohesive. She protests that he had said logic leads to clichés, that they were in a muddle again, and that maybe they needed more rules to stop that happening so much. He asks teasingly whether she would rather play canasta than talk, and the two agree on the greater fun of the conversational game, particularly if both have the "game idea."

The daughter persists in thinking that the difference between a game and just playing is that a game has rules. If there are rules, who makes them up? If it is a game, is he playing against her? He tells her that to some extent he does make them up and confesses that he sometimes competes a bit, but essentially they are playing together against the blocks. The purpose of such conversation is to discover the rules, and that discovery, he affirms, is the purpose of life itself. (We could say that therapist and patient "play together against the blocks" and that their purpose is discovering the rules.)

Bateson (1955), in a later article, concerns himself with metacommunication, in which the subject of discourse is the relationship between the speakers. He observes that human beings have a number of ways to signal to each other that "this is play." In speech we convey it by intonation, as well as by lexical means. We also make "play faces";

we smile, posture, employ mock irony. These signals announce the premises from which the person is operating; they make a frame, which is itself metacommunicative. (These are among the ways we know that we are in a dialogic playground in the clinical situation.)

In playing, as in dreaming and fantasying, one does not operate with the concept "untrue"; in these activities there is something like a combination of primary process and secondary process, the terms psychoanalysis has used for wishful and logical thinking, respectively. Like Winnicott (1971a), Bateson observes that this sort of frame thus involves paradox. I would add that the ability to tolerate the ambiguities of paradox is closely connected with an ability to play with dialogue.

The playground of psychoanalysis and analytically oriented therapies is made up of frames within a frame. There is the overall frame, ideally negotiated by therapist and patient conjointly and consisting of the constants that comprise the background of their interactions: the time and place of their meetings, the frequency and duration of sessions, the fees and methods of payment, understanding about vacations and interruptions for whatever reasons, confidentiality. Included in that frame are the being and behavior of the therapist, who becomes, in many respects, part of the context, the "holding environment" of the dialogue as well as a participant in it (Winnicott, 1986). There are also the metabehaviors that signal playful moods and that also signal both time-outs and endings of playing episodes.

In many ways there can be tension between the constants of the situation and the variations that may be introduced by playfulness. Balint (1968) tells of an analytic patient whose complaint was a crippling uncertainty whenever she had to make a decision or take a risk. Some years into the analysis he made an interpretation to the effect that she had always found it important to keep her head up and her feet firmly on the ground. She responded that from early childhood she had longed to do a somersault but never could. Balint asked, "What about now?" She leapt from the couch and executed the acrobatic stunt with no difficulty. He reported this event as a "real breakthrough," and, indeed, it heralded further changes toward greater freedom and elasticity (p. 129). Critics of that scene might accuse the analyst of "breaking the frame" and accuse both of "acting out." It did happen in the context of a transference, which at that moment must have been experienced as a playground by both participants. It was not, strictly speaking, either regression or repetition but represented a new beginning, the therapeutic result of which depended on the work that both preceded and followed the incident (pp. 131–132).

Many and varied are the transference reactions to the overall frame, including reactions to the institution of psychoanalysis itself. As Bleger (1967) has written, "Institutions and the frame always make up a 'ghost world' " (p. 460). To keep up the frame beyond necessity or to avoid any change in the relationship with the frame could – like maintaining an unchanging relationship with parents – result in a "paralysis of development" (p. 464).

Later I illustrate such transferences to aspects of the frame to show how playfulness works to violate unnecessary fixities and thus to contribute to the analysis of the overall frame itself.

CHAPTER 5

Playgrounds for Transference and Countertransference

TRANSFERENCE AS A PLAYGROUND

Freud (1914b) wrote of the "transference as a playground . . . an intermediate region between illness and real life through which the transition from the one to the other is made" (p. 154). He was still thinking of transference as part of the compulsion to repeat, and he wanted to turn it into a motive for remembering and an intention to repair. He affirmed that the mode of accomplishing that was to allow the transference "to expand in almost complete freedom," so that a "new condition" is created, manifesting "all the features of the illness, but it represents an artificial illness at every point accessible to our intervention. It is a piece of real experience, but one which has been made possible by especially favorable conditions, and it is of a provisional nature" (p. 154).

Freud (1905) had already observed that the unconscious idea, wish, or affect that is transference could take "advantage of some real peculiarity in the physician's person or circumstance" (p. 116); yet he maintained that we could detect its nature because it is "entirely composed of repetitions and copies of earlier reactions" (p. 117).

Those who succeeded Freud have been increasingly less sure that it is possible to discriminate repetition from what is, indeed, evoked by the real peculiarities of the therapist. Perhaps that uncertainty is why we sometimes glibly refer to the entire relationship as transference. My thesis here is that Freud gave us a way of thinking that awaited further elaboration from both the emphasis on the "intermediate area" that Winnicott (1953) introduced and the findings from the last several decades of infant research.

We may now be enabled to look at transference as manifested in therapy as a transitional process, a distillate of past experience without which the person could not change from one state or form to another. When we are confronted with a new experience, we would be quite lost unless we could "transfer" to it some of what we have learned before. Previous learning might or might not be a good guide to the challenges of the present. It may be, but is not necessarily, inappropriate to the here and now. The baby's use of the transitional object may especially prepare her for coping with what lies ahead, although at the time it may look to adults as irrational of the baby to cling so closely to blankets or teddy bears. When the baby herself decides that to employ such objects is no longer appropriate, the thing will be abandoned and its soothing functions transferred to other sources. The capacity to create for oneself what can represent both the "me" and the "not-me" of experience to date is ideally never extinguished.

For some years psychoanalysts and many, or perhaps even most, psychodynamically oriented therapists followed what they understood to be Freud's belief that patients had to be capable of stable transference neuroses to be treatable. Those not so capable were seen by psychiatric social workers, whose therapeutic function was "therapy of the kind that is always being carried on by parents in correction of relative failures in environmental provision" (Winnicott, 1963e, p. 227). These therapists worked largely intuitively and did not write for us much of their theories and approaches. When Kohut (1971, 1977) came along, they were often attracted to his ideas about mirroring and idealizing transferences, long familiar to them but part of their "unthought known" (Bollas, 1987).

Then infant research offered us rich new information about what clinicians had called the preoedipal period and hence gave us new ways to look at archaic transferences. We needed data about the first years of life very much, because by then therapists in all the mental health professions were seeing patients who were not quite like the classical neurotics, and we presumed that we were dealing with problems that originated in early privations and deprivations. Interestingly, those researchers were, unlike clinicians, focused on healthy development, and it is just possible that that focus moved therapists, too, away from their preoccupation with pathology and hence from their viewing transference as inevitably inappropriate. Gill (1982) asserted that we could not distinguish transference from nontransference on the basis of its incongruence with current reality. He reiterated what Freud had once said, that "transference is usually organized around significant contributions from the analyst in the here-and-now" (Gill and Hoffman, 1982). Schafer (1982) declared that transference is "new experiencing and new remembering of the past that unconsciously has never become the past" (p. 220). He emphasized that "transference, far from being a time machine by which one may travel back to see what one has been made out of, is a clarification of certain constituents of one's present psychoanalytic actions" (p. 220).

This view implies that the patient may well remember a different past with different therapists and over time may create new versions of earlier times in life. Freud (1896) observed this latter fact in one of his letters to Fleiss; he wrote that our memories are "subjected from time to time to a *re-arrangement* in accordance with fresh circumstances – to a *re-transcription*" and that "the successive registrations represent the achievement of successive epochs of life" (p. 233). We could see Schafer calling our attention to the new version that the patient may arrange with this therapist, at this particular time of the patient's life and in the situation that is therapy. It may be of significance that Freud used the term "epoch," which, in Greek, means "pause," or a kind of time-out, as for stock taking, very close to what may occur in the therapeutic situation.

There have been interminable debates about the meanings of transference (Ehrenreich, 1989), and it is not my intention to offer one further definition. My thesis is that if we can create a suitable playground with our patients, they will play out and redo any past experiences from birth to the day they appear in our consulting rooms. They will test both therapist and themselves in this process of revising, to ascertain whether old ways of knowing, feeling, and acting are or are not appropriate to this new situation. If we take seriously the conclusion of the infant researchers to the effect that there is a powerful self-righting tendency in the human being and if we see play as perhaps the most suitable modus operandi for actualizing that tendency, then we will work to enable the person to convert what seems all too real into partial make-believe. The patient then becomes an actor, so to speak, playing out with the therapist the drama of his own life and simultaneously rewriting the script. The action's disengagement from its consequences in the patient's everyday life is the new condition under which the person can permit former patterns to "expand in almost complete freedom," as Freud prescribed. Here I differ from Freud, however, for I think that for the therapist to be mainly on the lookout for "pathogenic instincts" hidden in the patient's mind would be likely to render the playground unsafe. Instead, I suggest looking for the "instinct" to play.

Play and Freedom

Freud was quite right to observe that a sense of freedom was essential to his idea; however, the therapist's "allowing" the expansion of what the patient is repeating is more complex than it sounds. It is clear that the person must experience a subjective sense of that freedom and that this experience can happen only in an interpersonal world felt to be safe. Often the "theories" carried over from the past may themselves be in the way of perceiving the analyst's "allowing" freedom. A number of our patients seem, instead, to be seeking "escape from freedom" (Fromm, 1941); instead of availing themselves of the potential leeways offered in the therapeutic situation, they may demand to be advised and told what is best for them.

Other patients present themselves as so besieged by such urgencies that they cannot lend themselves for some while to attending to what may not serve their immediate adaptive goals. Even curiosity behavior, the exploration of the unknown, can occur only when one is relatively free of the motive of appetite (Lorenz, 1971). We see the original constellation in infants' requiring some satisfaction of literal hungers before they are ready to engage in play and to let mother be a playing mother and not just a feeding one. It is possible that with many patients there must be analogous transactions with the therapist before the play spirit can be liberated.

Fear is another obstacle to the subjective sense of freedom and can, of course, stem from many sources. Some are internal—apprehensions whether one can contain powerful emotions or whether their very force will be fragmenting. Some concern the reactions of the other person, apprehensions over how safe it is freely to express one's feelings and thoughts. Specifically, in the therapeutic situation it is common that patients are anxious about how pathological the therapist is viewing them. Like the infant, they engage in recurrent "social referencing" (Emde et al., 1978) and look to the therapist for an appraisal to see whether their feeling states are or are not matched by those of the other and hence to know whether it is safe to proceed.

What they discover in scanning the therapist's demeanor may or may not be what the latter assumes is being transmitted. Sometimes we may find ourselves in the predicament of those parents who avidly read the books written by the experts and think themselves to be following the recommended procedures in their interactions with their offspring. We try to imitate the techniques of our mentors, be they supervisors or lecturers or famous authors of current professional literature. There is a question whether the very word "technique" has any place in our vocabulary, if by that we mean some systematic procedure to accomplish the complex tasks of psychotherapy. Some of us prefer the term "approach" to signify an attempt to draw near to the other – inevitably influenced both by our own predilections and by those of the patient and hence not precisely describable in advance. From the styles of the two persons will emerge unique ways of being with each other. When, as therapists, we are less than authentic, attempting approaches not congruent with our basic values and beliefs, our patients often detect the dissonance. Even when we may be saying words that seem "right," their gut feelings make them uneasy about doubts and contradictions within us.

Stern (1985) declares, "At the level of intersubjective relatedness, the authenticity of the parent's behavior looms as an issue of great magnitude" (p. 214). He goes on to observe that the issue can be only the degree of authenticity and that babies must learn to discern the necessary blendings of sincere and insincere behaviors. I recall one scene from a film of Emde's on social referencing. The mother had been instructed to put on a scared face so that the researchers could ascertain what effect that would have on the baby's approach or avoidance behavior. The mother happened not to be a very good actress, probably because she could not bear to render her baby fearful unnecessarily. So a slight smile escaped her while she was trying to frown in an apprehensive way; the baby correctly read the smile, which determined his selecting to advance rather than to retreat.

In the course of a session, we therapists may send out a number of contradictory messages, perhaps via different channels (Labov and Fanshel, 1977). We may say one thing, and our body language communicates something else. Freud's method of sitting behind the couch may have minimized the likelihood that the patient could detect these inconsistencies, though it is just possible that, like blind babies, analytic patients develop alternative ways of finding out what their analysts "really" feel or think. If they can feel sufficiently free, they will discover the "area of negotiation, rather than of signalling, of the status of intersubjectivity" (p. 218). They will then mention their conflicting impressions and check them out with the other and in the process expand the sense of freedom.

Persons approach treatment with certain ideas about what the therapist will expect; these ideas are part of their "transference predisposition" (Sander, 1980). A main means of diminishing the tendency to conform is to render that inclination conscious in a context that does not, in fact, demand conformity.

The Playground

In alluding to the playing field in which the patient could experience the necessary sense of freedom to reenact and to retranscribe the past, Freud was, of course, referring to metaphorical space. I think he would have been delighted with Winnicott's (1971a) further description of the special place and time for playing and of the way in which they become established and with the observations of infant researchers whose findings so complement Winnicott's ideas.

The original model for potential space (Winnicott, 1971a) is between the baby and the mother and is intermediate between reality and fantasy. It comes into being at a time of particular advance in the baby's ability to create a representational world. The evidence for this capacity is in the infant's making some soft blanket or toy into the transitional object, which stands for the "me" and the "not-me," the mother, and the relationship with her.

Winnicott's description of how potential space is generated is relevant for a clinical approach that makes room for playfulness. To paraphrase that author, like the good-enough mother, the therapist does not impose but is a "to-and-fro" between being what the patient has the capacity to find and being herself, waiting to be found.

Winnicott is similar to Erikson (1963) in affirming that trust, combined with the infant's confidence in his own creativity, makes the playground.

Like the writers on infancy, Winnicott (1971a) sees playfulness as intensely exciting, but not primarily because the instincts are involved. The excitement is always "the precariousness of the interplay of personal psychic reality and the experience of control of actual objects" (p. 47). When the other is experienced as sufficiently reliable, the "clinical infant," as Stern calls the adult patient, can then enjoy being "alone in the presence of someone" (p. 47) and finally enjoy the overlap of their two play areas. So potential space both joins and separates the participants.

In the paragraph from Freud with which we began, it seems clear that he was describing a dialectical process—a sort of make-believe generated out of what felt "real"—and that reality itself was to be created differently in this new context, so that it could lead to immersion in an "artificial illness."

We are increasingly aware that the sense of the real is always created and that, from the start, fantasy also entered into it. As Arlow (1969) states, "External perception and internal fantasy were intermingled at the time of the experience and together they formed the reality which to the patient was the record of his past" (p. 30). At the time the event was laid down in memory, it was with a sense of "real reality," and to the extent that this sense was not subsequently questioned, it was the premise on which reactions to similar events were based. What Freud liked to see happen in therapy was that the patient's conviction of reality would be diminished, even that the scale would be tipped toward an openness to the perhaps equal role of imagination and fantasy in the original and ongoing constructing of reality. There then exists the paradox of which Winnicott has been so fond: what is constructed is not less real, although the person's attitude toward it is tilted toward an emphasis on the part played by imagination in the drama of interplay with the therapist. Freud's stress on the "provisional" nature of this situation seems to be to reassure us that the patient will not stay lost in the world of make-believe but will remember and correct his memories and move ahead to a truer view of the real.

From this immersion in playfulness, however, may emerge the capacity to oscillate much more freely between what is outside and what is inside. The person will not just be internalizing but will have a renewed sense of being able to modify realities by flexible ways of viewing self, other, and self-with-other. Fixities will have been violated, the repetition-compulsion, if not altogether overthrown, at least seen as overthrowable.

Playgrounds, Inner and Outer

Play makes lasting impressions on the human psyche, even when the play experience may have been brief. As Huizinga (1944) noted decades ago about play, "Once played, it endures as a newfound creation of the mind, a treasure to be retained by the memory" (pp. 9–10). In this sense we glean a hint that there is something about play and playfulness that renders them peculiarly capable of being remembered, not susceptible to repression, as is much of human experience. They must then contribute powerfully to learning, including the learning that takes place in the context of psychotherapy. They are meaningful, especially because they contain that creative apperception that, says Winnicott (1971a), "more than anything else makes the individual feel that life is worth living" (p. 65). They combat compliance, which is a sick basis for life and which leads to a sense of futility.

Whereas in real life we are aware of time as linear, past, present, and future delineated from each other, in play we have some sense of timelessness. In the social play in psychodynamic psychotherapy, reconstructions of the past and their enactments in the transferential present are mutually interdependent. As Schafer (1982) put it, "What was, is, and what is, was" (p. 196). This dialectic between past and present renders both more meaningful. It is very much the core of a therapy based on psychodynamic principles and hence is a main reason that extracting an anamnesis at the beginning and ignoring what the patient may choose to tell us is contraindicated.

At its best, psychotherapy can afford the patient a benign illusion of time as unbounded possibility: the past as resource rather than burden, the present as full of significance rather than empty, the future as open rather than closed.

We could well worry about a trend on the current scene, often imposed on clinics due to financial limitations or on private providers by third-party payers, to abbreviate the number of sessions. This trend is likely to lead not just to a quantitative diminishing of the therapeutic experience but to a qualitative change in the nature of that experience.

A strict goal-directedness will usually result in a more constricted time and space for playfulness, with the result that only urgent needs are addressed. Just when those needs are felt to be less urgent and some playfulness could begin to occur, the case must be closed. The most basic improvements entail the liberation of the play spirit; these necessarily brief therapies may not make the lasting impressions on the human psyche that are the potential of play. When the rules are imposed from without, from whatever authorities, the two potential players may be deprived of participation in creating the playground. It is work that is prescribed, and there may not even be sufficient time for its entering into a dialectic with playfulness. The very safety of the therapeutic space may be in jeopardy in some of the current systems of delivering mental health services and also in some institutes that in their training programs take it on themselves to prescribe matters such as frequency and duration of treatment for their students.

When, in spite of obstacles, sufficient safety can be experienced, there will be a "natural evolution of the transference arising out of the patient's growing trust" (Winnicott, 1971a, p. 86). Winnicott admonishes us not to break up this natural process by our personal need to make interpretations, lest we prevent or delay deep change.

This thought leads to a consideration of features of the countertransference as they enter into therapeutic choreography.

A PLAYGROUND FOR COUNTERTRANSFERENCE

The term countertransference is as differently defined and regarded as is transference. Coined by Freud (1910), it was for some while thought to be a hindrance to the therapy, hence to be recognized and overcome. Freud (1912), however, very early observed the possibility that the therapist could "turn to his unconscious like a receptive organ toward the transmitting unconscious of the patient . . . so that the doctor's unconscious is able to reconstruct the patient's unconscious" (pp. 115–116). He thus allowed for the dual meanings of the suffix "counter"; it could signify opposition or reciprocation, dissonance or harmony.

As with transference, the meanings of countertransference have been extended, the broadest being that "it is the totality of the therapist's experience in relation to a particular client" (Grayer and Sax, 1986). Racker (1968) so uses the concept, and his ideas are compatible with current views of the therapeutic interactions as interpersonal.

I want not to enter into the debates about definitions but to observe that both parties to the transactions in therapy come with their transference predispositions; that is, each participant will have had unique life experiences and will have evolved a somewhat typical way of understanding and ordering those experiences. In some sense, each will be capable of both transference and countertransference experiences with the other. Ideally each also comes looking not just to validate previous conceptualizations but to discover something new. Each may therefore manifest what psychoanalysis has called resistances, that is, not only wariness that the schemas that have been tried and tested so far may have to be questioned, but also a wish that those formulas might be emended since our very complaints are testimony to their not having been good enough or complete enough.

Therapists, like patients, bring their entire life experience to date to the situation. The circumstances and events that characterized their years may or may not have been similar to those of the other. Usually the main difference is that psychodynamic therapists, operating from an ethic that demands that they approach their work with as full self-understanding as possible, will have made themselves fairly conscious of the ways in which they have been shaped by and have shaped the so-called facts of their lives. Sometimes even this difference does not pertain, as when patients are fellow professionals who have engaged in therapy of various kinds and seek to extend their self-knowledge via a fresh exploration. Perhaps these persons had analysis and now seek briefer therapy; or, having dipped into the vast grab bag of therapies now extant, they may be ready for the deeper and longer look (Shor and Sanville, 1978).

Whatever the remembered life experiences, there will be basic commonalities between the members of this newly constituted dyad. Students of infancy are now convinced that babies the world over are born with the capacity to express a wide range of emotions and that their mothers, by and large, have the capacity to read those affects as communication. We have all lived through a period when we conveyed without words what we were feeling, and we counted on significant others to interpret our body language correctly, especially our facial expressions. Across all cultures infants manifest in their facial muscles emotions that can be recognized by others whose languages and ways are quite diverse (Ekman, 1973; Izard, 1978).

Wherever they may live, some mothers and babies are more facile in developing satisfying communication than are others. In the clinical setting, therapists also differ in their aptitudes in reading the nonverbal cues, but to some extent we all do read them, albeit perhaps not as consciously as we read and interpret verbal content. We find ourselves responding emotionally to the patient's facial demonstrativeness – or sometimes to the lack of it. This is perhaps the most important cue in face-to-face therapies. The use of the couch, of course, diminishes our recourse to that information as well as to some of the motoric cues that are more in evidence when the patient is sitting.

We still do attend to certain metacommunication, such as tempo and tone – the "phatic" aspects of language – and even in a reclining position the patient will manifest some body movements that will register, consciously and unconsciously, with us.

With many of the patients whom we see today it is a long while in the course of psychotherapy before the therapist can free up the person's most playful reactions. In the beginning there is something analogous to "primary maternal preoccupation." Some of us might testify that it begins even prior to our seeing patients, when on the basis of the initial phone call we tentatively identify with their sense of what they are seeking and of the ways in which they are able to express their felt needs and wants. Ideally we recognize that this "projective identification" (Winnicott, 1960b, p. 53) on our part is just that – imagining ourselves in the position of the potential patient and then imagining our own responses to what we have projected. Just as the mother's fantasies of her unborn child and of her mothering self may be modified when the baby actually appears, so as therapists we have to be willing to relinquish the aspects of our imagining that are not realized when we have our first meetings with the patient.

Like the mother, we ideally manifest primarily an adaptation (Winnicott, 1963d, p. 86) to the ego needs of the other. It is one of the Winnicottian paradoxes that if the mother is able to give herself over to the care of the baby, the infant does not even have to be aware of this environment. This idea is akin to Balint's (1953) idea that the mother is more like a "substance," such as the oxygen in the air, that the infant can just take for granted. It is to this unconscious dependency with which life begins that we enable those patients seeking profound characterological change to regress. Only later will the infant – or the patient – come to recognize that dependence on the "holding environment" for that sense of "going-on-being" and, better still, for that sense of emergent self that such an environment facilitates.

What is required of the therapist is akin to what is demanded of mother, namely that she subsume personal needs and interests for the time being, and for some patients that "time being" may be quite extended. It does not sound as though there is much of a playground for countertransference in such a description. Indeed, Winnicott (1947b) wrote of "hate in the countertransference," and posited just what we are saying here, that the therapist in some ways finds herself, in the position of the mother of the newborn, having to love that infant, "excretions and all," and, in spite of being quite dominated by the baby's array of needs, having to wait for "rewards that may or may not come at a later date" (pp. 201–202).

Characteristically, Winnicott does not portray the mother as just repressing her hate; rather her very owning of it is part of why she does not have to "do anything about it," (p. 202) other than perhaps singing "Rockabye Baby" to her infant! Maybe there is something analogous in this situation for therapists. Their real hate is partly converted into make-believe, and if they discharge it at all, it is in some playful fashion, as by confessing to supervisors their sometime wish that the cradle might fall. Perhaps the best insurance against their acting out is precisely their awareness that they are, in any event, acting.

While patients in their use of the playground create an artificial illness, therapists create an "artificial healthiness," a way of being in this situation that they could not enact in the rest of life. Their knowledge that they are enacting a role is what enables them to take the patient's behaviors both seriously and not seriously and to take their own behaviors likewise. They know that they are neither as good nor as bad as patients may variously see them. To play their parts well, they must be ready to improvise those responses that allow the patient to be in the agent role, like the newborn, to be essentially in charge of the dialogue. The satisfactions they derive are from their relative success in this part, from their ability to let themselves be part of the scene, the necessary environment in which playfulness might occur and in which patients use them as agencies, as resources for achieving their own ends.

Schafer (1982) writes of the analyst's "second self" and likens it to that of the creative writer, whose authorial second self is infinitely more sublime than that employed in everyday life. We readers recklessly create illusions of what these writers are, he says, and those illusions may bear little or no relation to the writers' actual qualities as observed by those who know them personally (pp. 43–44).

An important difference, however, in the clinical situation as compared to the reading room is that the other is physically present. We therefore do not have quite the same opportunity as the writer to conceal what we really are, and it may be that we must really have quite a bit of playfulness in our characters to be able to enact the role we are hypothesizing here as desirable without our "first selves" putting in an appearance and spoiling our acting. Schafer speaks of the "second psychic structure" as akin to Fliess's (1942) "analyst's work ego." I am likening it much more to a "play ego." While Schafer finds partial explanation for the second self in Kris's (1952) "regression in the service of the ego," I resort to Balint's (1959) "progression for the sake of regression." Unless therapists have a certain confidence in the progressive elements in their psyches and in the tradition of psychodynamic thinking, they may find such regression dangerous and may take haven in a stance that keeps them fully in charge. I heartily agree with Schafer (1982) that "the appropriate analytic [or therapeutic] attitude is one of *finding out,*" although I would add to his comment about "where the principal work will be done" something about where the principal play may take place. It takes a certain playfulness to see the treatment process as "a study of itself as it is created in and through the analytic dialogue" and not to need to know ahead of time "where one is going, how, why, and with which consequences" (p. 21).

This absence of clear goal-directedness is likely to be initially somewhat disconcerting to patients who want quick results and who may not yet realize that the shortest route is not necessarily the best. If psychodynamic therapy can be said to have a purpose, it is to enable the person to be aware of her own purposes and to acquire ways of moving toward them. In the beginning patients may present their complaints urgently, want the therapist to offer solutions, and pressure for guidance. The therapist has to decline the authority role in which the patient would place her, to resist the temptations to be seen as a sage, and to maintain the genuine not knowing that offers the greatest transformational potential for the patient. So, whereas therapists in their ordinary lives might seek or even relish being seen as experts, in the clinical situation they try to eschew that role and follow the lead of patients, who, after all, have the most relevant data about their own lives, past and present. Perhaps we can view the pleasure therapists may attain in being able to submerge their personal predilections in the service of enacting their professional role in a way suitable to the situation at hand as gratifying some of their wish for playfulness.

Some writers have seen the role of the analytic therapist as twofold: setting up the structure and routine that are to be the frame of treatment and then becoming the medium to be used by the patient in the search for a better sense of self. They see the therapist as leading in the former, and the patient as leading in the latter (M. G. Fromm, 1980), the distribution of authority always unbalanced. Some of us have been questioning whether, from the very beginning, the patient might not have a sense of at least equal participation in setting up the arrangements for fees, time, frequency, and general approach (Shor, 1990). Therapists, of course, have their own limitations, which have to enter into initial negotiations, concerning their available hours, the fees that they consider necessary, the manner of payment, and even the method of treatment that they employ. But in their negotiating they can show the concern for patients' preferences that lets the latter feel that their circumstances are also being taken into account and appreciated. Something of the reality of each of the two will inevitably enter in, but the therapist who can best enable the patient to feel some sense of her own powers even initially may best ensure the gradual use of the frame as a playground in which a different reality will become possible because it will be enhanced by creative illusions.

The idea of therapist as medium implies that we are a kind of "culture" in which the patient and the process could exist and thrive, analogous to the "substance" that M. Balint (1953) thought might be the baby's experience of the mother. It also implies that we are an agency for transmitting energy and the means by which something is accomplished or conveyed. In the model being developed here, it would then be up to the patient to use us in either of these senses, as she might be inclined to alternate between times of just wanting an ambience in which to relax, remember, think, and feel about whatever seems to occur at the moment and times of wanting some active dialogue with us. Shor (1990) goes so far as to believe that we should engage in interpretation only when rather explicitly invited by the patient and that meanwhile we should simply deepen empathy; otherwise, we are in danger of intrusion into private space and could deprive patients of understandings at which they might arrive by themselves and of the enormously enhanced sense of self that can come from so doing. Like the mother with the not-yet-verbal infant, I believe there are clues other than specifically verbal ones that also constitute invitations. Our hope is often to enable the patient to become explicit about what is wanted or not wanted from us, but again, just as the mother's sensitive response to the myriad of non-verbal communications from her infant is a necessary foundation for later language unfolding, so the therapist's attunement to the moments of the patient's wanting by responding to the sensed message is part of the patient's ultimately acquiring the "words to say it" (Cardinal, 1983). Much that we know about disabilities of the verbal self, if we assume that there is no organic pathology, suggests origins in the period before speech (Bullowa, 1979).

I am, however, in essential agreement with Shor about the importance of not barging in with uninvited interpretations. There is evidence that many therapists find this philosophy a constriction of their play. Psychoanalysis has long thought of interpretation as the main mutative factor in therapy. Also, in this area they have a great deal of fun – seeing whether and how cleverly they can translate the patient's material into the language of psychoanalysis. Increasingly, however, we are realizing that such self-indulgence on the part of the therapist may deprive the patient of a sense of discovery and of creating. Many of us thus discipline ourselves, as Winnicott (1971a) described himself doing for extended periods, and feel our reward when patients essentially make interpretations for themselves. As is so characteristic of Winnicott, he found a way to gratify his own narcissistic needs by writing down the interpretations he withheld.

Moreover, when we do offer comments at the patient's invitation, we do so tentatively, so that the person is quite free to ignore, to modify, or to build on what we have said. If we imagine that there are different qualities of playfulness, depending on the relative proportions of narcissistic and of social components, then what is happening is that we are moving toward gaining greater pleasures from our success in rendering the therapeutic process a collaborative one. Perhaps paradoxically we even take pride in our very ability to relinquish the authority role or, at least, to share it with patients.

The original paradigms for such pleasures are in play situations between mother and infant. When the mother defers to her baby's inclinations and lets him lead, then the baby soon naturally seems to allow her a turn also; in time, together they enjoy the reciprocity that is social play (Call, 1968, 1980; Stern, 1977). The mother's delight is both in the sense of contributing to this exciting unfolding of the baby's capacities and then in the enhanced dialogue that their play makes possible.

In this approach, the therapist avoids one of the dangerous shoals of countertransference – succumbing to the patient's projections of "good" parts, long thought to be one of the obstacles a positive transference might entail. Instead, the therapist keeps giving back to the patient capacities not felt to be fully owned.

What of the negative transference and the feelings that can be aroused by patients who often show us their difficulty in believing that we can be any help at all and who project their "bad" aspects onto us? We often feel ourselves in negative countertransferences with such patients and in danger of acting in ways that are antithetical to enabling the patients to use the transference as a playground. As Heimann (1950) said, violent emotions, whether of love or hate, tend to impel us toward action, rather than contemplation. She did not see the answer lying in our revealing to patients the feelings evoked in us, although there are those on the current scene who do advocate that. In general, the answer has been thought to lie in interpretation (Rosenfeld, 1971), which, I believe, can best take place when there is a playful ambience. Since bodily excitement attendant on strong emotions is not conducive to play (Winnicott, 1971a, p. 52), to attempt interpretations when angry would most likely result in the patient's feeling them as force-feeding and in their being indigestible.

Bion (1962a) suggests that we go into "reverie," as the mother does when she becomes aware that her baby is imagining his bad parts to be in mother. She "contains" the bad stuff, thinks about it, and "responds therapeutically" so that the infant feels he is "receiving [his] frightened personality back again, but in a form [he] can tolerate" (p. 115). I like that word, "reverie," which derives from dreaming. In the dream, we may also experience strong emotion, but our motor equipment is not connected, and so we do not act on our feelings other than in the dream script. From my own experience and from my supervision of others, I can testify that we may actually dream of our patients in times of struggling with our negative emotions. The reverie of waking life, however, has advantages, for it can include all that we have learned to date about the course of development and about the psychodynamics of such situations. We can reflect on ourselves and our responses in ways we do only imperfectly in dreams. So in the play that is psychotherapy, we can stay in our role in spite of the impetus to abandon it.

Bion offers the paradigm of the hungry baby screaming in such a way that the mother experiences some panic, but she manages to feed the baby anyway. Her infant tolerates the emotion in her because the milk is forthcoming. Building on this, Carpy (1989) hypothesizes that some acting out, whether by mother or therapist, is inevitable but must be minimal, lest the "badness" that the infant/patient senses in the other be more powerful than the "goodness" of the milk or the ongoing safety of the relationship. What the therapist usually does is in the realm of the verbal, like putting forth an interpretation that is not itself mutative but that does communicate to the patient that he has "got to" the therapist. Essentially the therapist stays therapist, primarily motivated not by the temporary anger (and it is anger, not rage, which might be more likely were there not some safety valve such as a misplaced interpretation) but by an ongoing commitment to being there to be used eventually by this patient. So one fear, that of provoking the other to abandonment, is quelled. The patient sees someone not knocked out of commission by emotion, able to keep it within bounds, and willing to keep the dialogue going. So this person tones down a self-image about the hugeness of his own destructiveness and may arrive at a new view of the other and hence of the potential of this relationship for purposes of psychic repair. The playground will have been rendered safer, possibly to the extent that the patient can now make some use of what the therapist has to offer.

Winnicott (1971a) saw something like this testing of the other as developmentally necessary if the child is to be able to use the human "object." Projective identifications are, in some measure, not just to get rid of bad stuff but are ways of finding out about the self and the other. When the child provokes the parent to anger, if the latter neither retaliates nor is destroyed, then he can be seen as distinct from the self, a "real object" (p. 94). Identification can then take place on a new level and can contribute to the growth of the senses of positive self.

But, we might ask, does the therapist not "retaliate" in this, albeit verbal, "acting out"? There is certainly that element in it, and it is a delicate matter whether such comments as we may make are too much for the patient, in which case we will not have detoxified (Bion, 1963) the projection but maybe increased its frightening aspects. In my own experience, if I have managed to keep a sort of "playground in my mind," I have been able to say what I have to say with a touch of humor. Although the patient may or may not be able to appreciate it at the moment, I have felt simultaneously angry and amused at my anger—as, indeed, I can recall feeling as a mother. So what happens is that my real countertransference anger is converted into partly make-believe, not nearly so lethal. It is analogous to the "'artificial illness" of the patient.

We might think of it as a temporary regression on the part of the therapist, essentially intended for purposes of repair of the professional "second self." How well it works may depend, in part, on the strength of this therapist's conviction that regressions, whether in patient or self, are motivated not by such things as death instincts or primary hostile aggression but by the eternal wish to re-create fresh editions of that primary illusion in which there was no conflict between self and other, only a gentle oscillation between attention to self and attention to the relationship (Shor and Sanville, 1978, 1979). If the therapist has quite consistently conveyed such an attitude to regressions in the patient, the latter may be more ready to comprehend an essentially positive motive behind the therapist's "negative" behavior in this instance, and the therapist may be more ready to forgive herself.

CHAPTER 6

The Work

Building a Playground
With an Unplayful Adult

Among our adult patients we find those who, like Katie, seem singularly unplayful. Descriptively, they may in a number of ways have much in common with autistic children, although within certain narrow limits they do function in the world. Their complaints have to do with not finding life meaningful, and one has the impression that one of the reasons is that they are somehow out of touch with both their own and others' feelings. The one emotion they describe is anger, which is experienced as out of their control and hence in eternal danger of alienating others. They do not manage to find or make significant relationships, although they tend to keep trying. They rarely report events that have been experienced pleasurably. When they do, we sometimes observe that they then flee from the very pleasure, particularly when it stems from moments of positive connection. Even their dream space is not experienced as safe, for there, as in waking life, anxieties and dreads seem to prevail.

With Katie, my hypothesis was of a probable deficit in the child herself, a shortage of sending and receiving power that was, in large measure, responsible for the difficulty the mother had in relating to this offspring. There were evidences of "ghosts in the nursery" (Fraiberg, 1980, p. 505), the mother having had to take on a parental role with her own younger siblings early in her life. Her husband was dubiously supportive, either financially or emotionally, for he was beset with obsessions and depressions of his own. Yet, in the years of work with me, this mother proved a fine cotherapist and must be credited with whatever degree of success was achieved in enabling Katie to attain some relatedness to the human world. Moreover, with two children born later, she proved a fairly good mother. Whether her good mothering resulted, in part, out of gains in confidence about her mothering capacities, a sense of being "held" by me, or the fact that the other babies were, unlike Katie, not handicapped in basic equipment is perhaps debatable. Perhaps all these factors played some part.

With the unplayful patient whom I am about to describe, both the nature of the transference and the woman's own reports about current encounters with her parents suggested that the deficit may have been primarily in the early "holding environment" (Winnicott, 1974), in the inability of either mother or father to be sensitive to this infant's needs and to exercise a soothing function that their daughter might eventually make her own. We might well postulate that the results of such early privation can simulate those of organic or constitutional deficits. Whether the essential provisions are "completely outside the perception and comprehension of the infant at the time" (Winnicott, 1963b, p. 226) because the baby lacks the equipment to observe them or because they are not there to be sensed may not make a crucial difference. Hence, differential diagnosis, even if we could unequivocally make it, might not lead to a different treatment approach.

In both instances the damage seems to result from obstacles in mother-infant attunement, specifically from those that limit the arena of playing. When we are dealing with a child whose mother makes herself available as a participant in the treatment, we have some chance to remedy the situation, if not always to "cure." With an adult, the patterns may be more set, and, even if we could include the parents in the treatment program, the bulk of our efforts still have to go toward creating with the patient a new relationship in which some healing could occur. Specifically, we aim at facilitating a sense of safety, sufficient to enable the patient gradually to experience both stimulation and soothing.

My first impression of Nora, as of Katie, was of a person who avoided eye contact and whose face showed little expression. Her voice was flat, and the content of what she had to say was quite abstract. Her body seemed tense and tight, constricted in movement. I keenly felt the absence of what infant researchers call "cueing" (Stern, 1971; Brazelton et al., 1974). Lacking the usual signals one receives from an adult, one finds oneself speculating what the averting of gaze might mean. Mutual gaze in infants is associated both with feeding and with free play (Stern, 1974a; Trevarthen, 1979). Did Nora expect neither?

Looking away is one of the earliest coping mechanisms, used to control stimulation and to modulate states of arousal. The infant, as Shor and I (1978) have written, normally oscillates between locking eyes and looking away. In adulthood, while engaged in conversational exchange, most of us alternate between looking directly at those with whom we are speaking and glancing away. But here was Nora, who gave me the impression of being fearful to connect with me visually.

Nora came in following the breakup of a lesbian relationship, but she said she had not "had time to think about it yet." Her central complaint was that she was not finding life meaningful. Her work as an accountant for a big company was "easy" but not something she really liked. She declared that there was nobody to whom she felt close, and she volunteered that in this regard she was like her father, a suspicious and untrusting man. She was an only child and was "not close to mother either." She recalled that, sometime in her early teens, she went through a bad time, and was obsessed with death. A teacher suggested therapy, but her parents thought that one had to be "far gone" for that. About a year ago she had a brief period of psychotherapy but left it and did not want to return to that person. She wanted, she said, "someone stronger, who would hold me to my resolve." She had interviewed several possible therapists before seeing me, but she found it easiest to talk with me and would like to "really work" on problems with me. She was not able to articulate what made it easier, but whatever it was she had made her "diagnosis" of me or of some quality of potential connection that I felt augered well for our working together. As we talked of the details, we were able to set up an hour that would be possible for us both. She asked whether we could make the appointments every other week. I said that, of course, that arrangement was feasible, but I wondered what her thinking was. She said that she was feeling an eagerness to leave here even before the end of her hour. "So," I suggested, "although you want to learn to be close, right now you'd be more comfortable with a bit of distancing?" Now I received my first glance and a slight smile. She agreed and said she would like to begin with once-a-week sessions. I took hope from the smile, even though it was immediately followed by that flatness of affect that had permeated the session. Nevertheless, I took the smile to mean that for a moment, when I had gently commented on her dilemma about closeness and distance, she had felt my attunement with her. If the smile in infancy can be "credited with keeping the infant in the situation, thereby extending opportunities for continuing explorations and assimilating new information . . . and generally enhancing the transactional exchanges between infant and other" (Demos, 1982a, p. 542), perhaps it could predict such opportunities for this therapist and this patient in this situation.

There seemed a general "inhibition of responsivity" (Beebe and Stern, 1977). My only cue that something was possibly happening was the decision to come at least weekly. I thought of Beebe and Sloate's (1982) term "facial ambivalence" or of facial "ambitendency" (Mahler, Pine, and Bergman, 1975). I sensed Nora's reaching for something with me but simultaneously warning me that she was also capable of ending relationships. Yet she wanted me to help her "hold to her resolve." What, I wondered, could render our relationship meaningful to this woman, who complained of a lack of meaning in her life? What could enable her to experience the emotions that could lead to investment in positive meaning?

"Emotions," Sroufe (1982) writes, "always involve a person interacting with the surrounding environment" (p. 576). Quantitative factors of stimulation do not predict whether the resulting affect will be positive or negative. Each child will build up an experience-based meaning of events. Sroufe asserts, "It is tension, reflecting a transaction between infant and event, that results in affect, not the stimulation per se" (p. 576). In Sroufe's model, tension is not negative and is not to be avoided; it is connected with positive, as well as negative, affect. My guess was that Nora's complaint of finding life "meaningless" was essentially a complaint that she could not generate much positive meaning and that this lack was related to a paucity of playful episodes with parents or others in childhood.

The initial period of therapy was difficult. Nora was constantly "losing" herself, me, or both of us. "I feel nothing. I'm not here. I'm far away," she would say, or, "I don't know who you are." She would "lose," too, the ideas and thoughts that she had once seemed to grasp. She complained of almost chronic anger, which would "descend" on her and suffuse her for reasons unknown. Because of her affectless way of talking, it was months before we could even begin to construct a history that could afford us cues as to what had gone wrong. She had told me that her parents were both highly intellectual and undemonstrative and that she had been taught by percept and precept not ever to rely on another. Yet, perhaps by the very virtue of her continuing to come to me, I inferred that there was at least a modicum of that "regression to dependence" that Winnicott and Balint both felt was probably necessary for deep-reaching change to take place. All I can know for sure is that I was feeling attentive to her and that, because of the scarcity of emotion in her demeanor and her words, this attentiveness was not effortless. I was not pushing her, and certainly there was little to interpret. But she was, in this context, gradually doing her own explorations in an attempt at self-understanding.

One such attempt was when she told of a trip home to visit with her parents. She had reported to them an event that was of some current importance in her life. While she spoke, her father looked out the window, and mother busied herself with something about the room; neither seemed attentive to her message. This scene evoked memories of how regularly she had experienced this nonresponsiveness from them. She also recalled no emotional interactions between the two of them. Her father regularly insulted her mother in social situations, and mother would "just take it." Nora seemed rather surprised by her own "discovery" of this probable factor in her own problems, in her not knowing how to connect with people. She remembered having been a lonely, isolated, but "good" child, achieving in school but enjoying little satisfaction from that.

Here was an example of what Bollas (1987) calls the "unthought known." It was not so much that the data were unknown to her, but that their significance for her problems had never dawned on her before. The anger connected with the data was more acceptable to her in the context of the awareness of what had provoked it. Previously she had manifested fear of her own negative feelings and had seen both herself and others in danger from her affect storms. I thought it likely that no "self-regulating other" had enabled her to modulate and thus safely express emotions of this sort. Nora went on to evoke more memories that tended to strengthen her insight, which was both affective and cognitive. I could not know whether this awareness was possible, in part, because her experience of my attentiveness highlighted for her its discrepancy with the nonresponsiveness of her parents. It seemed possible that she had come to take my empathy somewhat for granted and that it was the background against which other experiences were then viewed.

Sometimes the contacts of patients with what they often call the "outside world" thus enhance the processes of therapy. Again, these contacts can be problematic for both patient and therapist. Nora, at the beginning of our work together, had been admiring at a distance a young intellectual woman who was herself in intensive therapy. That both of them would be having this experience may even have been some of the impetus for her own entering treatment. Indeed, they did draw closer, at least geographically, for Nora, albeit in a state of acute anxiety bordering on panic, moved into the same apartment building with Sally, at the latter's instigation.

From the start, this friend would query Nora about her sessions with me and demand to be told in detail what had transpired. Nora dutifully complied, to the extent that she could. But then, more often than not, Sally would castigate her for not having discussed with me what she should have discussed or for "not being honest" with me. Between us, there had been no "shoulds." I had never asked that she tell me whatever was on her mind, and she frequently engaged in silences that I did not interpret as "resistances" and, indeed, did not even see that way. Instead, I saw her attempting to plumb her own depths to see if there was something she wanted to share with me. But Nora attempted at that period to be "good" with her friend and to try to do what was asked and not even consider whether she wanted to do that or not. She "believed" that Sally was right, that she was doing this therapy wrong, and that probably she was not telling me what she should—although she did not have any idea what she was omitting. As time went on, her friend included comparisons of her own therapy with what Nora was receiving, with explicit opinions that her own was superior. Nora was repeatedly traumatized by these exchanges but was compelled—consciously by the urge to comply and unconsciously by wishes that we were later to identify—to continue her recounting of all that she could recall of our sessions.

With me, she often could not recall what had happened in the previous session, even when it had seemed to both of us especially significant. Sometimes she could not remember something important she had been intending to tell me. For example, there was the following sequence. She came in one day and said that she had had experiences that seemed important to her and that she had even looked forward to telling me since she had arrived at some insights. But now she could not recall what had been on her mind. She knew she had felt better after her last hour, but now she could not say what we had talked about. What we had talked about was that she had seen an old friend and had "kept the experience pleasant." When she had gone later to see Sally, the latter had commented on her improved demeanor; however, as had been her pattern, she shortly found herself suffused with anger again, and the two had parted in one of their disagreeable scenes. As she had come out from work the next day, she had noticed "not that spring was here but that winter had gone." She had felt a surge of energy and pleasure and a totally unaccustomed sexual feeling. Her dreams, unlike her usual nightmares, had involved men, penises, and a great longing for a penis of her own. She knew, she said, that this dream had to do with Sally, who, although currently living as a lesbian, thought she wanted to keep open the possibility that she may ultimately want a man. "No matter what I did," Nora told me that hour, "mother still turned to father, and no matter what I do, Sally and I won't be together always." The penis envy revealed in the dream seemed to us both to be essentially a wish for the "connector," and her seemingly unprovoked rage seemed to stem from her felt impotence to satisfy the mother/Sally.

Yet here, in the very next session, she was forgetting all that. I had by now learned to hold memories for her, so to speak. In due time she would remember events, and we would both recognize how they fit in with or elucidated something in later sessions. In this instance she looked at me helplessly, wordlessly pleading for some assistance. I suggested lightly that maybe, if we could retrace her activities of the weekend, she would find what she had "lost." To understand what she then retrieved, one has to know something of the kinds of reparative efforts Nora had been making.

For months and months she had made Sally her only social contact, in spite of recurrent ugly scenes in which Sally would tell her that she was the most disagreeable, the "sickest," "craziest" person she had ever known. During those months, we stayed close to the experiences she related and looked always for the reparative wish in the "craziest" behaviors. Such a wish was manifest in her attachment to Sally, her being "true" to her, in spite of Sally's several lesbian affairs and occasional rages at Nora. The affairs seemed to bother Nora minimally until much later. She was intent upon creating, as I had ventured to interpret, an exclusive relationship in which she very much wanted some of Sally's qualities to "rub off" on her. Her dreams confirmed this interpretation, and showed her seeking a mother, although conscious memories seemed to hold no good-enough mother whom she would want to emulate. As she began to realize that her "faithfulness" made little sense when it was not reciprocal and that some of her distress was a consequence of her recurrent disappointment, she began to seek out friends other than Sally.

On this occasion Nora had gone out to dinner with a couple, liked them, and felt they liked her. She came back to Sally and found her friend buoyant and optimistic on account of some felt gains in her own analysis. Nora had reverberated to that mood, especially as she had been experiencing some triumphant feelings of her own. For the first time in almost a year she experienced a sexual wish, and Sally, sensing this and happy that Nora had perceived her improved state, asked whether Nora would like to make love. Nora told me that they had, "somewhat." Although she "wasn't quite ready," it was a rather pleasant experience. Her own nice feelings continued until, on the arrival of another of Sally's lovers, Sally asked Nora to tell this other woman what she had observed, saying, "You can tell it better than I!" Suddenly Nora's anger came rushing back, and she could make only some feeble statement to the effect that Sally had been in an unusually good mood. Sally was manifestly disappointed and commented on the paltry communication of what had seemed so special. Nora could do no more with it. She fled to her own quarters and retreated to her bed. She did not know what she felt; it was one of her "blurry" states, often described as "a fog descending on me," a state that we had come to identify as a sort of auto-anaesthesia.

How long that lasted she did not know, but gradually she grew calmer as she said to herself, "Think about this situation. There must have been reasons you were so angry." This communication to herself resembled such lines from me, tone and all. Lying in her bed, she reconstructed the scene connected with the event and came up with insights that surprised her. When Sally asked her to share with this other woman her perceptions of Sally's state, she could find no words in which to capture how she, Nora, had experienced it, for it had included her own affective reverberations from a good, separate experience and had led to the sensual feelings that she was, by no means, ready to share. "I realized," she told me, "that I could not share what I did not yet own." This statement was an echo of insights that we had arrived at together before – often around Sally's demands that Nora "open up" fully about thoughts and feelings that the latter was only beginning to sense and form and tell them to someone with whom such intimate sharing was not reliably "safe." In this recent situation she had been asked to confide in a total stranger; she had resented that demand. With this self-understanding, Nora's rage and fog had slowly dissipated.

In the rest of the hour we dealt with her experience of telling me this story. I had commented on how pleased she must have been to do this reflecting and to have arrived at a far-reaching insight and thus to have changed her emotional state. Nora somewhat diffidently acknowledged that there had been pleasure, although, she noted, that was not part of what she had reported to me. It was as though she were commenting on my having gone beyond the material. Actually I had avoided praising her, for that action would put me in the role of authority, one who can give or withhold praise. I wanted to be communicating that my pleasure was in her pleasure. She sensed that and perhaps felt it to be more closeness than she wanted, one of those moments when there could be imagined fusion, some abandonment of usual defenses. So she took our discourse back to the scene with Sally.

She found she still could not articulate her feelings and perceptions of Sally's state and of her own reactions in those several hours. I commented that there had been precious moments in which she could let herself connect with her friend, even perhaps be imaginatively at one with her, and that they had not demanded words but were expressed in bodily joining. I reflected with her on what seemed the preconditions for that ecstatic experience: she was already experiencing a rather contented and happy sense of self, and Sally, also in such a state, was initially requiring no articulation about the situation. Then, with the entrance of the third person and Sally's ordering her to describe these special and private experiences, she had protected her privacy by opting not to communicate or even to be with the others. She responded by reiterating with intense feeling how mother and father, by their nonresponsiveness to her relating pleasures to them, "took away all that was good, everything that I valued." To speak of it was therefore to lose it. She had developed, as we already knew by now, a "defense" of nonrelating, noncommunicating. We added here that maybe she had hidden her feelings so deeply that it was, at times, hard even for her to find them again.

After Nora had reviewed her experiences with her family, I told her that she had just given me a possible insight into how it had been all this time that she tried so hard to comply with her friend's ongoing demand that she relate in detail all that transpired in our therapeutic sessions. It must be rewarding to have someone so intensely interested and attentive; Nora must have hoped in such sharing to "own" her therapeutic experiences more fully. I had in mind that, although one can inwardly generate meanings of events from the affects they arouse, to be able to communicate to others permits an enrichment of those meanings. What she had been doing seemed a combination of "self-traumatization" and "self-provocation" (Shor 1972), aimed at finding out whether this other person was or was not like her parents and hence at discovering the extent to which it might be safe to experiment with different reactions herself. Nora confessed to me and to herself that she was never able really to share the experience here with Sally; she overtly conformed, but "part of me went underground." In this moment she was aware that part of her was "not fully here." I observed that feelings of safety are always relative, but at least she was increasingly conscious that she could measure when and what and how much she wanted to share and with whom and in what situation.

Of course, there were regressions that were not of a benign nature, not chosen ones, and our conjoint task was to see whether we could move them toward something felt as less malignant. From time to time Nora catapulted herself into crises, especially around doubts about her therapy, which Sally recurrently questioned. There came a period when Sally changed her approach; whereas previously she had accused Nora of not really having to act as she did and hence of "not trying," she began to take an opposite stance, that is, that Nora could not help being as she was because she was "sick," needed help badly, and was not getting it. In her own words, Nora regressed to a "psychotic" state and manifested an almost paranoid suspiciousness in her relationship to me. What was I doing to her? Maybe I was weak like her mother, whom she saw as extremely vulnerable to her cold and humiliating husband. Maybe she should see a man, as her friend did, maybe the same analyst. She surprised herself with this idea, for she had never thought she could work with a male. She was angry with me that I might be failing her. It was a painful time. She assaulted me with her "craziness," her inability to sleep, her recurrent nightmares, her rages at everyone. I dealt with her doubts by suggesting that it was natural that she should have them in view of her seeming increase in tension and distress, when she had hoped to be feeling better. It was, I ventured, an important development that she could question me, and that she could consider whether some other source of therapy might be better for her.

One day she came in affirming that she had been "acting crazy" and that she had a fear that she could become crazy. She had, she said, done "something crazy." She had made an exploratory phone call to her friend's therapist, but the secretary had told her how she must be "screened" to see him. "It was stupid," she told me, "but I haven't really been working with you, so what could I expect elsewhere?" We both observed that she was returning to a former way of seeing the situation, namely that it had something to do with her investment in her therapy and not simply explicable by "sickness."

Nora informed me that her parents had visited her in her apartment for the first time, and Sally thought something "snapped" in her since then. Her own observation had been that since their visit, she had felt "presences" within her; her eyes seemed sometimes the eyes of her father, angry and cold, and again they seemed the eyes of mother, glazed and unfeeling. The presences felt "alien, not really myself." I mused about this feeling and shared with her my wondering whether the presences might not have been there all the time and whether the significant change might not be that they now felt alien. I suggested that her ascribing that status to them hinted at her wish to exorcise them. Could it be that she "externalized" the presences while her parents put in their visual appearance and that she became conscious of qualities of mother and of father that she did not want to have as aspects of herself? But, she told me, she was enacting their ways of being, even exaggerating their traits. Still musing, I wondered whether she might be thus trying to experience those more clearly, maybe preparatory to determinations whether to admit or expel or modify those traits.

Her response was to tell a story. She had complained to her father that her boss had talked rudely to her and said that he would "like to hire a goon squad" to do away with Nora and another employee, who were giving him some trouble over their rights. Neither father nor mother reacted at all. Nora said, "I would react with shock if a child of mine told me such a thing!" I observed that here she was distinguishing a difference from her parents, that her "self" would not be unresponsive as they seemed to be. Although Nora had often pleaded that she had no self, she was asserting one. She said that, unlike mother, she had no fear of her father, but she protected herself by "insulating" herself.

She went on to tell of complaining to her parents of the friction with Sally. Their response was, she thought, typical: "Why do you have to get along? Just keep to yourself." They were, she observed, that way with each other, enduring, not finding it important to relate warmly. We closed with my reiterating that we could see in her calling her friend's therapist her affirming an option that she had as an adult to choose the person or persons to whom she would turn. As a child, she had to cope with the parents to whom she was born. Now she could openly voice her doubts and opt for a change if she decided it was in her best interest. Once more, I suggested that she wanted neither "helpers" whom she would experience as uncommunicative and unrelated nor those who would intrude and take the decisions into their own hands as to what was indicated for her. In leaving, Nora asked if we could increase the frequency of appointments, and we made the arrangement.

It is always difficult to recapture the textures of some of the most meaningful sessions. There were a number of them as we continued to work over or "play out" some of the themes we had opened up. The hour I now want to report followed one in which Nora had related some positive experiences; these had to do with feeling that she was developing some new relationships, ones that she valued and with persons who valued her. She was even partaking of some cultural events that interested her. She had reported "an almost sexual feeling of connectedness." Then she had been dismayed to find herself with the old "No, no, no" to her own outgoing feelings.

At the next session she acknowledged a reluctance to come. She mentioned that at the end of the last hour she had looked at and seen me for the first time (after nearly two years of our working together). But she had not, she said, felt like mentioning this occurrence to me. She reported "a dream that wasn't a nightmare":

> I am outdoors with the grandmother that I liked. We see a cloud forming into a funnel shape and realize a storm is coming. I say we must seek shelter, and I rush to lead the way. At some point I look back and see my grandmother, who looks old and weary. I feel a surge of

conscience that I have not considered her welfare, so I go back and help her. We arrive in a neighborhood which is like one where I lived with my family as a child. But the house is not occupied by mother and father; just grandmother and I are there.

She was not sure she could say anything about this dream. So I assumed my contemplative mood and, speaking slowly, so that she could add, subtract, or whatever, I wondered whether she thought I might be the grandmother. She had mentioned suddenly seeing me, and maybe she had had some sense that what we had been going through was a strenuous ordeal for me, too. (Inwardly, I was thinking of Winnicott's [1963] "capacity for concern," which "is at the back of all constructive play and work" [p. 73]. He hypothesizes that the "object" is used by the baby ruthlessly to the extent that "instinct" enters in, but alongside this is the "quiet relationship to the environmental mother" [p. 76]. So anxiety appears, modified by the baby's sense that it has a contribution to make. He emphasizes the importance at such times of being the "reliable mother-figure to receive the reparation gesture" [p. 82] so that guilt does not reach intolerable proportions.)

I recalled how often Nora had referred to her own rages as "storms descending," and perhaps she had feared that I would also be hurt when they did. She wanted both of us to be safe from her destructive feelings. In the dream she experienced her own strengths; she would save us both. So her reliance on me had not taken away her own capacities but did make her feel she wanted nothing adverse to happen to this "grandmother." I also mused about what she might make of the "grandmother presence." I reminded her that we had sometimes guessed that there must have been positive presences, too, to account for her own strengths.

Her response to my musings was that her eyes welled with tears, and she was silent a long while. She then said, "I am hearing in my mind 'No, no, no,' but that is not all of it." I said I could see that it was not. She commented then on her own silence, "I don't know if I don't want to talk because I might persuade myself to drop the 'no' or whether something would be spoiled by the talking." So we sat quietly for a few moments until almost the end of the hour. Then Nora said that she had had some trouble with my being willing to see her this time at an hour that was not her regular one because of something that had come up for her and how it was always hard for her when people did special things. She also mentioned that the grandmother of whom she dreamed was actually coming to town, and she had debated whether to see her. What if she felt her old affection for her, with her being very old? "It would be painful to lose her," I said.

There ensued a period in which I saw Nora trying to regain and hold onto the capacity for concern. Her cat had been run over and had to be hospitalized, and she had been suffused with an unaccustomed feeling of love for him. She described to me how he had come to her as a kitten, and she had not wanted or cared for him at first. But he kept playfully reaching out, and she had been "won over." The week he had been in the hospital she had told people about him and elicited much concern from others. "I felt almost like a regular person," she said. Then she found herself without feeling again and unable to relate to colleagues at work. Even though she recognized that they were still nice to her, she felt like rebuffing them. Her eyes felt "glazed over"; the presence of father had returned.

She was suffering nightmares again, only now – in contrast to her usual report that she could not remember them – she could describe the content, and she could offer her own associations. There were scenes with slaves who were being mistreated; the slaves were all women; the tormenters, all men. These scenes blended into scenes with her parents, in one of which she learned that she had a brain tumor. Her parents had known it but withheld it from her. The slave scene, she thought, represented well her view of the relationship between the sexes, especially as she had observed it between her parents.

We speculated together that the caring "mother in her" had been awakened by the experience with her injured cat, for she had been aware of tender, solicitous emotions, but now the "father presence" was attacking that mother. Maybe that "father presence" was, I ventured, one reason for the difficulty in hanging on to the good sense of self she had briefly enjoyed? Perhaps that difficulty did, at times, make her feel that something was wrong with her brain. She agreed but added that the fear of a brain tumor was Sally's; it was from her that she got that idea. I commented on her wanting nothing withheld, even potentially traumatic ideas; she always wanted to know what I was thinking, even the previous hour when I had wondered whether the "mother presence" had been activated and it had been so unpalatable a thought that she had wanted to "puke it out."

The next session Nora came in announcing that she wanted my feedback on some experiences but that she knew she was "looking for a quick breakthrough." It seemed that a certain cat had been rather regularly making his home with her, although he belonged to the woman next door. When the latter went on vacation, she asked Nora to keep her cat. Nora, however, decided he would be better off with another neighbor and gave him to this person "for a trial visit." He did not, however, get along well there; there was already another cat in the foster home! Nora and Sally went over to get the unhappy animal, only to find that he had disappeared. She found herself with absolutely no feeling about him, whereupon Sally chastized her for her indifference and declared that she would be remorseful had she done something irresponsible like that.

In this context, Nora had the following dream. She was in a hotel room with mother and father, each sleeping in single beds. Hers was lined up at the foot of mother's, and father's was parallel to theirs but centered, so that half was against mother's bed and half against hers. Nora prefaced the next part by saying that she was not going to be able to tell this in detail. She had felt father making sexual overtures, about which she could not be explicit. In the dream she "woke in a rage" and bit him. He demanded why she had bitten him, insisting that he had done nothing. Mother commented to the effect that Nora should not blame him for what he did in his sleep and that it was "like Nora" to make up such an accusation.

In her spontaneous comments about this dream, the patient said that she thought somehow she did collude with father against mother. Although she had no memory of his making any sexual advances, this was not the first time that such a thought had occurred to her. Maybe, she hypothesized, here was some root of her feeling such a bad person, unworthy of any good thing. For the first time, she acknowledged that she had been afraid of her father. Moreover, she speculated, when she had told me of being afraid of Sally, she may have been identifying Sally with her father. Like him, Sally was dominating and humiliated Nora at times. But, she guessed, when she was afraid of losing that relationship, she must have been making Sally the mother. She doubted that she ever worried about losing father, but certainly she had terrors of separation from mother.

Thus, Nora moved toward a capacity to dream, to remember her dreams, and even to work and play with possible interpretations and to invite me to do likewise. We could usually see themes that related past with present.

A few sessions after the "incest dream," she brought in the following one: "My dog is there, the one that my parents gave away when I was eight or so, and I want to know whether she recognizes me. Then there is a little eight-year-old girl, and I realize she is the child I gave up for adoption. I have some feeling for her, but not enough. I think I should have more feeling." She spoke a bit about the dog, which had been given to her when she was four or five, "one of the few good things." When the family moved, it had to be given away. "I suppose I cried, but it was no use protesting," she told me. I commented on the importance to her that the dog recognize her and recalled that this recognition had also been what she wanted of her cat when he was injured and in pain. The experience of being known by those animals, then and now, must have afforded her some sense of "going-on-being," we thought, one that seemed harder to come by in the people world.

Nora claimed to have no idea what the child given up for adoption could mean, and she invited my thoughts on that puzzle. I associated to her recent story about giving the neighbor's cat to a "foster home" so that it would have a better chance for loving care. Maybe, in some sense, the animals were her children, although at times she doubted her ability to parent them. She nodded. "And maybe," I went on, "you got to feel a bit of your child-self in your play with that dog. So that when it was sent away, it was as if that part of you had been 'given up.' You became the unrecognized child." Nora's eyes welled with tears, but there was no "No, no," as had sometimes been the earlier response. She seemed comfortable to be with her thoughts, perhaps, I hoped, allowing herself more feeling for the child-self that might yet be retrieved. There were now emotions that I could read and that may enable more movement in therapy, too.

DISCUSSION

One is impressed with the strength of the reparative intent in patients such as Nora, with the power of the wish to make things better. There seems to be in such persons an image of what "better" could be, in spite of long histories of dissatisfaction and disappointment with self, with others, and with human relationships. Shor and I (1978) have developed a hypothesis about the origins of the notion of the ideal; we find it in the original gratifications at the beginning of life, in the primary illusion (from *in ludere,* in play). We have seen the newborn enjoying a "blissfulness in both the elemental feeling of self and in the primordial sense of home" (p. 121), with no conflict as yet between self-interest and connectedness with an other. We see this experience as imprinting a model of perfect fulfillment and imagine that subsequent efforts at repair and re-creation will aim at new editions of that primary illusion.

Of course, there is for the infant an inevitable fall from grace. Both maturational forces and environmental provisions and pressures make necessary the management of tensions and opportunities. The path of development can be described as a spiral dialectic between the two lines of development, that of the self (the "narcissistic" line) and that of togetherness (the "object relations" line). The infant with a good-enough mother first feels adequately supplied, with both the material and psychological nutriments necessary for going-on-being and for the sense of emergent self. Out of imagined "fusions" with the transformational other, he supplements his evanescent sense of self with identifications with others. As his own capacities and skills unfold, he uses these in participations with caretakers. As the core self begins to take shape, he exercises his abilities for affective cueing and movement to engage in the playful dialogue that Stern (1977) describes between an infant of several months with the mother, and his successes in regulating the interaction contribute to his self-esteem. The satisfactions derived from this interplay lead to ever more elaborate communications in the period when the senses of subjective self and of intersubjectivity are becoming evident and lead to still further refinement when language makes possible new sorts of exchange but also new complications.

Throughout life the person continues to emend images of self and of relationships in something like this original pattern. She seeks out sources – persons or ideas or cultural experiences – in the hope of taking in some wished-for qualities. Then, feeling those to be aspects of the emerging self, she wants to try them out in separate functioning and, by discovering that they are, indeed, now hers, to hone them for her own purposes. When she experiences a richer sense of self, she wishes to engage in exchange with others, both to share her new treasures and to explore still further possibilities that others may have found. There will be, at times, felt deprivation of needed supplies, suppression of functional capacities, and frustration in communications with others. These experiences motivate the search for what will set the dialectic once again in motion.

What of persons such as Nora, whose descriptions of relationships with her primary caretakers do not permit us to surmise that she enjoyed much of that illusion on which the reparative impulse might be based? Some sort of leap of faith is involved, perhaps, in our assumption that every living adult has had some modicum of the positive feelings that result when there is just an easy flow between autonomy and intimacy; if it were possible that there had been none, it is doubtful that the person would have survived. Certainly in those who make themselves patients for psychotherapy, the very cry for help signifies a hope. When the deprivation has been very early, as is likely for Nora, the restorative route will usually be a fairly long one, and there will be considerable work before a playfulness will be attained. These are the patients in whom some "regression to dependence" (Winnicott, 1954) is necessary to the self-reparative effort, but for whom reliance on the other is also fraught with risk.

Nora's story, to the extent that it can be reconstructed from what she either remembers or recognizes in current encounters with her parents could illustrate some of the recurrent efforts at repair in her life and could let us speculate on the possibilities and limits of those particular acts when they are performed unconsciously.

The other story is of this patient and therapist at this here-and-now time as they work toward a situation in which some playfulness might generate a revised edition of the primary illusion. This story can illustrate ways in which constant attention to the reparative intent in all symptoms and complaints may help to render potentially malignant regression relatively benign.

Nora described an ambience in her original home and family in which emotional responsiveness was minimal, and it left her with grave uncertainties about her ability to engage in meaningful dialogue with others. She seemed to have grown into an isolated and lonely little girl. Her reparative efforts included being nondemanding, perhaps even "disappearing" from the scene; as bad as the solitude felt, it was preferable to recurrent disappointment that the "supplies" for which she longed were not forthcoming. Her behavior of avoidant attachment led to a relative stuckness of the potentially spiraling dialectic. It became skewed toward the self and a premature "autonomy" that was not well grounded in imagined fusions of infancy or benign illusions of omnipotence.

Equipped with good intelligence, she managed to function well in school and achieve good grades, but this accomplishment was not particularly pleasurable to her, nor did it win any evident approbation from her parents. As we might expect, there was little joy in learning itself. Her desperate attempt to make school performance a substitute for other wished-for experiences may even have rendered the intellectual Nora something of a false self (Winnicott, 1960a). We could guess that some sense of this led, in her early teens, to the preoccupation with death, which also may have expressed the hidden hope that her despair would bring needed help. Only a teacher responded, with a suggestion for therapy, which the parents could not accept.

As Nora and I have reconstructed the story, she plodded on, going through college and getting a job that used what she had learned, but the work was infused with little pleasure and with no rewarding relationships either with employers or with peers. Her occasional attempts to make meaningful connections apart from work met mainly with failures. She felt consciously that she did not know how to be intimate, either emotionally or sexually. Her one previous attempt to use professional help ended with her quitting it, and she hoped that I could "hold her to her resolve this time."

The wish and the fear that this relationship could be meaningful were immediately apparent, both in her demeanor with me and in her suggesting appointments every other week. The transference, too, began as an avoidant attachment. When my recognition and articulation of her conflict about it enabled her to accept once-a-week therapy, I felt a certain optimism that she might, indeed, come to use me as a needed source, a provider of an ambience in which she might experiment with some new modes of repair and re-creation, and just possibly a provider of ideas she had not yet been able to formulate on her own, in part because feelings had been omitted. She brought me her affectless self. There was no evidence of grieving over the recent loss of a relationship, and she was inclined to "lose" me between appointments, since eros seemed as yet unavailable for creating a bond. Yet she did want to come.

In the therapeutic context, Nora was able to renew some functioning as a researcher gathering data for her own story. She visited her parents, observed and reported what she saw, and let herself consciously know the limitations of turning to them, either for emotional feedback or as models for meaningful connectedness.

Then she turned to a new hoped-for source, an admired woman, and for a while tried to comply with her request that Nora tell her the details of her therapy hours. At no time did I admonish her not to comply, but I empathically commented on the difficulty the demand posed for her and on the felt dangers of the recurrent, intense angers that beset her and that she tried desperately to curb, fearful lest she disrupt the valued tie to Sally. There were some risks of a "split transference" for a time, since Sally was admonishing Nora that she was not doing her therapy right, not telling me everything. This admonishment evoked some shame in my patient, but she did not know how to do other than what she was doing. I valued her going by her own measure of what she might want and be ready to share with me.

With Sally she felt some identification in that they were both patients of analysts. But she longed for more than that basis, especially for a kind of wordless closeness such as she imagined could occur in a sexual relationship.

Only after Nora experienced some capacity to connect with others could the pull to Sally include sexual feelings. As Winnicott (1958) observed, "an id impulse either disrupts a weak ego or else strengthens a strong one" (p. 33). Or, as Tomkins (1981) put it, a "drive" alone cannot motivate behavior; it must be amplified by affect. Nora achieved a degree of positive affect when, in her exploratory relationships at museums and cultural events, she experienced a bit of "ego relatedness," which is, Winnicott (1958) said, "the stuff of which friendship is made" and "the *matrix of the transference*" (p. 33). Perhaps she could generate those samplings of friendship out of transferences from her therapeutic transference. In any event, the resultant self-confidence let her at least tentatively be open to Sally's erotic advances. Their lovemaking did not feel like full exchange but was "pleasant."

That pleasure was spoiled, however, by Sally's demand that she "open up" verbally to a visitor who was a stranger to her, and her black cloud of fury descended on her, wiping out for a while her ability to see or say anything. In her retreat, she revived in the present the old experience of things being ruined when she was verbally relating to those from whom she could not expect empathy. She came, in sessions with me, to comprehend something of why she had been so compliant with Sally's requests that she share details of her therapy and why what she sought, namely a mutual exchange, could not be found when sharing was not spontaneous.

It was almost inevitable that Nora's difficulties managing the differences between relating to Sally and relating to me would, in time, catapult us into a crisis. She began to express doubts about me and this therapy. She was angry with me because she still felt crazy. She could also label as "crazy" her actually calling her friend's therapist for a possible appointment. It was an important test of me, and I passed it by interpreting her reparative impulse and by saying, in effect, that she had had no choice of parents but that she did have a choice of therapists, and it was important that she feel free to do what seemed best for her. The result was an increase in the margin of safety for some playing.

It is true that the "play" took the form of a brief dip into a psychotic episode. It followed the visit of her parents and her sense of their malignant "presences" within her. She experienced herself magnifying their behaviors in herself. Once more, there was relief from my interpreting her possible reparative motive, in her exaggerating their traits in herself, to make a conscious determination about identifications hitherto unconsciously made.

The test of this hypothesis might be in what ensued; Nora began once more reaching out for new relationships, and her dream revealed a growing awareness that she had been testing me in an array of potentially provocative behaviors. Neither had I been destroyed nor had I retaliated to her angers or "unfaithfulness," and so she could develop the capacity for concern about me as a separate other, valued and cared for. We discovered a positive "presence" among the negative ones that had crowded her psyche: a grandmother. In the process of arriving at possible meanings of the dream, she did not resort to her usual retreat as she experienced a felt closeness to me.

Now there was some playing out of themes of caring and not caring, of being cared for when one is caring, and of not being cared for when one is not caring. A new theme appeared—abuse of the caretaker role when an adult takes advantage of closeness for his own sexual purposes. She took that dream as a clue that perhaps her rages had active provocations but that there may have been prohibitions against knowing what she knew, prohibitions that would have included putting the lid on feelings.

As Bettleheim (1967) writes, "What probably heralds the extinction of all feeling, including pain, is an utter repression of hostility" (p. 62). He also observes the reverse, that when an autistic child begins to become interested in the external world, there is at first "an unfreezing of hostility" (p. 62). If, as Winnicott (1959–1964) believes, aggression is "evidence of life" and not of a death instinct, and it "makes objects feel real, and makes objects external to the self," then when patients like Katie and Nora can manifest directed angers, they are on their way to self-healing.

This freed aggression goes on to be shaped by interactions with the human environment. Libido and aggression are not for Winnicott (1950–1955) essentially different instincts; what will develop will be dependent upon environmental responses. Aggression is a part of love, but – as can be seen in Nora – after the "stage of concern," it can also evoke guilt. For Nora some of the defenses against concern have also been defenses against guilt. She probably did not have the help of a "personal and live mother" in discovering her own "personal urge to give and to construct and to mend" (Winnicott, 1950–1955, p. 206). In therapy she required a therapist who believed strongly in the reparative intent and at every opportunity enabled her to discover it in herself. Accompanied by love, aggression then can become a source of energy and spontaneity; accompanied by hate, a source of conflict, guilt, and fear.

As Nora began to play out many conflicts in her search for loving feelings in herself, she made use of cats to experiment with identifications, participations, and exchanges.

In the course of hearing Nora's cat stories, I found myself free associating to Milner's (1969) patient, Susan, whose earliest memory was of sitting by a piano and trying to feed her kitten at her breasts and "not understanding why the kitten didn't suck" (p. 6). At the point in her analysis that she began to turn up as a person, she had begun animatedly to talk of her various cats and of her cruelty to her present one. She would hit it hard because, like herself, it was greedy and insatiable. It would cower away, not understanding, she said. Milner thought this insight to be the first sign that Susan could attain "two-fold vision," that is, that the cat was both itself and yet also a representation of herself (p. 55). At about this time Susan was relating a dream of having a baby and wondering whether to do away with it or not. Her analyst thought the baby to be the frightening stirrings of what had previously been projected onto the outside world, and the cat, through such projections, had symbolized a split-off bit of herself.

Like Susan, Nora had some difficulty consistently caring for her cat/baby, but – indeed, like many babies with good "sending power" – he had, via his playfulness, elicited some caring and concern. It seems possible that he portrayed a "split-off bit of herself," too, in this instance a lost playfulness she could partly reclaim in attending to him. Then, after he was injured, his wounds perhaps facilitated an identification with him, since this patient was herself a walking wound. The gratification she felt from the solicitousness of coworkers to whom she told her tale gave her a sample of what the cat could never give her: human compassion and communication. She could speak to people of her cat's hurtings, but she had never been able to speak of her own.

That sense of verbal self and of exchange with others could not sustain her pet's recovery. The loss of a topic that could foster a conversation with others catapulted her again into nightmares, the image world, but now her ability to remember and report the contents and emotions in her dream life constituted a bridge between us. Our conjoint interpreting was increasingly a way of serious playing together, guessing at the role of her inner "presences" in her apparent loss of capacity for concern.

It would seem quite likely that Nora was not able to care for the cat that had been left to board with her and that her giving him to another neighbor was by way of sparing him her indifference – or even her potential cruelty. She could not yet stretch her empathy to feel the grief of the owner/mother who might have lost her pet/child. Nor could she herself grieve for the vanished cat/baby for whom she had been unable to become a good-enough foster mother.

Milner's patient dreamed of pregnancy, and Nora dreamed of an incestuous encounter with her father, of sharing perhaps in the "primal scene" in the way that a child seeking to regain something of the lost primary illusion might do. Instead of the hoped-for sense of fusion, sexuality under those dreamed circumstances led to rage and oral aggression. In her "memory bank" she did not find an image of father as much more capable of full mutuality than was her cat. So what began as assertion, as seeking for experiences of a transformational other out of which she could enjoy a sense of self in emergence, ended in hostile aggression.

We could view the dog/baby dream that followed the one about father's sexual approach to signify that Nora, like Milner's patient, was experiencing some long ago relinquished child aspects of herself. Her reparative thrust kept her looking for a situation in which there could be mutual recognition, in which the locking of eyes could be felt safe with human beings as well as with animals. Milner's patient had complained that she was "not behind her eyes," and Nora experienced alien "presences" behind hers. She seemed to sense that to be "there," she would have to be seen, really seen, by the other–whether in her "external" or in her "internal" world. Then she might really see the other as not alien to herself. To put it in Winnicott's (1971a) terms, we can claim as part of ourselves what we have the illusion of having partially "created" in the playful "omnipotence" afforded by potential space.

In the potential space of psychoanalytic psychotherapy, Nora may come to experience some benign illusion of fusion, out of which she could reclaim neglected potentials for participating and communicating with others. The dialectic between narcissism and human connectedness could resume.

CHAPTER 7

Re-railing the Dialogue

THE DIALOGICAL PRINCIPLE

Many of us see psychoanalytic psychotherapy as involving narrative (Schafer, 1980, 1982a; Spence, 1982). Weaving stories about our lives is one way we human beings attain a sense of continuity through change, of "going-on-being," as Winnicott calls it. I have long been of the opinion that education in literature might be a better undergraduate background for clinical education than the courses that are often specified. It could be fun to turn to some of the thinking of a writer who is other than a mental health professional and who is especially known for his absorption with the dialogical principle.

Mikhail Bakhtin has been called "the most important Soviet thinker in the human sciences and the greatest theoretician of literature in the twentieth century" (Todorov, 1984). He, too, has experienced the natural bond between his field and the human sciences. To shore up his theories about literary texts, he made forays into psychology and sociology and concluded that the methods in those fields were essentially the same as in his, namely the study of texts and their interpretation. Our science had to be different from those sciences that study objects – and of course he defined objects as "things." "Thingification," he declared, was not personification. When one studies persons, the object is not an object, but another subject. For Bakhtin, the sense of "being" human comes into existence only when there is responsive dialogue, and one's beingness throughout life is shaped by dialogue. Hence there is no understanding of human beings other than dialogical. While accuracy may be what matters in natural science, in human science it is depth that is essential. That, he said, is possible only with close attention to context, and, as we know, in the human realm one person is context for another.

Bakhtin's definition of interpretation is not based on the assumption that one person in the dialogue knows what the other "really" means; rather, it is essentially responsive understanding. The kind of dialogue he would advocate would be in a form in which the "thou" is equal to the "I," yet different from it.

For Bakhtin, not only human sciences but all artistic creation involves dialogue in its two aspects, which he calls *empathy* and *alterity*. The novelist, for example, puts himself in the place of his characters via identification with them. Then he must return to his own position, one of alterity, of otherness, difference. Only then can he give form to them; only then can aesthetic creativity begin.

Empathy, so much featured in professional literature today, must be complemented by exotopy, vicarious introspection with direct self-introspection. Our dialogue with the other increases our capacity to gain perspective on our externality for the other. Winnicott (1963d) would add that we cannot use the other until we have succeeded in creating that externality. So long as we imagine only identicality between us, there could be no growth on the part of either person. Creative understanding comes from the oscillation between the two aspects, imagined fusion and imagined separateness. Such understanding does not imply indifference, but it enables the viewer to be disinterested, that is, free of bias and self-interest. Says Bakhtin, it makes for an "assured, calm, unshakable, and rich position" (Todorov, 1984, p. 101) and for the preservation of the exotopy of the other, with the other's particular vision and comprehension. If we were to stop with empathy or merging, we would, he claimed, only deepen the tragic character of the other's life or of our own; in either instance we would double it!

Even if we creatively understand other cultures or persons of other cultures, we engage in the two aspects of the dialogue, empathy being always only preparatory, the second task being to use one's temporal and cultural exotopy. All knowledge has the status of ethnology, the study of socioeconomic systems and cultural heritage, in which the discipline is defined by the exotopy of the researcher in relation to the subject. Here, too, the dialogue is ongoing, and no understanding is final. Even past meanings are never finished; they will change in the course of further dialogic development. Forgotten things will return to the memories of the persons, and "every meaning will celebrate its rebirth" (p. 110).

I have been particularly intrigued that Bakhtin finds a role for fantasy in the dialogic process, for he writes that each participant in the dialogue imagines a "super–receiver." Neither the hypothetical author nor a patient can fully surrender himself, his work, and his ideas to the present and nearby receiver but instead imagines another with absolutely appropriate understanding. There is a third person hovering over the two participants, one imagined to understand even better than the watchful listener who is here now. (I am inclined to fantasize a fourth person, for in the clinical situation, the therapist may well entertain images of an ideal patient. Of course, those of us with leanings toward object relations could people the consulting room with hordes of "invisible guests" with whom we might be developing "imaginal dialogues" [Watkins, 1986]. I will stay for now, however, with the idea of this third person, since the patient whom I will be mentioning recurrently produced this never present but imagined other, with history and qualities more identical to her own. It generally had the effect of underscoring my alterity and my exotopy.)

As far as I know, Bakhtin left it to psychoanalytically oriented therapists to speculate on the sources of this fantasy of the ideal other, and some of us have done so, positing some traces of benign experience in even the most sordid of lives, experience from which the imagination takes off (Shor and Sanville, 1978). Bakhtin affirmed what we are increasingly confirming: "All that touches me comes to my consciousness–beginning with my name–from the outside world, passing through the mouths of others (from the mother, etc.) with their intonation, their affective tonality, and their values. . . . I cannot become myself without the other" (Todorov, 1984, p. 96).

INFANT RESEARCH ON THE DIALOGUE

Spitz (1963a), ever impatient with terms such as "object relations" and feeling that they were in the shadowy realm of abstract terminology that would likely lose its impact with time, preferred the language of dialogue, which makes us visualize a process between two persons. Writing at about the time that Bakhtin was writing in another society and another culture, he declared that life begins with the dialogue. Without it, maturation might proceed, but development would be arrested, for "dialogue constitutes the contribution of the surround to the inception, the development, and the subsequent establishment of ego, self, character, and personality. . . . Life, as we conceive of it, is achieved through the dialogue" (p. 174). It was through "derailment of dialogue" that all pathology was to be understood.

Yet, in 1965, Spitz published his book *The First Year of Life,* with a chapter on the objectless stage, essentially one of primary narcissism. The baby was, he said, shielded by an extremely high stimulus barrier so that the outside world was virtually nonexistent. Indeed, when the intensity of stimuli exceeded that of the barrier and shattered the infant's quiescence, she reacted violently with unpleasure. The counterpart of unpleasure was not pleasure, but quiescence. The infant could not, Spitz affirmed, be assumed even to perceive. She could receive, via "sensing," primarily in the viscera, and thereby attain a coenesthetic organization. Attaining diacritic, that is, discriminative, organization, would depend on later maturation, the use of peripheral sense organs, the cortex, and cognitive and conscious thinking processes. Such unfolding would rely on a reciprocity with the mother, on the dialogue. This was a dialogue of "action and response which goes on in the form of a circular process within the dyad, as a continuous mutually stimulating feedback circuit" (p. 163). It was not, however, a repetitive process; each interaction produced new constellations of ever increasing complexity. Traces would be left in the memories of each partner; these would modify subsequent reactions.

Like Bakhtin, he saw dialogue as possible only with an animate object, and in fact in his 1963 article he was explicitly examining the baby's attaining the ability to discriminate between animate and inanimate. He regarded this discriminative capacity as one of the more important ego functions, with a major adaptive role (p. 172). His experiments showed that infants became anxious when toys did not behave as the infants expected. Later researchers have emphasized that babies become distraught when mothers maintain blank expressions, devoid of affect.

Clearly, a paradox was involved in this dialogue since, in Spitz's schema, there was in that first year no self and no object. The self is a product of awareness, not manifest until around the 15th month of life. Until then, exchanges were somatic relations with the "non-I" (Spitz, 1983a, pp. 279–280), and they would remain as such within the personality.

So we can understand that Spitz was half-apologetic about asserting dialogues from infancy; he even expressed his willingness, if readers objected too strenuously, to call them precursors to dialogue (1963a, p. 163).

Probably no one who has viewed the film *The Amazing Newborn* (Hack, 1975) or who has studied in detail the vast literature describing the inborn capacities to connect with the other would demand that Spitz alter his language. If one's reading has included Piontelli (1987, 1989) and her study of twins in the womb, one might be ready to think that dialogue begins in utero, at least when a companion is there. Certainly one would also be ready to attend to the role of the caretaker, be it mother or father or other, in facilitating dialogue by playful interactions with the baby.

DE-RAILMENT OF DIALOGUE

So powerful is the "drive" toward social connectedness that one wonders how, under "average expectable conditions" (Hartmann, 1964), the dialogue could become de-railed. There is little evidence for primary narcissism, unless one redefines it, as did Winnicott (1971a), calling it the "original success condition," that is, the illusion of omnipotence enjoyed by the infant whose mother accurately interprets and responds to her baby's signals. That sort of benign narcissism simply lays the foundation for healthy self-esteem, and it grows out of the primary intersubjectivity (Trevarthen, 1979) between infant and caretaker.

If one wants to use the language of drives, then we might posit two: to develop the self and to connect meaningfully with others. The two are sometimes complementary (as in the earliest months of life when there is a good-enough mother with a good-enough baby) and sometimes in conflict. Dialogue, at its best, moves them toward mutual reinforcement of one another, while absence or scarcity of dialogue intensifies conflict and calls for defense.

How might dialogue become de-railed? The most obvious answer is that there could be deficits or obstacles in either sender or receiver or both. It has been common among mental health professionals to blame the original caretaker, usually the mother. At one time, we even coined the term "schizophrenogenic mother" and justified it by the aberrations in communication we could witness in families of psychotic patients. Some of us never subscribed to such a notion; especially if we had treated autistic children (such as Katie, the little girl in chapter 2), we suspected that there were deficits in the child that never let the dialogue get railed in the first place. We could stay open to the possibility that an especially inept mother or one who did not enjoy mothering might produce a child with similar symptoms, since the biological and the psychosocial are not strictly separable.

Grotstein (1989) hypothesizes that when there is a neurobiological impairment that leads to an absence of ties to objects (other human beings), there results a primary meaninglessness. He distinguishes this from secondary meaninglessness, which is due to decathexis or withdrawal of emotional investment because of conflict. He ventures that there may be a nonpsychotic schizophrenia, which begins with an experience of psychical death in infancy, with a subsequent "pathological but compensated restitution" (p. 266), perhaps manifest only in a subclinical affective disorder.

For the great majority of patients seen in outpatient settings there is probably not a demonstrable neurological underpinning. It may be that medical science does not yet have the tools to discern such factors when they exist in minimal ways; nevertheless these factors exert influences on the extent to which persons can actualize their dialogical potentials.

We are, however, on more solid ground when we note that there are temperamental differences among us human beings and that the match or mismatch with caretakers will exert a considerable influence on our developing personalities. How parents meet and interpret our inclinations–whether they can both identify with us and allow us our individualities–will influence both the selves we become and our later relationships in life. Although derailment of dialogue in the "sensitive" periods when the early senses of the self are in the process of forming will be harder to re-rail in later life, there is the unquenchable search for repair and re-creation, for the violation of the fixities into which one feels one has fallen. Many infant researchers have noted this self-righting tendency. Just as the body knows its own wholeness and, when ill or injured, tends toward restoration of that intact state, so does the psyche have a sense of its integrity and, when damaged, will instigate measures intended to be self-healing.

Sometimes the very measures themselves can appear to be the problem. As Freud (1914b) affirmed, every symptom is an attempt at restitution; the processes of recovery can give us the impression of being a disease (p. 86). This is perhaps true also of the so-called character defenses, those ways of being in the world that each of us adopts as a result of some disappointment with the dialogue of early life. Patients do not often come for treatment with specific symptoms, but rather with complaints about life in general, uncertainties about self, and restiveness about existing relationships.

Balint (1959) somewhat playfully describes two possible reactions to severe disillusion with primary love and makes it clear that no person fully takes on either mode in pure form and that both are attempts to regain a sense of harmony between one's own wishes and satisfactions and those of the other. But his definition of primary love is "a relationship in which only one partner may have demands and claims; the other partner (or partners, i.e., the whole world) must have no interests, no wishes, no demands, of his or her own" (p. 22). Such a state of affairs could exist only as illusion, and its very one-sidedness precludes the dialogue essential to psychic growth and development. So Shor and I (1978) choose instead to speak of primary illusion and include in that term both primary narcissism and primary love, coexisting under conditions that do not yet demand sharp boundaries because there is as yet little conflict between them.

We do find merit in playing with Balint's two possible ways of reacting to felt imperfections with this initial state of affairs. The first he calls *ocnophilic,* the love of clinging. The ocnophil likes to stay in touch with objects or persons; so long as she can be in physical proximity, there is a felt safety. Having discovered that the other, however kindly, may go away or may "drop" one, one has a chronic sense of possible danger. So the person with ocnophilic bent attempts at all costs to preserve the object. The second reaction is the *philobatic* way, to regard the world as full of friendly expanses but dotted with dangerous or unpredictable objects. The philobat needs to watch, to stay at a safe distance. Confronted with empty spaces, she feels very much alone. Philobats engage in the illusion, Balint says, that apart from their "own proper equipment" no objects are needed; the attitude is one of acceptance of separation. The equipment tends to consist of objects over which the person feels a certain control.

Both ocnophils and philobats entertain fantasies of their opposites; the ocnophil has dreams of venturing into the wide open spaces, and the philobat has dreams of home. I wonder whether in some persons, the ocnophilic stance may be akin to a version of the "false self" (Winnicott, 1960a), the "real self" inclining toward philobatism. In the following case, we could think that the philobatic self was the one presented to the world, seemingly adventurous and fearless, while the ocnophilic side, because fraught with anxieties, is the one most generally suppressed.

The story line in which we will be most immediately interested concerns the obstacles to, and potentials of, the developing dialogue between this patient and me and how we navigated the open spaces between empathy and alterity.

The patient's own unfolding narrative will have to do with discovering the features both of temperament and of early experiences that led to the predominant development of one of Balint's patterns and the relegation of the other to a more covert role and with achieving a more satisfactory balance between the two.

Initially asking for analysis, Andrea did not have very clear indications of what she might want to accomplish, and she certainly had doubts whether she and I could do anything meaningful together. For a long while she emphasized the differences between us and how they were likely to preclude my being able to understand her. In view of her long list of these obstacles, it was something of a mystery that she had chosen to see me. I was, she imagined, from an upper-class family while she was from the working class. I represented, she thought, "the establishment" while she was a rebel, rather outside the pale. Our sexual orientations were different, as were our religious backgrounds. I was a "lady" while she was a delinquent! I was a psychoanalyst, and she was not at all sure that she believed in psychoanalysis. She had had some previous therapy, lasting many years. Retrospectively, she was critical of that therapist for rather consistently "breaking the frame," and she was manifestly vigilant over my every move and only gradually decided that I could be trusted to respect the frame. The only hypothesis we could both entertain about her seeking me out was that she was aware of a certain reputation I had in our community and perhaps that there were some ways in which she hoped to transcend the confines of previous sociocultural, personal, and professional self-definitions.

In the beginning she recurrently complained of no particular attachment to me. One day, appearing in a very low mood, she reiterated her feeling that I could not possibly understand. I said something like, "You think I could not feel your pain?" She promptly corrected me. "I don't feel pain. I just feel I do not exist." What I chose to comment on was that in this instance she had expressed this feeling to me and had thereby helped me to comprehend the state she was in. We were then able to elaborate on that state, to see why, in spite of what to the world could look like a considerable degree of accomplishment, she went about with a feeling that she was a sham. None of the praise that often came her way seemed to alter in the slightest her very low self-esteem.

Our relationship was punctuated by sessions in which there seemed to be some breakthrough. She would manifest feeling and even arrive at seeming insights, but the very next session it would be as though the breakthrough had not occurred. There was little continuity or "working over" of themes that seemed important. Her way was to introduce some subject, usually some event in her current life, and shortly declare that it was not useful to talk about it or that it was something about which I could not be helpful to her. I usually think of analysis as a sort of journey of discovery, with the patient leading the way. But when I attempted to enable Andrea to pause and look at the scenery on the path she had taken, she declared it either uninteresting or too distressing, and we had to keep turning back. She was, at times, able to express a wish that I would take the lead but then would quickly warn me that if I did, she would give me trouble. There was in this ambivalence, as I experienced it, a humorous perspective on herself that promised playfulness to come.

With this pattern of interrupted dialogue, it was inevitable that periods of silence would ensue, often silences "loud" with angers. I felt very like a mother with a hurting and restless baby whom I could not successfully comfort. One day Andrea complained that she knew analysands who acutely missed their analysts over weekends, but she rarely even thought of me when she was not here. She supposed, she said, that she had a "resistance to the transference." I heard this statement as an invitation either to confirm or to deny her hypothesis, and so I allowed myself to say that perhaps what she was describing of her distancing me, not trusting, and not letting herself feel any needing of me was itself the transference. I invited her to review with me some bits of her history (gleaned not at the beginning but over the hours) that might support this idea. As I spoke, I noted (not for the first time) a steady trickle of tears down her cheeks. I mentioned something to which she had often referred, namely, that she was quite ill the first couple of years of her life. Mother had told her that she cried constantly and was inconsolable. I said that I felt rather like that mother, unable to soothe or comfort her, and, trying to imagine what the baby might feel, I guessed that she would not have the experience of complaining and seeing the other as able to do anything about her distress. Andrea wept more overtly, and softly said she knew I did understand.

We went even further with this topic. She allowed herself a bit of curiosity (the apparent absence of which had puzzled me all along in this very bright woman) and thought she might ask her mother more about these first years. What she knew was that the "stomach difficulty" cleared up after age two or so, and then she became superindependent. We both speculated that, on her part, she was freed for the first time of a condition that had rendered her futilely needing, since mother could make no helpful intervention. Perhaps mother was also relieved at the disappearance of the distress she could not alleviate and so welcomed the separation-individuation. Here Andrea added a note that it would, in any event, be in the character of mother to discourage dependence.

I wish I could report that after this session, there was some follow-through, that our dialogue began to flow. But no, instead there was a session in which Andrea was furious with me. As I had sampled before, her rages could be extensive. This time the complaint was that she was aware of the presence of a cleaning woman in the house, and where did I "get off" to allow that when she had her appointment! It was bad enough that there were sometimes noises of construction from a nearby house, but here, where I should be able to control things, I allowed gardeners outside, cleaning women inside, and "that man" (my husband) often around, unseen but sometimes heard. After all, a patient paid for a quiet surround, where meditation could occur. (As her tirade went on, with abusive language thrown in, I was struck by the noise coming from the couch and the tranquility of the rest of the space outside of the room. She was being so provocative that I had to allow myself some silence before making a response to her. I comforted myself with the memory of many patients who say that they love coming here because it is so peaceful.) Andrea continued with her critique of the quality of space I provided her, saying she did not know what other patients did with it, but for her it was intolerable.

I reflected inwardly that, indeed, there might be some reason that she could not filter out irrelevant sounds. My thinking took me to the idea of the "stimulus barrier," which was being rethought by current infant researchers. Freud (1917) and indeed some of the earlier observers of infancy (Spitz, 1965b) had posited that the baby at birth responds only to sensations in the body, but Spitz had redefined this stimulus barrier as the uncathected condition of the sensorium, so that stimuli had as yet no meaning. Current writers were emphasizing the stimulus hunger, especially in states of quiet alert. They were noting, however, that infants can be selective, block out unwanted stimuli, reach for others. Mothers play a dual role, on the one hand as stimulus givers and on the other hand as regulators of the dosage so that the baby is not overstimulated, by unassimilable stimuli either from within or from without. Whatever internal "structure" enables one to tune in or out, to filter out what is relevant and to let go of the irrelevant may also depend upon early relationships with caregivers.

I should mention that all along I had noted that this woman rarely came in and began talking at once, as do many patients. She more often seemed to scan the room, to look about as though to see whether anything had changed, rather like Balint had described of philobatic behavior. She would but briefly glance at me on entering and leaving the room. She had a ritual for both events. As I described earlier she would come in, sit down on the couch, lay her purse and her keys on the coffee table, take off her shoes, empty her pockets of any change, and then lie down. At the end of the hour, she would reverse these actions, again casting a brief look at me before her exit.

After allowing myself to turn to my theories for some cues, I said to Andrea, "I am hearing your distress that I do not provide for you the ambience you need. I know that it is hard for you to get away from those daily events and to make the journey into inner space, and when you must be aware of things going on in daily life here it seems to make it even harder." Then I wondered whether, as soon as I could manage to work it out, she would like to come early in the mornings before any of the goings-on that disturbed her would be occurring. She seemed surprised at this offer and said that it would be hard for her to rearrange her own schedule and that it sounded to her as though I was taking too seriously what she was saying! We parted, with my commenting that she could think about the suggestion, and if at some time she wanted, we could try for earlier sessions.

The next hour the topic was gone. Some mundane concerns were preoccupying her. She herself observed, however, that she was not returning to what she had been saying the day before. She informed me that she was not going to let such things interfere with our work together. She began to talk of a forthcoming trip home to see her parents and to ask herself whether she might try to find out more about what had turned her so decisively against her father.

Close to the beginning of our work she had said that she was convinced that she had been sexually molested, although she had no idea by whom or when. She suspected her father, and she told of literally years in which she utterly refused to talk with him. She had no idea why. Day after day she would sit at the table and stubbornly refuse to speak in his presence, and she would retreat to her room after meals.

The few dreams she brought, always written down, were usually of being chased by unidentified males, but included one in which father was pursuing her with intention of rape. There was also one in which her brother was having intercourse "a tergo" with her, and she admitted, to her chagrin, she was enjoying the experience and did not want him to leave. There had been some intensely emotional sessions, one in which she had pounded on the wall and declared that if she ascertained that, indeed, her father was the guilty one, she would have to kill him. That fantasy filled her with dismay, since mother, whom she loved, would also be hurt.

In the next-to-the-last session before she left for her visit home, she came in saying, "I don't feel like talking today." Shortly she said she was trying to put herself into a calm state before seeing her parents. She had a strong premonition that something calamitous could happen, though what, she could not say. I simply commented appreciatively on her wish to generate in herself an attitude that would facilitate her meeting with whatever was to be. She was silent a while, then said, "If I were going to the guillotine, I would turn off all feeling as I am doing now." I wondered if she wanted to play with that image a bit and said, "If you were, you would not be going to it of your own volition?" She picked up this thought, and said she did not know where the compulsion came from; it was just something that had to be. She seemed to be setting up the scene for tragedy, some inevitable and not necessarily wanted ending to her story. I commented that she did seem to fear losing her head. My comment missed a bit. She denied fear and was not inclined to say any more. Instead, she fell silent again for some while.

In such periods I tend to allow my own mind some of the free play for which the patient is not ready, in this instance about the theme of tragedy. Andrea was disclaiming that whatever was to occur would be of her own agency; instead, she was seeing herself caught up in something bigger than she and out of her control. I wondered whose head was likely to fall; after all, the executioner also approaches the guillotine, and there were those fantasies of having to kill the father – and of the possible death penalty, were she convicted. Indeed, she had talked of that possible ending, not as a fear, but as part of a story inexorably unfolding, her self not the center of initiative.

There played in my mind the strains of the chorus in Stravinsky's *Oedipus Rex*. Like that one, the chorus in Andrea's mind seemed to be ominously predicting for this female protagonist some profound disaster or ruin. Like the classical heroes of tragedy this one saw herself as engaged in a morally significant struggle; her high principles were to be her greatness and her downfall. Yet, although she had been an articulate defender of females against corrupt and untrustworthy males, I remembered that in her dreams there had sometimes appeared a rescuer, in the form of a man. My gut feeling was that eros would triumph over thanatos.

I began, as when I am part of the audience to a play, to try to imagine whether the father, whom I had met only through his daughter's descriptions, could possibly be guilty of what she suspected. As much of the literature on incest informs us, however, and, indeed, as many patients had already taught me, the view from the outside is never a complete one; many seemingly fine and high-principled men have made quite unfatherly advances to their young daughters. As an adult, Andrea had maintained what could be described as a cordial relationship with her father and even averred that she loved him and knew that he loved her. There was a side to him that she liked, a warmth, a concern, a generosity; indeed, she identified with these aspects. Yet she took great care never to be alone with him nor to tell him anything that was deeply important to her. But then, with mother, too, she tended to be most circumspect about the content she allowed to enter their dialogue and rarely spontaneously shared personal feelings. For reasons not yet clear, she experienced a degree of irritability when mother was around, so she regulated their togetherness to relatively brief times. She admired a quality of forthrightness in her mother but did not credit her with great empathic capacities. She identified with mother's strong, vigorous, lusty qualities while seeing herself as more sensitive than mother to other persons and situations.

I also let myself dwell briefly on the relationship with her brother, with whom, when she was a child, she had shared a room. When she was about seven, why had he left home abruptly, never to make himself part of the family again? Neither she nor her parents talked of this situation. With me, Andrea seemed either uncurious or unwilling to ponder this topic much.

So, I was letting myself concoct these possible plots when, at the end of the hour, Andrea decided to comment, just to say that it was going to be hard to face things alone. She was disappointed her lover could not accompany her.

The following hour she was feeling better; she had had a long and helpful talk with her lover. She did not want to tell me of that; in fact, she did not want to talk at all. "I'm not mad at you. It is only that you are irrelevant." I replied, with a touch of humor, "That's a pretty complete dismissal." She said, "I don't want you to take it personally, or as permanent." She shortly went on to assure me (and herself, I thought) that she was not feeling guilty about the way that she was treating me. "I don't feel responsible for you. If I loved you, I'd have to feel responsible." I said, "You want to feel that I don't need you, and so you don't have to take care of me. That could be a relief." She was silent a while, then said her lover would go on a vacation with her next year. They were talking of a trip to some islands, where Andrea could take lessons in scuba diving. She would take them alone, since the lover "would be claustrophobic" about going to those depths. I could not resist this one; I said, "One could be claustrophobic about depths." She turned her head to look at me directly, laughed, and declared, "I am speaking about scuba diving!" But the tension lightened.

She went on to a fantasy of walking alone on a long trail to a certain spot on the island, where her friends, having arrived by helicopter, would meet her. The only thing she would fear would be sexual assault, not the steep and slippery trail. Now she mentioned her good walking shoes. She imagined that I did not even own a pair of sneakers; at least she had never seen me in such. Mother never owned any either until last year when Andrea bought her a good pair. "Maybe," she joked, "I will have to take you out and buy you some." We both laughed.

She fell silent again. She ventured at one point, "You must be bored." I replied, "You hope that I have lots of things to think about, having read all those magazines." (I was alluding to a previous session when she had, in one of her further illustrations of the differences between us, observed the variety of publications on my table outside and compared them to their total absence in her original home.) She smiled. "And," I added, "you give me lots of images about which I can fantasy, and that could let me stand by until such time as you find a use for me." She was quiet again. Then she asked whether we were close to the end of the session. I told her, "Two minutes." In a voice so soft I could barely hear it, she thanked me for not intruding. She mentioned receiving a card from her former therapist and not reacting so resentfully as she had last year when that event had happened. (I remembered how she had viewed that as an unwarranted intrusion and thought she might obliquely be telling me that, given enough time, she could "mellow out.") She said I must notice that she brought her own coat today. At the end of the preceding hour she had reported that she had been cold and that she was well aware I kept an afghan near by. But she could not bring herself to ask me for it or even to use this thing of mine. "I can't let myself need you," she whispered in parting.

Can we consider any of this therapy as play? In a way there was something rather like "deep play" (Bentham, 1840) in the whole enactment going on in this psychotherapy, play in which the stakes were felt to be high but by this woman's felicific calculus may have made it worth the risk.

When she first came to analysis, she professed no belief in it as her "defense" against being hopeful, lest the endeavor fail. She seemed to me to be reaching for an experience that might restore a sense of emergent self, for she had been accusing herself of "stagnating" and especially of not using her rather considerable intellect. Difficulties in nearly every area of the core self were manifest. I have cited situations in which she seemed to disclaim a sense of agency, of feeling. Discontinuities were in evidence, big and small. Some years before I saw her, she had been left by a lover with whom she expected to share the rest of her life; grief about that loss kept recurring, especially since she was forced at that time to see the abandonment, in large part, as a consequence of some rather abusive behaviors of her own. She consciously feared that she could have a break, so a sense of coherence was not solid.

When she returned from her visit home, she reported that it had been relatively uneventful. Now she told me that, prior to her trip, her lover had advised against opening up old issues with parents and said that it was unlikely to be helpful. I explored with Andrea whether she had thought I might have wanted her to confront them. She fumbled a bit in her answer and joked, "Sometimes English is my second language," but she managed to say that she never felt I pressured her in any way. Whatever pressure she may have felt, she attributed to herself, to a wish to move this analysis along. As she described some of the interactions at home, however, I was aware that she cited examples of father's temper with mother, of his constant "picking on her." Mother always seemed to field these verbal assaults well, so Andrea stayed out of the frays. But sometimes she was guilty that she did not defend mother. If he had ever laid a hand on mother, Andrea and he would, however, have engaged in mutual mayhem. I suggested we could play with a hypothesis that Andrea protected both herself and him by her withdrawal from him. She could entertain that idea better, she said, than another we had thought of – an identification with mother and "carrying" the hostility for her, since mother seemed never directly to express hostility. She did not think that she was identified with mother nearly as much as with father. She thought mother's ability just to remove herself from the situation over the years had prevented more serious open warfare between the parents. Andrea herself had father's temper and often exploded when someone stepped on her narcissistic toes.

There was one more possibly significant scene during her home visit. Mother had offered her money for her plane fare; she had declined, although she was not without financial worries, as both parents knew. Father then made some crack about how they hoped she would come to their financial rescue when they were old. She thought that comment "weird," implying an incompetence on her part, so had asserted her ability to help them if necessary; she had investments. She was glad to have declined mother's offer in view of this development. I thought of her reluctance to take from me. There was almost no comment I could make that she would not correct in some way or, worse, fall into a silent anger that I had imperfectly understood. It was far easier to deal with the first; dialogue could then keep flowing. The alternative seemed to connote a despair on her part and a concomitant mistrust. Here was a clue, perhaps; if she accepted from me, she would prove her own insufficiency.

There were extended periods in which nothing I could do or say was right, but also nothing she could do or say was right either. She tended to rule out events in daily life that evoked strong emotional reactions, forced herself to speak instead of what she "should," and then declared it devoid of feeling and meaning. For example, one day she announced, "I should talk of my father" and informed me that he had never wanted another baby. In fact, she thought babies were not important to either parent; they waited a long while to have their first child. When the second one came, she was somehow defective. Andrea had previously told me of this fact and also that mother had not told her for a number of years that she had this institutionalized sister. She guessed that father may have been apprehensive on this account. Mother, not wanting her son to be an only child, insisted, and "this squalling, sick baby who was me arrived." Her mother had told her that before the children, she and father used to have fun; afterward, fun stopped, including sexual pleasure. Andrea told all these things as "facts," shrugged them off, and said they were what they were and seemed irrelevant now. In the next session she was angry at me and at herself again.

One day she came in with one of those rare, subdued smiles and said she had been wondering how I had been coping with her behaviors; they must be "frustrating." I observed that she might be wanting to check that I was all right. (I had in mind Emde's social referencing, needing to know whether it was safe to engage in such modes of conducting herself, even within an analysis.) She then went earnestly into her reluctances to care for me. Our relationship was, she declared, a relationship with no future. She was not one to long for what she could not have, and she had no time for brief commitments. (I was experiencing her becoming literal about the therapeutic relationship; it was either "real" love or nothing.) She hated imbalance, that is, that she should depend on me and that I did not need her. I ventured that she had managed to establish that "balance" in her previous therapy. She responded with surprise; she had never thought herself to have had any part in creating that; she had attributed it solely to the therapist.

She did not want to be a baby; babies were useless. Mother told her that she only cried and that babies seemed "totally uninteresting." "So," I mused, "a crying baby and a mother with little time for infants?" (The then and there and the here and now seemed to me one and the same.) One of those big tears ran silently down her cheek. "Someone should have put me out of my misery," she said. "If you had thought someone might want to, it would have been terrifying," I noted. "How?" she asked innocently. I reminded her of the time when I had referred to her pain and she had corrected me, saying she was not in pain, just "not being."

She had forgotten. Indeed, her memory seemed to be scant not only for much of early life but for much of our attempted dialogue. For a long while that fact made for feelings of discontinuity, incohesiveness.

Slowly, slowly, Andrea's reluctance to let our relationship matter was giving way. As she began occasionally to enjoy some relatively tranquil sessions–analogous, perhaps, to quiet alert states–she would report, "I felt good about last session, but I hated to tell you." In such states she could work over–or perhaps play over–data that she had previously dismissed. She began to grieve that she had never experienced a mentor in her whole life. This feeling revived her wishes that I were a lesbian; then I could be a model for her. Among the dreams she began to bring in, sometimes now unwritten, was one in which I was–and yet was not–a lesbian. (I thought that the "super-receiver" was being identified and, at least to some extent, now fused with this dream representation of me. The corollary was that she was becoming something like a "super-sender"–although Bakhtin had no such category! In any event, it seemed evident that the dialogue was moving toward re-railment.) Andrea thought in the dream that I would not know how to have an affair of this kind, but my not knowing would not matter. In still another dream she learned I had a spiritual life, and she thought she might want to look into that for herself some day.

Then, to her astonishment, she began to have dreams of children (although she had always told me of her intense discomfort and unfamiliarity with children). In one such dream she encountered an old friend who had a child with him, and she experienced a touch of envy. In another, she herself was playing with a child, quite pleasurably. (I felt these dreams signified that she might be approaching some readiness to bring her child-self here, to allow expression to those early senses of self, to rework and replay them.)

At the time of this writing, we tentatively summarized things to date by observing that in childhood her behaviors were centrifugal; she was forever going away from people, either psychologically (never confiding in anyone her feelings and thoughts) or literally (she eventually ran away from home.) In adult life she had tried to remedy that extreme mode and had become centripetal, removing herself pretty much from the social world and gravitating to home. We both hoped that the future could include flexible movement in both directions, so that there might be further delight in the dialogue that flexibility permits. Occasional derailings were to be expected, but it was now likely we could learn from them in ways that promised to restore some meaningfulness to her life.

DISCUSSION

There were, of course, recurrent derailings of our dialogue. As Bakhtin well knew, the dialogic sphere is fragile, easily destroyed (Morson and Emerson, 1989). The facilitating context was, I think, the absence of any coercive feature, even in the form of instruction to free-associate, and the willingness of both of us to re-rail when there were rifts. Although at times it seemed Andrea despaired of understanding, given the differences between us, there were also times when there appeared moments of felt identification, and these tended quickly to be followed by episodes that generated a distance. On several occasions Andrea was relieved when I acknowledged in words that a "gap" existed between us. Although she longed for a richer experience of identification, it was not to be at the expense of her own exotopy.

Like Bakhtin, Andrea was a realist and, like him, probably would not have gone for Shor and my (1978) dialectical ideas about the oscillating states of fusion and separateness, both of which, in our view, are illusions. She was the kind of analysand to provoke in the analyst some questioning of cherished assumptions. In this instance, I kept thinking of what I knew of Bakhtin's description of the limits of empathy, that to identify totally with the other – if that were possible – would be to reproduce what was already there and contribute nothing new. Yet I was continually reminded in the dialogue of her felt necessity for a sense of identification with me, simultaneous with a felt necessity to keep her separateness.

I began to rethink ways of describing for myself the dialogic process. Perhaps Bakhtin's *vzhivanie* (translated as "live entering" or "living into") was a better concept than our empathy. "In *vzhivanie,* one enters another's place *while still maintaining one's own place,* one's own outsideness, with respect to the other" (Morson and Emerson, 1989, p. 11). It seems a kind of double vision, requiring both "insight" and "outsight" simultaneously. The creative understanding that results is productive of something new and enriching, because it is simultaneously of self and of other. One glimpses oneself in the eyes of the other, with her particular singularity, and enhances one's sense of the uniqueness in this and every clinical encounter.

Bakhtin saw the opposition of the social and the individual as a false dichotomy; rather, the two constitute a "live entity" that transcends synthesis (Morson and Emerson, 1989, p. 7). This view seems in keeping with much that infant research is revealing about the beginnings of life and with the trend toward the interpersonal model of psychoanalysis and psychotherapy. We are, I think, fundamentally ready to acknowledge the interdependence of self and object, although our theories may not have kept pace with our clinical experiences. We may, however, not be ready to do as Scharff (1988) challenged us, to write protocols that include the analyst's own reactions and internal experiences alongside those of the patient. I am aware that I have included some, but by no means all, of my own in the case vignettes in this book.

Bakhtin would emphasize the absolute unrepeatability of each dialogic encounter. Although we hunger for a theory that might tell us "how to do it" in each instance, such a theory is highly problematic. Andrea, treated by someone else, would have had a different analytic experience; the same could be said of any patient with any therapist. Her own, somewhat jaundiced view of psychoanalysis was, in part, because of what she perceived as its theories about women and their development, but also because its method deprived her of knowing anything much about me. The dialogue of psychoanalysis is not an equal one, as Bakhtin would see "true dialogue" to be. In that way, too, he would take, with Andrea, a stance against Freud, but equally against Pavlov or any theoretical school.

He was against our deriving norms from our generalizations about human actions. His ethic features a profound respect for the individuality and singularity of the other, much as one finds in some current writers (Shor, 1990). To theorize is to lose the "eventness" of the event, the particular, never-to-be repeated aspects. For many of us, part of the pleasure of our professional lives is precisely that no two narratives describing our therapies will be the same and, indeed, that we find ourselves not the same therapist with one patient as with any other. One of the attractions of this profession is that we find it meaningful to play at being coauthors of so many stories of psychotherapy.

Andrea was seeking for meaning in her life. She felt a persistent sense of obligation to do something for the world, something bigger than her work and her personal life. She seemed motivated not by any rules that she might be violating but by some existential sense of "oughtness," by a wish to make a commitment that was her own. She had a sense of what Bakhtin calls "potential meaning," born out of a realization that she had unused abilities and that she could somehow address some of the many social problems that dismayed her. To transform that potential meaning to actual meaning would take some act to which she could inscribe her own signature, as Bakhtin puts it, thus making the act her own (Morson and Emerson, 1989, p. 16).

Patients such as Andrea, who imagine that they could accomplish something that no one else could, challenge psychoanalysis to contemplate issues of moral choice. We might, traditionally, suspect such an aspiration to be motivated by narcissistic needs or perhaps by guilt. Bakhtin would, I gather, say that "one could think [in that model] but one cannot accomplish an act in it" (Morson and Emerson, 1989, p. 10).

Bakhtin does not offer to explain the origins of this sense of obligation or of what enables the person to act on it. Nor does he deal with what gets in the way of such action. If superego is the motivator, it must be of the sort that arises in earliest infancy, in the pleasurable exchanges with the mother that make for a delight in one's sense of self and of reciprocity with the other. But, if Andrea and I, to any degree of accuracy, reconstructed her infancy, it seemed more distressful than happy. There appeared to have been experiences in childhood that left her without a solid sense of agency. So we must posit a basic reparative or recreative intent in her expressed dream of making a singular contribution.

Andrea impressed me as having considerable ease with her own body, as evidenced by the way she made herself comfortable on the couch and her awareness of body sensations, including breathing. Such "primary self-enjoyment" can be, as Milner (1969) writes, "not a rejection of the outer world but a step toward a renewed and revitalized investment in it" (p. 383). She posits that some persons seem "to be aware, dimly or increasingly, of a force in them to do with growth, growth towards their own shape" and that this force can move them toward "a kind of creative fury" that will also be feared "because of the temporary chaos it must cause when the integrations on a false basis are in the process of being broken down in order that a better one may emerge" (pp. 284–285). Andrea was conscious of such fears and, indeed, of the myriad ways in which her relatively comfortable exist-ence would be suspended, if not abandoned, were she to move toward some new and different commitments. Added to this were some anxieties stemming from her not having experienced clearly choosing a goal and then successfully attaining it, although to an outside ob-server it would seem that she had some noteworthy accomplishments to her credit. Even in the period I knew her, she reported many episodes in which others lauded her performance, but these did not add up to an increase in self-confidence.

There seemed to be hovering residuals from early years. There were severe constraints about translating into words some probable trau-matic experiences. Perhaps, she thought, she may have tried to talk with mother, who then simply dismissed her story. Or perhaps to have given voice to these experiences might have confirmed an unwanted reality, maybe catapulted her toward an action felt to be destructive of self and others. So there were years of silence, especially with father. That these experiences were now felt as "lost" may, in part, have been due to their never having been articulated and hence "kept."

In our sessions Andrea recurrently manifested reluctances to put into words what might enable me to understand better. It was not always that she thought I might not comprehend but rather that there was just no point of telling me something that she already knew, so the texture of daily life tended to remain somewhat hazy. One of the differences between us to which she did not call direct attention was one of which I am constantly aware and which can make for some sense in me of delimited space for countertransference – playing with language itself. I have always loved the language of poetry, which Bakhtin calls "a unitary, monologically sealed-off utterance" as contrasted with the language of the novel, preferred by him for its prosaic qualities (Morson and Emerson, 1989, p. 53). Whereas with some patients both their tropes and mine emerge freely, to be used as playthings between us, with Andrea I learned to stay close to the "warmth" of everyday language. Fortunately I love the novel, too, and appreciate that "warmth" – not in the sense of its feeling qualities, but in the sense of its not having been formed for aesthetic purposes in any primary way. There was much playing with ordinary talk, sometimes a gentle teasing, and again – from Andrea – an experimenting with hostilely tinged testings, followed by manifest relief in my survival and in the going-on-being of our essential relationship.

I encountered another countertransference problem when Andrea pronounced broad generalizations and universalized from her particular experiences. For reasons that I unearthed in my days on the couch, I have always had an allergy to anything smacking of dogma. Thus, I have to contain myself when I hear flat pronouncements, as about the virtues of the female of the species versus the offenses and offensiveness of the male and various extensions that have to do with implementing such beliefs. In such moments it was easier to go with Bakhtin's idea of "living into" Andrea's worldview and simultaneously to stay with my own than to get lost myself in empathy with her. At least it was easier when I did not experience her wanting to extract some agreement from me; some of our troubles were when she could not experience that as forthcoming.

What seemed to be getting repaired was our mutual confidence in the reparative urge, in our ability to re-rail the dialogue when it was off-track, to commit ourselves to this ongoing process that is psychoanalysis. Like Freud, I suspect the process is essentially interminable or – in Bakhtin's terms – "unfinalizable" until death itself makes it so, and then the survivor will have the last word.

CHAPTER 8

Primary Trauma
Work, Love, and Play
Toward Repair

PRELUDE

The concept of trauma bears constant rethinking. As with many words in our psychoanalytic lexicon, we throw it around easily, glibly even, perhaps hardly noticing that its referents subtly change in different historical periods and that it is influenced both by sociocultural events and by the shifts in our clinical theories.

In recent years, those who have been impressed with Masson have tended to believe that Freud, after abandoning his seduction theory, concerned himself only with the internal fantasies and ignored the possibility or even probability of external events. Those who trouble to read Freud himself, however, realize that all his life he was recurrently preoccupied with trauma and with the interactions of inner and outer that are involved in the experience of trauma. Particularly if one reads what he was writing at the time of World War I or at the onset of World War II, with the massive persecution of the Jews, one sees him again and again giving cognizance to actual happenings. Moreover, he seemed constantly to be expanding his idea of the traumatic beyond the sexual.

Part of what troubled him about attributing to traumatic experiences a role in all neurotic disturbances was the assumption that these were the fate of only a few human beings, while his notions of drives included us all. In his recently published *Phylogenetic Fantasy* (1985), originally written (1915) during World War I as one of his 12 inter-related metapsychological papers, he was making an effort to integrate trauma and drive theory (Grubrich-Simitis, 1988). He was, as he himself acknowledged, engaging in his own fantasies, invoking the even-then discredited Lamarckian theory of the inheritance of acquired characteristics to posit that our ancestors who had suffered the ravages of the Ice Age had genetically bequeathed to us a disposition to neurosis. In 1915 he wrote, in a letter to Ferenczi (Jones, 1957), "What are now [psycho]neuroses were once evolutionary stages of the human species" (Grubrich-Simitis, 1988, p. 5).

In 1924, he manifested an initial enthusiasm over Rank's idea of the birth trauma and celebrated it as the most important step since his discovery of psychoanalysis. But then, according to Grubrich-Simitis (p. 26), he later wrote to Rank, "You are the feared David, who will bring about the devaluation of my work with his birth trauma." (I cannot help but draw analogies to the reactions of some analysts to the burgeoning information about infancy, information often seen as threatening established doctrine.) Yet, Freud himself, in the 1915 paper he had elected not to publish, had widened his concept to include events in the period of primary structuralization. He included not only "impressions of a sexual and aggressive nature" but also "early injuries to the ego (narcissistic mortifications)" (p. 74). Later he further pondered, "A small living organism is a truly miserable, powerless thing . . . compared with the immensely powerful external world, full as it is of destructive influences. A primitive organism which has not developed any adequate ego-organization, is at the mercy of all these 'traumas' " (1926, p. 202).

Grubrich-Simitis describes Freud as steadily moving toward a theory of causation that includes both trauma and drive, or event and fantasy (1988). Today's clinicians may not have much trouble embracing that view, although they would be more likely to speak of "drive-affects" (seeing drive as a metapsychological term and affect or emotion as the driving power.) Our increasing sophistication has led us to recognize that it is a basic attribute of the human mind to interpret all events according to the maps or models created out of individual experiences. We do not perceive directly but via the concepts that we have organized to enable us to find meaning in life's events. Many of us do see herein a cue to what is mutative in psychotherapy – that meaning schemes are modified and expanded in such a way that old fixities are undone and new flexibilities become possible.

I want herein to maintain that this mutative factor is operative even when the experienced trauma is very early, provided we can enable the adult patient to engage in what I will call a "developmental regression" and – like a child in play therapy – use this to reconstruct or perhaps to construct more satisfactory life narratives.

A CONCEPT OF PRIMARY TRAUMA

"Trauma" comes from the Greek, meaning a wound or hurt. It refers not to what inflicted the injury but to the effect on the person. What is wounding to one person may not be to another, or what is hurtful at one age might not be at a later age.

The concept is, on the one hand, an economic one, being concerned with the power of the assault vis-à-vis the resources (inner and outer) of the person at the time. It is, on the other hand, a hermeneutic one, involving the schemas available to the person to comprehend the event, its meaning and significance. The link between the two could be seen as the emotional factor. We presume that the experience of trauma exposes the emotive system to stimuli of high intensity (Spitz, 1945). If that intensity reaches a level so high as to disrupt the individual's adaptive capacities, then the power to organize would be dissipated. Were this disorganization to happen in the earliest months of life, the infant's relationship with caretakers would be seriously affected. As I have said, the baby learns the dialogic mode best in playful encounters with parents, but if, for whatever reasons, there are "derailments of dialogue" (Spitz, 1964), there will be little playfulness and much danger of later psychopathology.

Babies learn best when there are no pressing inner or external (social) needs (Sander, 1983a). "Normal," that is, predominantly pleasurable interactions, are the stuff of representation (Sander, 1983b). When, however, the infant experiences overstimulation, that is, stimulation beyond his abilities to make order of the chaos, there is likelihood that something may be omitted from the mental maps that are being formed; they will consequently be less good guides for action. Demos (1980) says that the bulk of psychic structure is created when "I" and "we" are going well. If this is the case, then when there are the inevitable empathic breaks with caretakers, the infant is challenged to test out adaptive capacities. The baby who experiences good-enough mothering has some confidence in his restitutive capacities.

Ferenczi (1931) was of the opinion that it was the non-communication after the event that rendered it really traumatic. He was writing explicitly then of sexual seductions, but we could extend his concepts to apply to what I am calling "primary trauma," that is, the wound to the psyche in the period before there is speech to discuss it. At its worst, even prespeech, the dialogue of affective exchange, can be retarded and rendered inadequate when the baby is subject to such high-intensity distress that caretakers, no matter how eager to be of help, cannot alleviate the misery. So, in addition to the original trauma, there is added the trauma of the failure of the reparative effort.

What might be the reasons for primary trauma? Clinicians often have a tendency to find the parents somehow to blame, and our literature is full of stories of the ways in which children are deprived or mistreated by their parents. Here I will focus on the baby's sensibilities and behaviors as they shape and are shaped by the caretakers' behaviors.

Today we could go back even further than did Rank and imagine the injuries that can occur in the womb. Babies born with AIDS or already drug-addicted are not easily able to contribute to the formation of the bond with mother. But also, when there is illness, abnormality, or prematurity of the baby, there may be distortions in initial contact.

In the "normally competent dyad," preadapted complementary behaviors ensure mutually produced contingency experiences. The competent infant "roots and sucks efficiently, alerts to stimulation selectively, modulates states of arousal, cries loudly when uncomfortable, quiets when comforted" (Brazelton, 1989, p. 418). If the infant's abilities to elicit comforting responses are weak or distorted, parental behaviors will become so. This consequence is true to such an extent that babies later discovered to be brain-damaged elicit anger and rejection from their parents even before an official diagnosis is made (Prechtl and Beintema, 1964). It is reported that a large number of premature babies become battered children (Klein and Stern, 1971). Some observers attribute this result to the early separation of newborns and their mothers (Klaus and Kennell, 1970), while others, such as Brazelton (1989) would add the effects of maternal depression after the delivery of a sick neonate. In any event, failure to thrive is common; deficient parenting patterns exacerbate an already compromised start.

One is struck with the artificiality of attributing the problem either to "inner" or "outer" factors; particularly in the beginning of life the "inner," to a considerable extent, creates the "outer" as much as the other way around. Although human beings in time develop defenses that enable them to minimize their projections and their introjections when necessary, we could also acknowledge that the intrapsychic and the interpersonal are intricately intertwined, not separate lines of development. Indeed, the very concept of trauma connects events in the external world with those in the internal world (Haynal, 1989).

I like Brazelton's (1989) model for early infant learning, perhaps especially because it is a fresh way of describing a model that Shor and I (1978) proposed as that of a "spiral dialectic" between intimacy and autonomy. Brazelton sees the baby as coming into the world equipped with reflex behavioral responses that he soon organizes into complex patterns – first for warding off threatening feelings of disorganization and then for interaction with others. As the infant achieves each objective in turn (that is, internal cohesiveness and external connectedness) his feedback systems say, "You've done it again. Now go on!" (p. 421). So the baby keeps moving from a state of "homeostatic" control to the next stage of disruption and reconstitution and is also rewarded for these risks by social cues. There is a "bimodal fueling system": a sense of achievement from within, freeing the energy to reach out and incorporate reinforcing signals. Shor and I hypothesized that this system fuels repair and recreation, so it is a model for all growth and development as well as for psychotherapy.

Brazelton notes that something analogous goes on for parents. With each new stage in the infant, they discover the excitement of the gratifications and the pains of the disruptions; they learn about themselves simultaneously with learning about their babies. They, too, manifest spurts in development and periods of regression for the reorganization and digestion of newly achieved skills (McGraw, 1945). In pondering this analogy, I wondered whether parents, already "traumatized" themselves by their imperfect infant, might become unduly perturbed by "regressions" and regard these as setbacks, rather than as essential to recovery. Are there perhaps therapists who regard as evidence of their own failure the regressions of their clients?

THE CHALLENGE TO EMPATHY
AND TO REPAIR

What I have just said is part of the challenge; for the parent and for the therapist who endeavor to facilitate the healing of the "basic fault," as Balint (1968) termed the primary trauma, there must be some comfort with regressed states, which are part of the tendency toward self-cure (Winnicott, 1959–1964). Winnicott believed that families could often recognize their having "let down" the baby and could see the child through to recovery by a period of "spoiling" (1963, p. 207). This could lead, he thought, to the baby's being able to play, to use an object as the "symbol of a union" (1969, p. 97), so that separation would not be separation but a version of togetherness.

Even Winnicott, with his tendency toward faith in the parents, acknowledged that early trauma can lead to an ongoing pattern of distorting influences. To the original failure there may be added the failure to heal the effects, and—as clinicians are sadly aware—later failures of society may well further exaggerate the problem. One of the failures on today's scene is to be seen in the paucity of services for those wounded in the beginnings of life, sometimes the virtual nonexistence of clinics and hospitals or—at best—limits of treatment to so few sessions that no basic repair is possible. It is as though we are adopting a policy of triage and simply abandoning those we know to be beyond the paltry resources we are ready to allocate.

Those clinicians who do attempt to work with patients who persist in their self-reparative efforts are often impressed with what the latter have been able to accomplish. These are often persons who, although manifesting to the external world significant accomplishments, yet harbor within a haunting fear of breakdown. Winnicott (1959–1964) would say that "the breakdown that is feared has already been" (p. 139). In his often poetic language he tells us that the original break was at a time of total dependence on maternal care; now, however, the child, as adult, has "a capacity to be a person-having-an-illness" p. 139). The original environmental failures were unpredictable and so resulted in "*annihilation* of the individual whose going-on-being was interrupted" (1963b, p. 256). Now, in treatment, "profound regression offers an opportunity to fulfill, in the transference situation, primitive needs which had not been met at the appropriate level of development" (p. 256).

The regression that Winncott believes essential for any profound repair is not, of course, the old id regression, but rather an ego regression. For, as we are now aware, the newborn manifests more ego instincts than ones related to drives. There is even a rather playful quality to the very regression Winnicott is advocating, for in their daily lives, persons able to do this are not for the most part behaving regressively. But in the special time and space of the therapeutic sessions, they discover the possibilities of imaginative "regression to dependence," the playing out of old themes and the invention of new ones.

For some patients, such regression does not come easily. In her own terms, Andrea, the patient in the last chapter, "resisted the transference," firmly rejected for a long while any sense of depending on me, and indeed, avoided the affective connection that could lead to the dialogue on which the success of her analysis depended. Like those patients whom Winnicott has described as needing for their sense of aliveness to be forever reacting to impingements, she seemed virtually to invite such intrusions from me. For instance, she complained that I had not instructed her to free-associate and that if I had, at least she would have been able to show me what a futile approach that method was and to defy the "basic rule." She explicitly rejected any signs of the "infantile," and it was not until she began to make some peace with a hidden "true self" who longed for just being and for spontaneity that we could both experience the "transference as a playground" (Freud, 1914b).

We might observe, however, that not only the patient manifests such resistances. Therapists, too, perhaps those who prefer directive approaches, may not tolerate well the sometimes long periods when the relationship itself is the most important factor, or those who like to exercise their interpretive skills may become restive in periods when language itself may be misunderstood. M. Balint (1968) wrote of working in levels prior to the oedipal: "Words – at these periods – cease to be vehicles for free association; they have become lifeless, repetitious, and stereotyped. They strike one as an old worn-out gramophone record, with the needle running endlessly in the same groove" (p. 175). Balint did not believe that it was only with profoundly regressed patients that such an approach was desirable. All persons should be allowed to discover their own ways "to the world of objects – and not be shown the 'right' way by some profound or correct interpretation" (p. 280).

Winnicott's (1971a) advice is similar: the therapist ideally waits until the patient is ready to reach for our hypotheses rather than too eagerly offering his own. "The patient's creativity can be only too easily stolen by a therapist who knows too much" (p. 57). And, we might add, by one who does too much. Omniscience and omnipotence are both to be avoided. He would have us provide instead "the opportunity for formless experience, and for creative impulses, motor and sensory, which are the stuff of playing" (p. 64).

A RETROSPECTIVE: WORK, LOVE, AND PLAY IN THE SERVICE OF REPAIR

When there has been primary trauma, either unrepaired or incompletely healed, one hears cosmic themes of life and death, often in terms that are not immediately easy to understand. One has the impression of something not yet expressible. It is not only that the person seems not to have the "words to say it" (Cardinal, 1983) but that she has not yet discovered what there is to say.

I never take a history in initial interviews but am there to receive what the patient can or will tell me. From one patient, Elise, I learned very little for a long while. The main complaint was that she was unable to use language; she could neither express herself, she said, nor comprehend clearly what others said to her. This problem had existed since early childhood. Although I found this young woman appealing, in both senses of the word – attractive, interesting, and also reaching to me in an urgent yet shy manner – she seemed surprised that I would accept her as my patient. Happy and excited, she told the referring person, "I have found the therapist for me!"

In the second hour, she reported a dream: "I go into a shop and see a little old-fashioned, green-enameled oven, with flowers painted on it, just like I've always wanted. I ask the price and am told so and so many dollars, just the amount I have." (And just the amount we had agreed on as her hourly fee.) The dream did not ask for interpretation. My own guess was that I was going to get a grandmother transference. Goodies could come from that oven; maybe there would even be cookie baking together; and there could be some easy conversation about our mutual interests. It did not yet occur to me that products might be removed from that oven before they were quite done. In any event, I took the dream as a sign that we would be able, as Freud

(1914b) had said, to use the transference as a playground, and for me that ability has become the most important diagnostic consideration. Grandmothers both are and are not "real" mothers; although they perform some of the mothering functions, their responsibilities are usually somewhat time-limited, so they do not have to be so earnest about them and can engage in many activities with children for the sheer pleasure of them. I imagined that, via this imagery, I was being informed that historically and in the present, Elise had sought out a human object different from parental ones in order to activate a sense of emergent self (Stern, 1985).

The themes were not to be only connection, movement, and integrity. Their opposites were abundantly manifest. She alternated between allowing herself to feel good that I had accepted her and feeling terror that I would not keep her. Her agonies were so momentous that she feared they would infect me. Sometimes she thought she should postpone treatment until or unless she could cease feeling like "toxic waste" that should be expelled. I did not understand at the time but have retrospectively hypothesized that the danger for her was that I would give birth to her before she was ready to be born. From the start, separation seemed ever to be looming.

In every way she expressed a sense of stasis. "I am stuck up against a wall." "I don't know how to grow." She was frightened of the "electrostatic universe," which I took to mean potential energy that is not translated into motion. Although every patient seeks treatment because of some felt fixity, Elise's sense of nonemergence seemed intense. Interspersed with that, however, I heard of her grandmother, who used to say to her, "You could convert that energy to action."

Death itself was a prevalent theme. She had told me in the initial interview that a few years previously she had made a nearly successful suicide attempt, as a result of which she was in a coma for many days. She was suffused with guilt and shame because it had been her adolescent daughter who had found her. As I gradually realized, among the conscious reasons for not expecting me to take her was her belief that a therapist would not want to take a patient with suicidal inclinations, or, if she did accept her, would have no respect for someone who had attempted to take her own life. Yet, significantly, it was many months before Elise told me of the circumstances of that event; she at no time offered any self-defense against imagined recriminations.

Menninger (1967) once said that suicide is "a peculiar form of death which entails three elements: the element of dying, the element of killing, and the element of being killed" (p. 332). In addition to her humiliation about "the time I killed myself," as she put it, Elise suffered remorse about an abortion when, in early adulthood, she had an unwelcome pregnancy. The fetus was sufficiently developed that it looked like a baby, and she described herself as holding it for some hours and as weeping and horrified. At the time I heard the story, I could do no more than empathize with her anguish that she had found herself in that tragic situation. Later on, it was possible to see the workings of the old repetition compulsion, an identification both with the mother who did not hold her in utero long enough and with the infant who could die as a result, a classical "turning passive into active."

Related to the death theme, too, was her fear of going crazy, of disintegration. Again, retrospective insights about the origins of this fear are better than those we could discover at the time. I did imagine severe traumatic experiences in the earliest period of life; although their nature and extent were unknown to me, it did seem likely that they were related to a "failure of basic provision" (Winnicott, 1963b, p. 256) and that they had resulted in "the *annihilation* of the individual whose going-on-being is interrupted" (p. 256). Like Winnicott, I did believe that the patient holds to the hope that the environment will acknowledge and make up for the failure that did the damage; Elise's very seeking of therapy was testimony to that hope.

Counterposed against these themes of death and disintegration were the reparative notes. She would say to me things like, "I can talk with you because you do not demand that I make sense." She had a dream: "There is a space behind my head, and you said I could use it. Shapes of love came out of me. I felt love, then fear. . . . I'm suspicious of love because I also hate. . . . Mother would say to me, 'I love you' – but through clenched teeth." She had dreams of being in "animal-mouth rages," as in this one: "A woman approached three inches close to my face. I was furious. We wanted to kill each other. I called her a 'dirty slimy cunt.' And then I went limp." As we talked of this dream, Elise said, "I always handle myself with helplessness." She also reflected that dreams of this sort and proneness to angers were at their peaks when she was premenstrual. When her period was over, she was "glad to be alive, not dead."

My own thoughts were that there must have been, at some time, unwelcome and even felt-to-be-dangerous intrusiveness, perhaps connected with bodily affective "agony" (Winnicott's word). In her transference were evident the wish and even inclination to permit closeness and trusting, but for reasons we had yet to comprehend the sense of relative safety had to be protected by a nearly equal quota of distrust and anger. I thought of Winnicott's (1963f) hypothesis that an infant's inability to become angry would be one reason for traumatization (p. 209). As Freud (1926) wrote, "Anxiety is the original reaction to helplessness in the trauma" (p. 16), and anxiety was often hovering in this patient.

I saw Elise's dream space as something of a playground for her. She enacted parts that she in no way played in daily life. She never snarled at me, as many patients may, but kept our relationship a sort of haven. Her "demon-self" was manifest only in dreams. Like play, dreams can be antitraumatic; Freud (1926) had affirmed that they serve to reduce the effects of trauma. Ferenczi (1955) had seen every dream as an attempt to settle the unresolved consequences of past trauma. Eissler (1966) had attributed to dreaming a "traumatolytic" function, whether or not the dream was remembered. Through our work and play together Elise both played out and dreamed out extensively, and what we think of as acting out was virtually nonexistent.

At least we can say that there was no acting out, unless we see it sometimes as essentially reparative. Like many experienced patients, Elise knew our terms, and at one point she announced that she was "acting out the transference." She had met and become friends with a man, Saul, whom she saw as both spiritual and intellectual. They talked and talked, and she had "feelings of love" for him, she said, "like my feelings of love for you." There were sexual feelings, too, but she did not act on those. She feared that, like her mother, I would say, "This is a madness and I can't let you continue with it." She asked herself if this sense that communication that flowed between them to the extent that she experienced "feelings of oneness" could be a delusion. Could it "be just erotic discharge?" In that case, she would feel that she was "part of a gigantic energy field, and I'm only one atom."

I replied that I was hearing her "sampling" the possibility of integrating felt-to-be disparate aspects of herself. I had learned by now that her parents had ridiculed religious interests and that Elise had suspected a psychoanalyst might also take such a stance. So she harbored a yearning for a sense of belonging to something bigger than herself, but she had to keep that yearning secret. So, using her metaphor, I suggested that if she was but one atom, she wanted both to receive from and to give to that gigantic energy field in an active way. Instead, she had felt a conflict between the intellectual and the spiritual, a conflict not experienced by her new friend. Perhaps what she was calling "erotic" was a longing to "take in" something of that quality of integration she felt in him.

In the next session she told me she had missed me. "You say simple things that stay with me." But soon thereafter she engaged in what Shor (1972) has called "self-traumatization" by directly pursuing the transformational potential she was sensing in imagined fusions with her male friend. She elicited in herself what she called a "crib memory" of being in pain, unable to breathe. There were half-recalled miseries of many physical ministrations of a frightening sort; she had had asthma or some breathing disorder. Somehow the fear of closeness, of merger became intermixed with a terror of loss of self, of life. She concluded that being in love was like being psychotic.

She returned to playing out the yearning and the fear directly with me. She said, "As I get less crazy, I feel a partnership with you. It is scary, like morning sickness when you're pregnant, but at least you know there'll be a new little thing." We were, I thought, to give birth to a new Elise. Out of the sickness and maybe the pain of delivery, there would be a "new beginning" (Balint, 1932). She reviewed her relationship with Saul. "He idealized me, so I fell in love. I don't believe you idealize me," she said. I began to comment, but she could not hear me. "I just left the room because I said, 'I want you to love me.' " She had found at least some words that she wanted to say, words of desire, but they propelled her into a fantasied separation.

In the next hour, I learned for the first time the details of her suicide attempt. She had been very depressed. Her husband had had an affair and brought her a venereal disease. Her daughter was in a rebellious state, maybe on drugs. Her therapist had made sexual advances. There were worries on the job. Despite a great pull just to stay in bed, she dragged herself out, but when she tried to start her car, it would not go. She returned to her room and took some stiff drinks and a huge supply of sedatives. The whole event was not very clear in her mind, which had been "dissolved" at the time.

The stalled car became one more metaphor for the pervasive sense of stasis, nonemergence. I commented on her heroic attempt to maintain some sense of self as able to move and make something happen (that is, to claim agenthood) but observed the enormous obstacles she must have felt, including "helpers" who did not earn her trust. She told me of a dream: "I am in a store, see something I want and I try to take it, but it is bolted to the rack. A woman says, 'Don't take that.' She didn't trust me, and I don't see how you can. If I were a therapist with a patient who tried to kill herself, I would not trust her." "And so you think that the love you want is likely to be 'bolted down,' " I said, "because you believe you haven't earned my trust?"

Shortly after this session, an AIDS patient whom Elise had be-friended died. She remained at the hospital with him and his family until the wee hours of the morning. She had been conscious, she said, of both "wanting to melt into" the grieving mother and also rejecting her, since she had not protected her son from the sexual assault of the father. She told herself, "You must be a rock." So, she reported, "I found you in my brain, solid and warm," and she had "held my hand." As the man's life ebbed, she felt "pain and cold as though I had taken him in." She thought she had, over the months, "taken him in," including his "theater of masochism and sadism," his ways of "keeping violence inside."

She continued for some while to work on her experience of the man's dying—"the being trapped there." We both recalled a daytime image she had once produced of a spider trapped in a lucite sphere and immobilized. "I have no memory," she said, "of my own death." "So," I suggested, "you are making a memory, confronting death here and now." That suggestion appealed to her. It was strange, she com-mented, to be in that realm. "It's like a body seeing itself, and then while I'm in that I try to shape it, give it structure. . . . There must be a function that pulls images together 24 hours a day!" I was aware of pleasure on many levels when she made that observation, since I think so much that the central characteristic of the human psyche is this organizing process. My patient's emerging sense of self was, as Stern (1985) had described it, "a sense of organization in the process of formation" (p. 35). I had a strong feeling that Elise was at a turning point and was ready to convert the unthought knowns (Bollas, 1987) into words and to permit us to think and talk about them.

For quite a while she "worked over" the notion of "making a memory," the "body images" evoked in her. "If I think, I reduce the experience," she noted. "Most people attend to reality, but my strength is not in thinking but in perception." I suggested that she did think a lot in images, that, for her, words seemed to diminish the experience somewhat, but that she had been using words to share her images with me.

She saw herself in some ways as having done the opposite of what was done by that dying man, who had tried to be aware of the whole experience. When she left the hospital after her suicide attempt, she raged at herself for not having been more aware. At the age of 10, she had imagined herself on her deathbed and "looking back over my life, my soul complete." But, while her AIDS friend had died a "meaningful death," she came close to "dying as a false self." She was glad that she had not died that way. As though to underscore this wish that death be meaningful, she dreamed: "I am a noble but condemned man. I swallow the poison, and my eyes grow dim, and everything fades away."

I saw this patient reaching out for experiences that would, to some extent, re-create an old trauma, a time when her defenses failed her. What I was yet to learn was the nature of the primary trauma that I had thought might have been. This information came at a time when well-meaning advisers were pushing Elise to take a position for which she did not feel ready. They teased her, "You're being an infant!" "I am because I want to be," she said. "I want to grow up naturally." She was by now enjoying her sessions with me and expressing her pleasures about them and was no longer besieged with doubts about my wanting to be with her. So she was in no hurry. She had, she said, started life as a very premature baby. "Mother had no chance to get ready, and I have never been ready for anything," she told me. Now those crib memories could be explored, the actual problems with breathing, the painful treatments.

She remembered that, when she had regained consciousness after her suicide attempt, her mother had weepingly confessed her guilt that when Elise was crying so much as an infant, her father on several occasions picked her up and threw her. Mother felt that she should have left father but had been unable to do so. I had often heard about father's "throwing" her little sister, but never her, the "good child."

Elise pursued an exploration of her relationship with words, because, as she said, "I want to do something before I die." She had the courage to begin to write poems and stories. "It's like when one is little and everything is possible." Winnicott would say she was reclaiming a sense of omnipotence, an important feeling if one aims to be creative.

She told me: "There's a difference between words and drawings; the latter are inside me, and after they're out, they're still in. My body can understand without translation. . . . I've always felt I was not entitled to use words, but I just felt they never came from me."

She had most certainly communicated to me in words, words that, like poetry, were themselves imagistic. Perhaps the fit between us was my love for poetry, which seemed to me her natural language. Our words, perhaps not fully understood in initial exchanges, gained in meaning as our shared realm of intersubjectivity expanded and deepened and as we both found what we wanted to say to each other. They came to occupy much of the intermediate space between us and eventually to constitute a link, as Bion (1962a) would say, both between Elise and life experiences and between her and me.

Like Bion and Beckett, whom Simon (1988) calls "imaginary twins," Elise had a style that included "a willingness to experiment, to 'play,' to outrage, to push the limits, and a deep conviction of the absolute necessity to spell out and play out" the implications of her ideas. Simon imagines Bion to have been profoundly affected by his patient, Beckett, and he acknowledged his debt to them both. As he said of them, I would say of Elise: she enhanced "my ability to think more freely, more loosely, and more playfully" (p. 350), especially about the dialectic between images and words and maybe even about the meanings of life and death.

CODA

At the time Elise entered this world, there was still a belief that the neonate came equipped with a "stimulus barrier," so strong that the outside world was virtually nonexistent (Spitz, 1965b). Today, as we look at babies firsthand, we observe they actively reach for stimuli, and when they have "enough," they tune out. These self-regulating capacities are ideally both supplemented and complemented by a mother sensitive to the baby's affective signals. A sick or premature baby is likely to be a much less effective communicator, or the affects expressed may convey abject distress that the mother feels impotent to relieve. A baby of very low birth weight often must stay in the hospital; so separation is involved before a realm of relatedness is established.

We no longer think in terms of a "drive reduction" model. Affects in infancy are not automatically disruptive or "traumatic." They do not need to be "tamed." Instead, they are aspects of ego (Emde, 1989b), utilized for learning and transmitting messages to caretakers. They would constitute potential trauma only if there were to be a preponderance of negative affects. Since we now see the infant as essentially reality-oriented (Stern, 1985), there would have to be real provocations, external, internal, or both.

When, however, there have been breaches in the mother's role as protective shield, there is a likelihood of "cumulative trauma" (Kahn, 1963). Dialogue may not be securely "railed" in the first place so is vulnerable to recurrent "derailings," which can be pathogenic (Spitz, 1964). Breaches accumulate invisibly. They are not themselves traumatic, Kahn thinks, in the way that some gross intrusions from mothers suffering acute psychopathology might be. They become trauma only cumulatively and in retrospect. I have imagined that Elise's mother was herself traumatized by giving birth prematurely to this baby, whose very life was in danger for a long while. Her responses, as Elise experienced them, were so infused with anxiety and worry that her solicitous protectiveness managed subtly to diminish Elise's confidence in her own abilities. The mother's verbal reassurances could not mask her deep concern, communicated affectively. So "coming close" to mother connoted danger, vulnerability.

Although, as Greenacre (1967) affirms, trauma in the "pregenital period" exerts a "disorganizing influence on the maturational drives" (p. 283), there will be the ubiquitous self-righting tendencies. Mother could also be fun. Father, after her early crying babyhood, could be tender. She and her sister played endlessly, and I have no doubt that much of their play exerted its "traumatolytic" function. And, of course, there were the dreams.

There are many possible story lines for this tale of Elise and of our conjoint adventure in the search for repair and recreation. One could well resort to Lacan (1966), with his concept of "le Reel," the order that is impossible to name and represent. We could posit that a child born under these adverse circumstances must confront very early what every human being must confront at some time: issues of life and death. At the beginning, we assume the baby could not even "think in imagery" but would, indeed, be contending with "primitive agony."

This child was, I would guess, gifted with imagistic capacity, so images came to represent and organize experience for her, and she trusted her imagery. But this was not yet Lacan's "symbolic order," in which signifiers could "support the possibility of speech and of faith" (Davoine, 1989).

For all of us, when the sense of verbal self unfolds, there is a sense of split between experience as lived and experience as talkable about (Stern, 1985). The neonate who comes face-to-face with the unnameable, death, simultaneously with birth, must feel a considerable obstacle to identifying the source of such disruptive anxiety. Later images of separation and stasis and disintegration abound but are largely experienced as "unspeakable." Winnicott would say that this thing of the past has not happened yet because the patient was not there to whom it could happen. The tendency to look for death, to experience it fully in the present and yet to survive, is part of the need to "experience the not experienced" (Davoine, 1989). It could not be experienced in the past "because there was no other (belonging to the imaginary order) through whom this experience could be reflected, and no other (belonging to the symbolic order) through whom it could become a signifier" (p. 587). Until it can be represented, thought about, with the removal from the immediate that language can bring, the patient may herself have to represent the disaster. This solution, then, could be the tragedy of the reparative urge turned desperate, eventuating in an actual suicide attempt.

Winnicott (1967) writes that patients of this sort are "all the time hovering between living and not living. They force us to look at this problem, one that really belongs *not to psychoneurotics but to all human beings*" (1972, p. 100).

We have been letting ourselves learn from our patients, and as we learn, we have changed the paradigms from which we practice. We have moved from one based on Freud's instinct and defense, to Erikson's identity and the life cycle, and currently to one based on death and the continuity of life (Lifton, 1989).

I like Lifton's (1989) idea that suicide is concerned not only with death but with the quest for continuity and with the search for meanings at all levels. One kills the "dead self" to break out of despair. The quest is for future-oriented meaning, locating oneself in the "design" of the cosmos. He quotes a fragment of a poem by Levine

(1979), which alludes to new beginnings and the hoped for outcome of
the quest:

> Let me begin as a speck
> of dust caught in the night winds
> sweeping out to sea . . .
> a tiny wise child who this time will love
> his life because it is like no other.

CHAPTER 9

Dreams as Private Playthings

Dreams, by their very nature, invite a certain playfulness since their meanings are not inherent but have to be attributed by the dreamer, with or without the help of interpreters. It is, perhaps, this quality that leads psychoanalytically oriented therapists and their patients to persist in practicing a certain attention to dream life, in spite of goadings by brain researchers and others that our theories have been wrong. Many of us are ready to admit the necessity to rethink those theories and to explore what the new ideas might do to practice.

We can no longer think of the dream primarily as defensive in intent, but neither are we ready to buy into the notion that dreams are simply phenomena that result from specific brain activity at the cellular and molecular levels. Even Hobson (1988), with his fascinating laboratory reports on the workings of the brain in the REM state, develops a theory that leaves room for the creativity with which persons may often deal with their dreams. But he does seem to be admonishing clinicians to be somewhat less sure about meanings that they might separately devise by way of symbol interpretation.

I like to think that Freud would be intrigued with the findings of current neurobiological researchers, even those that might challenge his basic assumptions. Actually, some of his own ideas already pointed in the new directions. He wrote that dreams were but a particular form of thinking in the state of sleep and that the dream work created that form (Freud, 1925b). He declared that dreams were not one of the mental activities directed toward useful ends but, rather, toward pleasurable "play or fantasy" (p. 127). The writings of the dream researchers seem to be leading us very much in the latter direction.

They are saying that the form of thinking is made necessary by the conditions of the REM state, conditions they spell out in impressive detail. The dreamer is a creator working under a certain handicap, so, of course, he must work to organize and make sense of the pretty chaotic stimuli presented by the dream material. What they do not explicate is why the dream, at least as reported in the waking state, usually contains a discernible plot, and, especially, why a given dreamer directs the narrative as he does (Spence, 1982). We might assert that, to emend the not-yet-satisfactory dream stories concocted in a somewhat disabled state, the person ideally plays with them in a context in which fuller faculties are restored. In treatment, this playfulness will best be effected with a therapist who does not purport to know what the dream "really" means.

To play with dreams, we have to be aware of the linguistic and extralinguistic considerations that enter into the form in which we therapists receive the dream, translated into words and hence reflecting both the symbolizing powers of images and those of language proper. Images are potential raw material for imaginative elaboration, and such elaboration can be fun when there is, in the extralinguistic realm, a relationship context that facilitates playing with that material.

A CHANGING VIEW OF DREAMS AND DREAMING

Within psychoanalysis itself there is recurrent evidence of shifts in thinking about dreams and dreaming. As theory evolved from the topographic to the structural and ego psychology held sway, it came to be recognized that the dream was influenced by ego and superego as well as id. But free association remained the way of comprehending meanings. Then, for a while, the dream as the "royal road" to the unconscious was replaced by the transference (Blum, 1976). Some believed the dream was a communication similar to any other and so should not be accorded any special position (Waldhorn, 1967), while others held that it would always maintain its unique role in psychoanalysis (Greenson, 1970). With the growing influence of object relations theory, there has been increasing attention to the representational world. While Freud's model was of internal forces acting blindly and unilaterally, analysts have moved toward seeing people as interacting systems and the field as interpersonal. We might say that meaning was coming to have a different meaning, one more dependent on the person in a particular context.

Then, with the advent of self psychology, Kohut (1977) called our attention to the self-state dream, whose meaning was not to be uncovered by free association. The following could be seen as an example of such a dream.

Emma, a young college woman, reports that she has been having some "ups and downs" about her weight. For a time she had adhered to her diet and exercise regime and had lost "eight pounds of fat and three of muscle," but now she has put back on five of those pounds. She tells a dream: "I am in a school corridor, talking with another girl. A man comes along and asks me to come up with him on the elevator, and I understand that the purpose is to eat. I decline, but he seizes the other girl by the hand and drags her into the elevator. I cling to the corner of the corridor, but it is as though a magnet is pulling me. I am terribly frightened and wake with my heart pounding."

This patient presents her dream almost as an illustration of her current estimates of temptations and her own dubious powers to resist them. She does not spontaneously associate, nor do I ask her to associate. What is most significant for her is close to the surface and congruent with her central conflict and self-complaint. Her irresistible appetite, although consciously unacceptable, is not disguised in the dream. There may be, of course, other potential meanings in the symbolism that she has employed, but these are not immediately the most relevant.

It is possible to think of all dreams as self-state ones, usually depicting self-in-situation, and therefore not to seek for "latent" content so much as to discover what potential meanings could be derived from the manifest content. Although, to attend to language for a moment, the dictionary defines "latent" as "potential" and vice versa, their etymologies reveal subtle differences. "Latent" comes from *latere,* to lie hidden, be concealed, while "potential" comes from *potentialis,* powerful. Freud's use of the term "latent" has directed our attention to the disguised, the concealed, to what is not in evidence, rather than to the potential, the possible but not yet realized. Since patients usually come to us with the hope that they are capable of being something that they have not yet attained, the notion of potential may have greater transformational value, allowing room for the person's own discoveries rather than a reliance on the translational skills of the therapist.

CHALLENGES TO THEORY FROM BIOLOGY, NEUROLOGY, AND SYSTEMS THEORY

This rethinking from within psychoanalysis may render it more open to change, even to some collaboration with thinkers from other fields as we emend our theories. No science can long survive that does not attempt to integrate its concepts with those of other evolving sciences; we need them and they need us to further our mutual interest in the relationship between mind and brain.

In the past, although intrigued by what biologists, neurologists, and systems theorists were pronouncing about the dream/sleep states, for the most part psychoanalysts declared that laboratory studies contributed little to our psychological understanding or to the clinical significance of the dream. Nevertheless, as we try to think about the language of dreaming, it is not irrelevant to ask the questions with which Peterfreund (1971) confronted us: What information is available to the dreamer? What processing capabilities does he have in the sleeping state? What is his goal of portrayal? Peterfreund observed that there is a diminution of input from the outer world, that stimuli from somatic sources are present. Something was removed, as Hartmann (1976) put it: the possibility of feedback. The dreamer is, in effect, psychotic— experiencing emotions not necessarily appropriate to the hallucinated images or occurrences. Bizarre situations are merely accepted. As for the equipment available to deal with stimuli from within, there is a reduction in activity, availability, and sophistication of the "programs" that exist in the waking state. When it comes to representing, the dream has "low standards for detail irrelevant to the main theme" (Peterfreund, 1971, p. 259). Peterfreund seemed to throw out censorship as central, to dismiss condensation, and to declare that displacement was present in all learning and all generalization.

Current brain researchers are in agreement that the capacity to dream must have a broader purpose than defense. Dreaming is nearly ubiquitous in the mammalian species (the echidna, the spiny anteater, and the duckbilled platypus being exceptional!). It reaches its high point with homo sapiens precisely because there is simply too much information for the conscious mind to process, and therefore dreaming is necessary to supplement it. The frontal lobes, we are told, do "on-line" processing. Since there are sheer physical limits to the infinite enlargement of the frontal cortex, there must also be provision for "off-line" processing. Its purpose is to consolidate ecologically relevant experience and behavior (Winston, 1985). For Winston, as for Freud, dreams reflect lifelong patterns of experience. Unlike Freud, however, this biologist sees their significance as close to the surface, rather than seeing that symbolism is used in an attempt to disguise the true (consciously unacceptable) content. The dream simply employs visual means to express experience. Winston even ventures a new definition of the unconscious: "The phylogenetically ancient mechanisms involving REM sleep, in which memories, associations and strategies are formed and handled by the brain as a distinct category of information in the prefrontal cortex and associated structures, are in fact the Freudian unconscious" (p. 209).

It seems that during REM, there is, between the two hemispheres of the brain, a functional disconnection, allowing the right hemisphere dominance (Bakan, 1978). This permits "the exercise and strengthening of psychological thinking, stereopsis, perceptuo-spatial processes and music" (p. 300). Foulkes (1978) concurs with this view and adds that in normal human functioning there is an oscillation of frontal lobe on-line with temporal lobe off-line activity. In the dreaming state, the visual imaginal aspect, the surface representation, is generated by the right hemisphere, while the integral dream story is generated by the left hemisphere frontal system. The ability to recall dreams – or probably even to generate them – can be virtually obliterated by left hemisphere or frontal lobe damage.

Foulkes (1985) is saying that dream research should now move away from depth psychology and its psychophysiological underpinnings and should ally more with modern cognitive science. Evidently he sees little hope that psychoanalysis might embrace that, too, while I believe there is reason to suppose that many of us are already attempting to integrate a cognitive perspective. His new discipline, *psychoneirics,* would tie up with psycholinguistics, which in the last decade has been attending more to the form, the how, of saying something than to content. Foulkes declares that the content of dreams is basically meaningless but that their form can provide insights into the general functioning of the cognitive processes. Dreaming, he says, is never a playback of units from the past; instead, there is dream novelty, analogous to Chomsky's "linguistic creativity." In speech production, however, there is intention; a plan is chosen, followed by the selection of a syntactic frame and the words to fit it. In dreaming, there is no aim at communication, not even, according to Foulkes, intrapsychic, so there is no message plan. Instead, there is diffuse and random mnemonic activation, followed by the revving up of the dream production mechanism to make sense of what has been rendered active. The "syntactic plan" conforms pretty much to the formal principles of narrative development, and these "organizing structures" may themselves contribute to memory activation. "They take on a power of their own" (p. 61). We could hear in that schema the organizing propensities of the creative unconscious.

Foulkes's longitudinal studies of dreams from the early ages of three to five years lead him to question the idea of primary process, with its assumptions that dreaming represents some ontogenetic regression to preverbal cognition and that this entails condensation, displacement, and timelessness. The dreams of his little subjects were lacking in these qualities and in narrative, too. Perhaps Vygotsky (1962) was right, that to the extent that Freud defined these qualities as signs of primary process, he was, in fact, describing not primary but secondary process— undeveloped until the advent of speech and symbolism. Foulkes speculates that absent or inappropriate affect in dreams would be related to the dependency of feeling on symbolic knowledge, as yet not fully developed in small children.

At issue, of course, is nothing less than the meaningfulness of the dream and hence its value in psychotherapy. In Freud's model, the initial input contains meaningful information, which is subsequently degraded by primary process (although not always in the service of the censor). Then a semblance of order is imposed (secondary elaboration). The function of the dream is to preserve sleep by the hallucinatory gratification of potentially disturbing wishes from early childhood. A side benefit in therapy is the use of the dream as a symptom, to recover original information (or, perhaps more accurately, to recover the way some experiences were organized at an early time). In the *psychoneiric* model, the initial input is devoid of meaningful information; it is random.

So if psychological dreaming, as distinct from physiological REM, has any purpose, it has to do, says Foulkes, with programming our minds to deal with the novel or to integrate recent memories with older, evocative ones. In this idea, he, like the other researchers I have mentioned, seems to hint at what clinicians might deem centrally important. Although Foulkes admits that free association may track down these memories, he sees no diagnostic or therapeutic purpose in dealing with the dream. He concedes that since life is meaningful and interconnected, one can "start with the dream and end up with all sorts of more or less valid statements about the dreamer" (p. 207), although we probably will learn nothing we could not know from systematic study or casual observation of the patient in the wakeful state.

That attitude seems odd in one who is making such a point of attention to form, but he is evidently not considering the possibility of playing with dreams in psychotherapy and of the playfulness affecting the form of the therapeutic relationship itself. He writes as though the objective in attending to dreams were to learn something about the patient, rather than to facilitate the latter's imagination and creativity. We might be willing to concede with these neurophysiologists that the dream may not be meaningful initially; indeed, patients are often bewildered by their strange dreams and offer them with no idea of what they could mean. Sometimes they feel that there is some potential meaning, but it eludes them. When they and the therapist succeed in attributing meaning, they begin to experience the fun of dealing with the novel and consequently become less fearful of what is not immediately understandable.

A number of analysts have been attempting to integrate information processing into a psychodynamic model (Hartmann, 1976; Palombo, 1978; Meissner, 1968). Palombo sees dreaming as part of the memory cycle. The process that he describes includes a stage of matching, in which day residues are simultaneously displayed in a sensory projection system, in a kind of montage. Arlow (1961) previously entertained such a notion and proposed that if movies of unrelated content were projected onto a window blind from both sides, there would be chaos, but that if the images were synchronized in time and content, all sorts of fine effects could be achieved. For Palombo, one of the functions of dreams is to bring permanent memory into alignment with current reality. He does not throw out the dream censor; that is prevalent in dreams that retard the flow of information. He distinguishes displacement, which is a process of substitution, from condensation, a process of superimposition in which new relationships are created for the first time. He declares that condensation is "the primary creative act of the psychic apparatus: the act which lays out the structural foundations for the massive pyramid of conceptual thought" (p. 143).

Palombo would change analytic language and have latent content refer to the representations of experience from both present and past that are superimposed in the matching process. He believes that patients may have "correction dreams," in which they incorporate emotionally significant material that was originally excluded. Freud (1911a) had a similar idea when he advised that the best way to complete interpretation of a dream is to leave it and devote attention to a new one, which may contain the same themes in possibly more accessible form.

Provocatively, Palombo proposes that the dream can be seen as a precursor to developmentally more advanced stages of mind in which affect is experienced but action inhibited. In waking life, affect is both source of information about self-state and initiator of action, while in the dream, since the motor equipment is disconnected, affect is only a carrier of information. Thus the dream has an adaptive goal: the achievement of self-knowledge.

Psychoanalysts would seem to play with their theory's challengers and incorporate their findings in ways that enhance their own theories. At least one training analyst has put the work of Hobson (1988) on the reading list for his course on dreams.

Hobson's book, *The Dreaming Brain,* aggressively aims at the demolition of Freudian dicta about the causes of dreaming, but its author, a professor of psychiatry at Harvard and director of its Laboratory of Neurophysiology, clearly delights in his own dreams and does a most satisfactory interpretation of them all by himself. He hints at a new approach to interpretation that would, as I read him, primarily respect the narratives that patients can derive from their own dream material.

Significantly, Hobson introduces his book by informing us that he was born with mixed cerebral dominance, that he is left-handed and right-eyed, and that he attracted the attention of a dyslexia specialist because he did not have difficulty reading. He credits his mother: "If anyone's nurture could have overcome nature, it was my mother's" (p. xiii). So we do not expect and ultimately do not get an approach that is exclusively neurophysiological.

His activation-synthesis hypothesis is not totally different from the ideas of the other researchers I have mentioned. The brain has its independent source of energy and, during sleep, periodically auto-activates. The dream is simply the awareness that is normal to an auto-activated brain-mind; this phase is the activation part of his schema. Then the person attempts to make the best sense possible of intrinsically inchoate data; this phase is the synthesis phase. The dreamer, however, works under a handicap in the latter effort since two blockades are in operation: sensory input from the outer world and motor output. Both are, of course, involved in our usual testing of reality, so in the absence of this orientational framework, the dreamer accepts the extraordinary stories as reality. Dreams are easily forgotten when the "aminergic neurons do not send their 'remember instructions' to the forebrain" (p. 214). (We could wonder whether, when the patient decides to remember dreams, those aminergic neurons get busy.)

Like certain of the other writers, Hobson would have us distinguish form, which is determined by the particular state of the brain-mind in REM, and the content, which stems from our urge to make sense of whatever stimuli present themselves. He observes that form is important in shaping content. Bizarreness, in itself, has no special psychodynamic significance. Since it is due not to the censor's actively disguising unacceptable unconscious wishes but to the distinctive physiological features of the REM state, interpretation is gratuitous or even possibly hazardous.

Hobson agrees with Jung that dreams are transparently meaningful. But, unlike Jung, he is referring not to universal meanings but, rather, to the fact that each dreamer will synthesize dreams in an idiosyncratic way. This view is a "meaning-added" one, rather than the traditional "meaning-subtracted" notion.

If we are willing to relinquish our belief in the motive force of the dream as an unacceptable wish and to give up seeing that as the explanation of dreaming, then psychoanalysis, I think, can come in precisely where the neurophysiologists leave off. Those lab researchers have impressive data on the state of the brain that initiates dreaming.

Hobson admits that they cannot yet account for the thematic-narrative constancies of dreaming. He suggests that without a disguise/censorship model we should still be able to account for "enhanced associations" and "personally significant plot construction" because the coherence of the story derives from "the dreamer's biographical experience," and "its manifest content directly reflects the operation of personally significant meaning-attribution processes" (p. 271). He considers his mode of interpreting "broadly psychodynamic without being narrowly psychoanalytic" (p. 271).

Many of us psychoanalysts would counter that he takes a narrow view of psychoanalysis, which has undergone many transformations in recent years. His description of a "new" approach to interpretation is what many of us have long practiced. We, too, see thematic coherence as due to the synthetic effort. The dreamer may call on all that he knows, including the deepest myths, to create a suitable narrative frame. Dreams do contain meaningful, undisguised conflicts, although conflict is only one of many factors in dream plots, "persistent concerns" being also centrally important.

In his closing paragraphs, Hobson argues, "Why can't we accept the autocreative function of dreams as something given to us, among other things, for our own pleasure?" We have not been allowed simply to enjoy "these delightful home movies" because psychoanalysis has been shot through with the puritan ethic and with neo-Judaic authority, so we have to "cart them off to be sanitized via confession and analysis" (p. 279). Of course, since dreaming has a random aspect, the dreamer is prone to spontaneous error but for that very reason is also capable of imagination and self-understanding.

We could call his attention to the many analytic writers who have urged similar approaches. For example, Pontalis (1981) in France writes that we have paid too little attention to the dream as a "libidinal object," treated its narcissistic and aesthetic satisfactions vaguely, and thus often strangled the eloquence of dream life (p. 33). He also points to the satisfactions of both analyst and patient "in their search for an object that is evanescent, lost-and-found, absent-present and never completely reached by signs that render it distant at the same time as they point it out" (p. 28). Kahn, from the British Independent group, would have us let the patient tell a dream in a way that does not kill it and enable the person to feel astonishment in the process. He, too, would think of the therapeutic ambience as "play space" rather than "work space" and of the dream as unique play material.

Often patients, struggling to convey complex subjective experience, express a frustration with speech, which demands concessions to the objective. In a recent session, one man fell silent for a while and then mused, "Something happens when I try to translate my thoughts to words. I wish there were some way I could just lay it out for you, what's in my mind, like on a videotape. . . . There are so many intertwining things, and I don't want to sound too conclusive." This man is something of a dream amnesiac, and he consciously misses having opportunity to put themes out without having to take full responsibility, which dream playthings could allow. After all, as Rycroft (1979) wrote, there is an "innocence of dreams."

What the person can experiment with in the play space of dreaming can, in the therapeutic context, nevertheless lead to new organizational perspectives, new meaning schemes that may facilitate taking responsibility for what has previously been disavowed. The pleasure gain is high.

A DREAMER AND HIS DREAM

Jim is a young man who has been consulting me about a marital problem. His complaint about his wife is that she spends too much money and that she nags him about his use of drugs. He has a history of extensive drug abuse in adolescence, even hard drugs such as heroin. In his early 20s he had a break and was hospitalized for some months. Now he claims that he uses just marijuana, with occasional cocaine and not so occasional alcohol. He admits that his reactions to these substances is extreme; he gets a feeling of being dangerously out of control. "I haul out all the stops – wipe her out – get just like my father." The adopted baby, two, who has seen some of these awful quarrels, is manifesting disturbances, and that bothers Jim.

The day residue for the dream is that he and his wife have been away for the weekend. They promised each other in advance not to engage in the behaviors that create problems. But, he says, although he kept to his word, she "lied to her checkbook." So, on returning home, he went to the place of a friend and got "really stoned," smoked, and drank a lot. "I really enjoyed it," he admitted, "but the next day" he had awakened feeling terrible, hung over. So when his wife assailed him with accusations of having backslid, he "let loose" with her. That night he had this dream:

"It was of the Mansons threatening my family. I am driving down a freeway. Through my rearview mirror I see a hitchhiker who is picked up by a couple in a car. At first I think the driver is a woman, for the hair is long. Then I'm not sure; it may be a man. I somehow know that the hitchhiker is one of the Mansons, and sure enough, as soon as he gets in the back seat he hauls out a knife and stabs the driver in the heart. I drive on."

Jim spontaneously associates to the dangers to a hitchhiker who lets himself be picked up, to the dangers to a driver who would pick him up, to the appeal for him of danger, to "connections" that are fraught with it, to the drugs picked up in spite of possible consequences, to his later "hindsight," even to his uncertainties about his own sexuality. (We had previously talked of his original identification with the "soft" mother and her literary interests. He had majored in literature; then, just short of his dissertation, had shifted to business, his "stern" father's field.) He blocks a bit on Mansons, and I say gently that he had been speaking of being a certain "man's son." He reacts with startle and surprise, and responds as though we have found the key to the dream. His interpretation is that when he "picks up" drugs, they lead to that destructiveness that he associates with his father. It is "threatening the family," he says, because his wife may one day no longer stand for it, and he has guilt about the baby's being upset.

Now, what he did not include in these "superimpositions" was something I already knew and thought did fit—namely, that his sperm count was so low that his wife could not conceive and that he had been told that the likely reason was his years of substance abuse. He, however, continued after the session to add to the meanings that could be attributed to the dream, including the fearful one of the "killing of the pregnant mother."

Jim was profoundly admiring of his own dream. He declared that, just as Auden probably appreciated his own poetry more than any of his many readers did, nobody else could possibly appreciate this dream in the depth that he himself did.

In his dream this patient had concocted "homemade" raw material that he could employ in his creative process. In his treatment he had grown sufficiently reflective to be a sophisticated audience to his own production. His pleasure came from responses that enter into any aesthetic appreciation (Jackson and Messick, 1967). There was the sense of the unusual, with more dramatic appeal than in the mundane events of daily life. Yet this uncommon scene was somehow felt to be uniquely appropriate to represent his wishes and fears. A transformation had been effected; the form in which a conflict was expressed had been changed. Condensation was in evidence, especially to the poet in this patient. Maybe most of all, he could experience self as both entrepreneur and artist. In the felt safety of the therapeutic relationship he could spontaneously free-associate to his own home movie and come up with a personally meaningful synthesis of its content. He savored the dream and the experience of interpreting it and continued to attribute meanings after the session had ended, including those to which we might have thought he would be especially resistant.

IMAGES AND WORDS: POSSIBILITIES AND LIMITS

In our dreams we think in pictures, and this dreaming, as Freud (1923) said, "is only a very incomplete form of becoming conscious." In some way, he thought, "it stands nearer to unconscious processes than does thinking in words, and it is unquestionably older than the latter, both ontogenetically and phylogenetically" (p. 21).

Our interest now is in two alternative forms of thought: images, the so-called language of dreams, and words, or language proper. We are asking, In what different or similar manner does each of these modes form, express, and communicate thoughts and feelings, and what may be the relationship between the two languages? I propose that (1) dream imagery is uniquely suitable for communication of the self with the self, while speech, derived from language proper, is necessary for interpersonal discourse and even for supplementing the image both in the dream state and in the waking life, that (2) there is ideally a continuous interplay between these two modes out of which each is enriched, and that (3) these considerations are important for clinical theory and method.

In what sense are images different from words or true language? The first and, perhaps, most important difference is that the image is essentially individual, while language is social. The dreamer constructs dreams and uses materials from the realm of the senses, mainly visual, but at times supplemented by the auditory, kinesthetic, tactual, and even olfactory. The image has no fixed meaning; it is, as we say in psychoanalysis, overdetermined – its meanings are almost limitless. Therefore, with this instrumentality the dreamer can do many things otherwise difficult or impossible and can manipulate the what, when, where, who, how, and why of his personal drama in fantastic ways. He can represent his current state while simultaneously expressing wishes and fears from earliest childhood. Time seems irrelevant; there is no necessary contiguity or sequential order to events. Similarly, the dreamer may depict a setting but then shift it or convert it to other settings. He can manage artfully the personae of his dream; one person can be another or several others. He may handle these transformations by changing the character's physical appearance; again, he may not bother at all with physical resemblances, but, rather, he just knows that this figure is so-and-so. Indeed, the dreamer can hide himself in the various characters and secretly try out their roles. Actions, too, may be portrayed ambiguously, as may their accompanying affects; contraries and contradictions are not ruled out, for there is no negative, no "no." There is no urgency to decide either-or. If, in narrating the dream, the patient does express an either-or, Freud (1900) declares that we should regard the alternatives of equal validity (p. 316). The presentations of the dream permit, therefore, no genuine logical argumentation; reasoning is specious.

Logic and reasoning may not be the intent of the dream; indeed, it may be closer to the truth to suggest that the dreamer, innocently allowing the imagination utmost freedom, would avoid the constraints of reality and, instead, assimilate the world to self. With the excuse that the dream occurred in an unconscious state, the dreamer cannot be held accountable. Responsibility is an issue only in the social realm, and the area of the dream is a private one. Not having to share the contents of the dream, the sleeper can articulate without restriction what cannot be rendered discursively. With no necessity to communicate, other than to self, the dreamer may freely create a grammar of the ineffable.

In waking life, the person who wants to communicate with others must have mastered a very different grammar. Words, unlike images, have arbitrary meanings, defined in dictionaries and consensually accepted by the language group to which the individual belongs. There are a grammar and a syntax, a set of rules that determine the proper ordering of the elements in sentences. Whether these structures are innate, as Chomsky (1957) tells us, part of the biological heritage of the human being, or learned, as Piaget insists, part of the cultural heritage, the individual must have competence in these formalized aspects of language to function in the social sphere. Piaget (1951) tells us that even interiorized language is much more socialized than the image, and *"at all its stages* it is the draft of potential exterior language" (p. 72, italics added). That is, even those unspoken thoughts that we shape into words and sentences already contain concessions to the social world.

There are some decided disadvantages to these concessions. As Chase (1938) puts it, there is a "tyranny of words," so that erroneous identifications may be pickled and preserved in them. Chase humorously reminds us that human beings, in their dependence on language, can misinterpret their world in a way that Hobie, his cat, solidly grounded by his senses, never would! It is possible that children intuitively know this fact and for that reason often delight in nonsense words, reversals of meaning, or rhyming that ignores denotation.

Moreover, the translation from inner thought and from its nuances of feeling is most difficult and never quite satisfactory. Some persons, skilled in language use, do better than others with it, but most of us would concede that in attempting to express our innermost sentiments, we experience ourselves fumbling clumsily and are often frustrated with the results. The difficulties are particularly evident as we try to give voice to ambivalences. We say, "A part of me wants this, but another part of me wants the opposite." Even in the clinical professions we speak of "splitting." The language of spatial metaphor, of logic, does not permit us to convey that opposites can coexist in the psyche and occupy it fully and simultaneously. The dream image, as Matte Blanco (1975) is telling us, can allow two things to occupy the same space at the same time. Dream space is "multidimensional." The analogy he draws is to a film, exposed repeatedly, so that it shows many superimposed pictures. In this analogy, he is reminiscent of Palombo and Arlow.

Thus, it could seem on first examination that images and language are quite unlike. Piaget (1951) calls the image a "motivated sign" related to the signified by some resemblance, individually constructed. Words and language proper are conventional, socially determined, and arbitrarily represent the signified. Images seem to offer the dreamer an opportunity to break away from the fixity of language, the carrier of the collective unconscious. They are richer in associations than are words and thus lend themselves to innovation and change. Einstein (1955) wrote, "The words and language, as they are written or spoken, do not seem to play any role in my mechanisms of thought" (p. 25). He worked, he said, by combining the various images that existed in his mind; such "combinatory play" he saw as the central feature of constructive thought. There came a time when he could voluntarily assemble those images, and then he translated them into words. Only thus could the world reap the fruits of his imaginative genius.

So, there is a sense in which words and language can be regarded as freeing us from autistic fixities. The self cannot develop by itself, and the greatest ideas might die if never shared. Precisely because language and its signs are arbitrary, they emancipate us from physical constraints and let us deal with things and people and ideas that are far away in time and place. Images are rather more binding, in that they must resemble in some way what they signify.

In using language we do not and, indeed, cannot relinquish images. Piaget (1951) says that "there is in all verbal thought, a stratum of image representation which enables the individual to assimilate for himself the general idea common to all" (p. 164). This idiosyncratic imagery preserves, to some extent, the personal within the social, but, we should add, it also constitutes an area for interpersonal misunderstanding since, although we hear the same words, we may not conjure up identical images behind them. Moreover, there are symbols generally ubiquitous in a given culture. Most language is figurative, developing out of images containing "faded metaphors," as Langer (1942) puts it. We refer to the visible to explicate the invisible. For example, the word "analyze" means "to take apart" and thus refers back to what was once a sensory-motor act.

In our recourse to images and dreams, we probably do not and, at least as adults, cannot relinquish language. Piaget declares that the child does not dream until he develops language. I have never been quite convinced about that belief, unless we sharply restrict our definition of dream and even of image. Perhaps it is simply difficult for us to imagine the primary process by which the infant is already building up an image of his own body or of the core self by assimilating the coenesthetic, kinesthetic, or proprioceptive sensations that are elements in his first experiences. Of course, the baby does not inform us what is happening in his psyche during the 50% or so of sleep time he spends in the REM state; dreams become communicable only when the baby can hang onto his images by casting them into words and can hence inform us. Once language has developed, we identify the elements in our dreams by applying word signs, and we accompany the events by word thoughts. It is quite likely that we do not recall dreams unless, on awakening, we translate them into language for ourselves, and thus reevoke our nighttime images.

When we do translate dreams, we engage in inner speech, which I suspect is closely akin to speech in the dream itself. Perhaps it occurs when there is some swing to employment of secondary process. Inner speech does not follow the same lexical, syntactic, and semiotic rules as external speech does. As speech makes its transition from external to inner, it becomes much more fragmentary, condensed. Since I know what my inner speech or my thinking is about, I do not have to name it. The theme does not have to be signaled as it does when I talk with another. It therefore has a "predicative" character, rather than a "nominative" one. It can be devoted to pointing to something new – to what can be added, what action might be carried out. This aspect of speech the linguists call "rheme" (Vygotsky, 1962, p. 107). Talking to oneself can be abbreviated, amorphous. The symbolizer is not confronted with the demand for highly articulate representation such as is needed for communication with others. The speaker shares feelings, interests, prior awarenesses with the spoken to; the relationship between addresser and addressee is very close!

I find it useful in thinking about thinking to refer to Stern (1985) as he traces ways of knowing from earliest infancy through to the sense of the verbal self. In the very beginning, he tells us, the infant experiences the world abstractly. Perception is amodal; the baby experiences a world of perceptual unity. Affects are a component of each act of perception, and their shapes and intensities and temporal configurations are interwoven with the sights, sounds, smells, tastes, and touches into a global pattern, the first way of apprehending the world. When, however, during the second year of life, language unfolds, it grabs a piece of the conglomerate of feeling, sensation, perception, and cognition and makes it separate (Werner and Kaplan, 1963). Language, thus, always fractures experience. When we bind experiences to words, we isolate them from the amodal perception that was characteristic of infancy. Language, then, is a mixed blessing. Words can enable us to transcend lived experiences, can be generative, but they have an inevitable alienating effect both on self-experience and relatedness. When we speak, we must effect a compromise between felt meanings and texture of experience and the verbal syntactic forms of language.

In our inner world we hang on, to some extent, to the globality that characterized that first thinking. Perhaps we never lose the wish, expressed by that patient to whom I initially referred, that we could effect some kind of direct transfer from our mind to that of another and enjoy once more the sense of attunement we experienced with the good-enough mother. Indeed, sometimes in a state of benign regression a patient may talk aloud much as he might to himself, not specifying the topic but laconically and idiomatically speaking about something as though we would, of course, comprehend.

So long as we re-create the dream only for ourselves, we may still retain some of its aura, the sense of special significance that we have not yet had to justify. When, however, we decide to share it with another, we begin that process of interiorized speech that already alters the drama as portrayed in the dream, ordered now into the grammar and proper syntax for saying it aloud. In this process we refer back to the dream experience, but we also refer ahead to the act of telling the dream, to the person who will hear it, to the situation or scene in which the narration is to occur, and we rehearse the telling in a way that takes into account our purposes in that relationship. When we finally do recount the dream, we will have modified it, not only to conform with linguistic regulations but also to consider the felt safety or felt jeopardy in a relationship. The extent to which the dream will be violated will be a function both of the language competence of the dreamer and of his particular relationship with the hearer.

In therapy the dream will be violated most if the therapist exploits the authority position by requesting the patient to bring in dreams and to "work on them." Such intrusion can, as we know from certain dream experiments, even violate the felt safety of the dream space itself. It will be violated least if the therapist leaves it to the patient to decide if and when he wants to share data from his very private realm and to play with the images from his dream. When patient and therapist manage to create together an ambience nearly as safe as that of ideal dream space, the patient can avail himself of the "two kinds of thinking" (Milner, 1957), by embellishing recounts of daily life with imagery from sleeping states and enriching that imagery by infusing it with qualities derived from therapeutic playfulness. He may, even in this ludic situation, experience a sort of waking dream, a new edition of the primary illusion, an illusion that fuels hope itself (Shor and Sanville, 1978).

We postulate that life begins in a sort of dream, a state of benign illusion in which an evanescent sense of self gently oscillates with an evanescent sense of other, a state in which it is not yet essential to verify and distinguish what is inside and what is outside. There is no conflict so long as the infant's needs are supplied, his wishes granted. Reality, of course, intervenes, and the baby discovers that mother has needs and wishes of her own, not always consonant with his. The baby begins to devise ways of dealing with her and ways of modulating or curbing his own impulses, these defenses always having the aim of reconstituting some of the qualities of original bliss. Throughout life each person follows the dialectical pattern: first is a phase of attempting to obtain from a valued other what will nourish and protect the self; then, with a better-equipped self, there is a phase of "doing one's own thing," out of which one reaches once more for relationships and in this process always hopes to attain new and improved editions of the now-unconscious primary illusion. The shape made by these two intertwining lines of development will be unique for each individual, as the successes and failures at each phase affect the next. People seek therapy when their own efforts at restoration bog down, and they present problems of social relationships, of the self, or, more commonly, of both.

The wish expressed in dreams is both for repair and for re-creation, and the images symbolize the means by which these twin goals might be accomplished and the obstacles we have encountered and hence anticipate. The meaning of the dream is not given. In therapy it is created when patient and therapist can play freely with it in the context of the "transference of the playground" (Freud, 1914b). Meanings do not evolve best from close, continuous attention to the dream itself, as such purposeful effort can be self-defeating; rather, they unfold gradually, often over many sessions, when seemingly the dream is not at all the focus.

As in all clinical exchanges, both patient and therapist arrive at understandings through two modes. The first is something like Keats's negative capability, allowing uncertainties and room for the intuitive, or like Milner's (1957) reverie, a kind of absentmindedness. For this mode, however, a setting is required, one in which there is no need for immediate practical action and there is a tolerance for something that may look like madness. The second mode is a more intellectual approach (secondary process or logical thinking). Ideally, we freely oscillate between these two. As we listen to a dream, we restore it to images and "see" it as we listen, although, of course, it is never quite the same dream as the patient saw, for it will have undergone many transformations, and our connotations to the images described will be different from those of the dreamer. The inner eye of the dreamer, like a motion picture camera, catches more than the tongue can tell. The experience of dreaming is largely ineffable (Kahn, 1975). The elements recounted are not units with independent meanings; they are nondiscursive symbols that cannot be readily defined in terms of others; they have no intrinsic generality. Understanding can be only through the meaning of the whole and in the context of what the patient may be wishing to repair or to create at this particular time.

The best interpretations are probably those that neither patient nor therapist can fully claim, and, as with the transitional object, whether they were found or were created by the patient should not be asked. If the therapist does not need to see herself as having given the patient the interpretation, the patient may have a fresh experience of his own primary creativity. The dream is, after all, constructed in the "one-person area," the domain of the self, in which Balint (1959) locates the area of creation. Like a work of art, a dream may have generated "symbols for the life of feeling," ways in which inner life may become knowable (Milner, 1957, p. 226). Unlike the artist, however, for whom "out-there-ness" of the work is of central importance (Stokes, 1947), the dreamer is referring essentially to "in-here-ness." Since, as Hobson (1988) has written, his activation-synthesis theory "sees the brain as so inexorably bent upon the quest for meaning that it attributes and even creates meaning where there is little or none to be found in the data it is asked to process" (p. 15), some meaning will have been placed on the data even in sleep but will be vastly elaborated in waking life by those who are capable of playing with them.

The artist, Milner says, always idealizes the medium. Many of our patients also idealize their dreams, which—at least by themselves—are rarely works of art but require the application of processing abilities much more available in the waking state. The dreamer may sometimes, like the drug addict (Kahn, M. 1975) in an altered state of consciousness, have the experience of something of momentous importance, only to be disillusioned when, on awakening, he is unable to reconstruct that experience. Probably a number of such dreamers feel disillusioned because their inchoate dreams have not by themselves constituted paintings or poems. Some dreamers may even be motivated not to remember products about which they anticipate feeling ashamed and to practice a certain inattention to the dream screen (Lewin, 1946), which might allow them access to the creative unconscious.

Other persons treasure their dreams and, either in the imaginary dialogue of inner speech or in imaginative dialogue with a significant other, diminish their fears of those undifferentiated states in which distinctions between "me" and "not-me" are blurred. They come to allow in waking life recurrent moments of "blanking out" of ordinary consciousness, which can be the beginning of something new, a prelude to new integration. As Milner (1957) puts it, they may enjoy that "plunge into no-differentiation, which results (if all goes well) in a reemerging into a new division of the me-not me, one in which there is more of the 'me' in the 'not me,' and more of the 'not-me' in the 'me'." The dreamer may then experience self as "a dancing Siva creating the world" (pp. 221–223).

CHAPTER 10

The Psychomythology of Everyday Life

In his book *The Hero with a Thousand Faces,* Campbell (1949) observes that "in the absence of an effective general mythology, each of us has his private, unrecognized, rudimentary, yet secretly potent pantheon of dream" (p. 4). "Dream," he writes, "is personalized myth, myth the depersonalized dream. . . . But in the dream the forms are quirked by the peculiar troubles of the dreamer whereas in myth the problems and solutions shown are directly valid for all mankind" (p. 19).

We might surmise that, even if today there were a generalized mythology, individuals would still be dreaming their private dreams, which would, of course, be influenced by that mythology but ultimately would also exert an influence on it. In fact, in this era in which individuality flourishes, there is more than ever a likelihood that we might witness myths in the process of their creation and could speculate on the ways in which new human values are expressed in a new symbolism.

Both life itself and the processes of psychotherapy can be seen as having to do with the creation of narratives about the self. As Fischer (1987) declares, "Narrative fiction is the veiled autobiography of man, the quasi-domesticated beast that constitutes itself through fiction" (p. 343). Human beings are mythopoeic creatures who, from birth until death, engage in making stories that reflect their shifting views of themselves and their world. The form of the narratives will differ at different stages of life and at different stages of the therapeutic endeavor. Always they originate in a wish, and the way in which the therapist sees that wish will exert profound influence on her mode of collaboration with the main author.

At times the tale will be that of a *dream narrative,* which is perhaps the first form of story, whether in culture or in individual existence, and draws on images that have become metaphorical (Langer, 1942). The dream may be told only to the self or to one other person, such as the therapist, but as it "goes abroad," it must move into a higher fictional mode if it is to appear significant to those who may not know the storyteller so intimately. The next step is the *fairy tale,* with its comic mode, the wish barely disguised, if at all, the happy ending due more to favorable circumstances than to heroic deeds. Next comes the *legend,* with its "hybrid of subjective and objective thinking" (p. 181), in which the central character performs brave and worthy acts that benefit others as well as gratify his personal wishes. When there is "serious envisagement of fundamental truths" (p. 176), the *myth* comes into existence. Each form reaches the limits of its usefulness and passes on to the next. Myth, too, will give way as thinking develops further and will be replaced by a philosophic outlook. Perhaps the parables and sayings to which Erikson (1950) addresses himself will be distillations of the "truths" at which each of these diverse forms aims.

Although the developmental progression may be as I have sketched it, like all development the course will be one not of steady advance but of recurrent dips back into previous modes. These "regressions" need not be decried, however, for they may serve the purpose of remedying something that has gone wrong or of incorporating what was over-looked or not sufficiently taken into account. Each "advanced" mode probably still contains somewhere within it shades of the modes that have been transcended. Although the wish that was the prime moti-vating force for the unfolding may be less apparent in the more evolved fictional forms, it can always be unearthed by the discerning. There is much merit in staying in touch with it as a source of inspiration for perfecting our aesthetic productions, our personal mythologies. I will shortly illustrate this merit via a vignette from a patient with whom I am working and playing in the drama that is psychotherapy.

First, I will mention an event that seemed to me to herald the birth of a new myth. I was in England in the summer of 1981, when, on July

29, in London, there occurred a rite de passage of such universal appeal that, it was reported (Runcie, 1981), some 700 million people around the world witnessed it on television. It was, as the Archbishop of Canterbury said, "the stuff of which fairy tales are made: the Prince and Princess on their wedding day." But, he went on, while most fairy tales end with the words, "They lived happily ever after," we could no longer view the wedding day "as the place of arrival but the place where the adventure really begins." He declared that God intends people not to be "puppets" but to create their futures. This creativity has two aspects. First, the couple in their interactions transform one another. Here, Runcie (1981) quotes the poet, Edwin Muir, who writes that a happy marriage is one

> Where each asks from each
> What each most wants to give
> And each awakes in each
> What else would never be.

Then, having enriched each other, the couple turn to their task of "creating a more loving world." They shape their surround, and are not simply its victims.

I submit that this ceremonial represented a transition from a fairy tale version of marriage, in which the wish is fulfilled simply by the couple's having found or won each other and by having taken the vows "til death do us part," to a mythical version that takes into account changing social and psychological phenomena. Some further actions are to be taken if the couple are to bring to some measure of actuality the wish to "live happily ever after." The new symbolism had itself been formed by various societal transformations, and we can predict that it will be a formative influence in refashioning human ideas about marriage and family and hence propelling future alterations in our views of these institutions. The concepts the archbishop put forth were these: marriage as *adventure,* *change* as an ideal, the person as *agent,* and *creation,* rather than adjustment or conformity.

To term marriage an adventure is to acknowledge it as a hazardous and risky undertaking and to call attention to its suspenseful and exciting aspects. Bombarded with statistics about divorce, we can no longer deny the possibility that a marriage may not last. When it has become necessary to increase the marriage license fees to set up facilities for battered wives, we cannot pretend that even those marriages that do last are necessarily peaceful. Of course, not only does the encountering of dangers characterize adventure; there is also the hope of being stimulated and thrilled, discovering the unexpected, the surprising. Possibly the old fairy tales ended as they did because once-upon-a-time conjugal roles were strictly defined, and the choices of how to be a husband and how to be a wife were therefore limited. Today we are moving toward redefinitions of those roles, even of the parental one. (Perhaps significantly, the latter was not even mentioned in the television address of the archbishop.) It is not possible to foretell with any certainty what decisions a given couple will make and how they will allocate the duties, responsibilities, and privileges between them. We will have some clues from the personalized myths of each, but what will happen as they share their respective narratives, as they try to intertwine their stories into one? Here, indeed, there is suspense, each decision affecting both persons, their ways of being together, and their ways of being vis-à-vis the world.

The new mythology is of creation—not by gods but by human beings in the processes of changing themselves, each other, and their social surround. For each to ask of the other what the other most wants to give requires of the two individuals that they have developed some special qualities within themselves and that their choices of each other have been well considered. Each would have to feel fairly well "supplied," that is, not be in a state of urgent need, either materially or psychologically; feelings of deprivation can propel to demands that do not regard the state of the other. Each would have to experience self as capable of functioning effectively; feelings of suppression can engender rages, overt or covert, out of destructive envy. Each would be able to communicate with the other in a process of mutual exchange, for without this, misunderstandings can easily arise (Shor and Sanville, 1978; Shor, 1990). As Erikson (1950) has affirmed in his well-known work on the eight stages of life, identity must precede intimacy. That identity is established in the process of putting out to others some samples, so to speak, of our self-representations—or of our personal myth—to test whether the representations others have of us do or do not correspond with our own.

Fortunately, identity or the sense of self is never established once and for all; we continue our pursuit of self-creating as long as we live. One recurrent mode of building and modifying depictions of the self is via the image we glimpse of that self in the eyes of others. Herein lies the potential – and the danger – of that creation of each other to which Runcie alluded. The "what else would never be" can be a better version of the self, but, sadly, it can sometimes be a diminished version. It will depend both on what the mirror that is the spouse reflects back and on the firmness or fragility of the sense of self in the mirrored one.

One study of long-term successful marriages took as its definition of success the wish to remain in this marriage, the conviction of having "married the best mate for me," and love for the mate (Fields, 1986). Central to Fields's findings was that in unions that are the most satisfactory there is a high degree of ability on the part of each to perceive and reflect the other's self-concept, to see the mate in a way that is congruent with the mate's preferred self-perception. We could surmise that that sort of feedback could facilitate one's living up to one's ideals, and, well "supplied," one would want to do the same for the other.

Of course, change is not always in the direction of "better." In the clinical situation – and often in the social one as well – we hear personal stories describing a lesser sense of self-esteem emerging out of the marital relationship. We are aware of the dynamics that so often can lead persons to tear each other down; those with a fragile sense of self engage in what Klein (1946) called "projective identification" – attempting to dump unwanted qualities onto another to maintain the image of the self as the good one. The story tends to become stuck when this plot is activated, for the dumper does not actually get rid of the badness but often does manage to elicit counterhostility from the other. So – in Klein's terms – the dumper must then reintroject the bad stuff, and both participants tend to be the worse from this interaction.

Clinically when, in the context of the transference, the patient attempts this mode of defense, we see – according to psychoanalytic clinical mythology – an unconscious reparative wish at work, so we react not with hostility but with an interpretation aimed at transforming the wish into an intent, so that the patient is better equipped to realize implicit goals. In our most successful marital therapies, we may enable mates to recognize reparative wishes hidden in mutually provocative behaviors. Then, instead of always "reacting," they may come instead to respond to each other in such manner as to facilitate transformations in positive directions.

The third idea in the myth Dr. Runcie was developing is the idea of self as agent, one who has the power to act, who can experience self as able to cause things to happen. Often people seek out psychotherapeutic help because they have lost this sense of agency and therefore the sense of spontaneity and freedom. The image of self is of victim, at the mercy of forces over which they feel no control, although the sophisticated may imagine some of those forces to be within. Paradoxically, however, in the transference the person often manifests a seeming willingness to give over to the therapist the agent role; it is not hard to detect the fantasy that the latter possesses all those magic qualities felt to be lacking in the self. If the therapist will but impart the secrets, the patient will be healed and move on with full powers restored.

It is here that the myth of the particular therapist enters into the action – both the personalized myth and the mythical aspects of the theory to which this therapist adheres. There are those who like to be cast in the role of the wise one who knows what is best for this person. With benign intentions they advise, admonish, and direct, thus reinforcing the patient's mythology that answers lie outside of himself. There are therapies that bypass the patient's self-representations. Freud himself experimented with measures, such as hypnosis, that override the person's resistances and defenses. Playing the physician role thus was not, I think, in keeping with his preferred images of himself; so, on account of this dissonance, he went on to discover and describe for us a way in which the transference could be used as a playground in which the patient could imaginatively relive some of his past story in the service of creating better versions of it for the present and the future (Freud, 1914b). Psychoanalytic therapies, at their best, aim at restoring to the patient the sense of capacity to be agent. It is possible, however, to see a jeopardy to this goal in some of the prescriptive approach – for example, about couch, frequency, and duration – which may render the experience one of constricting ritualism rather than of ritualization, for which there can be no prescription (Erikson, 1977). The ritual that permits playfulness and experimentation must come from "shared visions." To the extent that the therapist does not attend to the patient's own pace and inclinations, the transference is contaminated and resistances and resentments are iatrogenically determined (Shor and Sanville, 1978; Gill, 1980). To the extent that playful improvisation is facilitated, the two participants may come to that ritualization that makes for "separateness transcended" and "distinctiveness" confirmed (Erikson, 1977, p. 90). This is the ideal for which we reach, whether in marriage or in psychoanalysis.

In other dyadic relationships, too, when one person arrogates to self the rights and powers of the agent role and the other is relegated to a relatively passive stance and endures what she feels unable to change, we can anticipate that hostilities will be part of the action. Indeed, in the social scene, when large numbers of people imagine themselves to be powerless, their furies are likely to mount against those whom they see as able to determine the course of events. It is possible, however, that, if the mythology depicts one's group as totally impotent to institute change, an apathy may ensue.

Today many persons in all walks of life are questioning whether the notion that they have a genuine say in decisions that may determine even the survival of their world may itself be a myth, in the pejorative sense of the word. Our tutor that summer of 1981 in Cambridge, while agreeing with us that the archbishop's words were "nice and poetic," yet declared them "sociologically irrelevant," his reasons being that economic forces outside the control of us all are the real determining factors. Whatever the "facts" of that issue may be, I would hold to the illusion that our sense of power or powerlessness will be as much a determinant of the future as will external factors. Our actions with another person or with the social world will be guided by the images and plots that we carry around in our minds.

Before illustrating this psychomythology of everyday life, I will go back to the wish that set the whole narrative propensity going and that motivates the thrust to keep producing improved versions of the story. Campbell (1949) proposed that the first ideal for us all is "that of the dual unity of the Madonna and Bambino," which is from infancy onward "retained as the unconscious basis of all images of bliss, truth, beauty, and perfection" (p. 6). Some of us, impressed by evidences both from infant research and from our therapeutic work, would propose, rather, that the first ideal has two component images: this one of the comfortable and comforting union of mother and child, but also another, of the comfortable and autonomous self, which gently, without conflict, oscillates with the experience of togetherness. In all of our later love relationships we are propelled by the wish to arrive at new editions of this primary illusion (Shor and Sanville, 1978). The ideal is of a close and warm relationship, but one that does not stifle the independence and growth of the self. We could put it another way: like

Odysseus, we want to be able to leave home, engage in trials and ordeals that test and strengthen the self, and then return, renewed and capable of imparting our new-found richness to others. This "leaving home" can, of course, be either literal or symbolic, and the rejoining can be in act or in thought.

While in the past it was Odysseus and not Penelope, his wife, who went forth to test himself in a grand adventure, today's Penelope often wants to do more than keep the home fires burning. We might even surmise that once upon a time each sex was somewhat limited to developing a personal mythology that emphasized just one aspect of the basic wish; males pursued the illusion of autonomy, and females, the illusion of fusion. Now neither sex seems satisfied with such a one-sided development; men and women are attempting to claim both images in the primary wish. When in therapy we can enable patients to be in touch with this basic, benign dream, they may convert the wish to a reparative and re-creative intent that may move the story forward.

The patient usually comes for psychotherapy at a time when the personal tale is stalemated and does not seem to be going anywhere. Such was the plight of Mr. B, a man in his 60s who complained repetitively over many sessions about his marriage of only several years' duration. He saw himself as having been deceived by his wife. Originally he had thought her to be an independent woman, but she had turned out to be abjectly dependent. Then, he had learned from other persons some months after the wedding about certain chapters in his wife's earlier story, and what he had learned had converted his idealized image of her into that of a wicked woman, not to be trusted. This circumstance emotionally repeated a very early childhood experience when his beloved mother had suddenly disappeared; only later did he realize this abandonment was due to her psychiatric hospitalization. When she returned, she appeared to him as bad, drastically different from the warm woman who had cuddled and fondled him. This connection between past and present he could understand, but he remained blocked about using this insight to modify anything.

He rejected any idea of trying to talk things out with his wife, who, he declared, only became hysterical when he tried to communicate on such matters. He could neither "work on" his marriage nor leave it. On one occasion he did move out for a few days, during which, interestingly enough, she had seemed to reclaim the autonomy he had once thought to exist in her. So they reunited, but after a brief new honeymoon the situation reverted to what it had been before. His complaints resumed. His wife chided him for "acting like a prince," soaking up all the limelight in social engagements and not sharing it with her. He saw her acting "like a greedy child," unable to countenance any frustration, wanting more and more from him, but giving him very little attention or consideration. Actually he indulged her materially to compensate for depriving her emotionally, and he could not miss knowing of her special vulnerability to his constant disapproval.

There was, of course, an element of historical truth in the image each tended to hold of the other; he had been a cherished only child, overprotected and taught to cling, while she–at least according to her personalized myth–had been unwanted and unloved. His parents had drilled into him the message that he should stay close to them, that the world was unpredictable and dangerous. Her parents had implicitly asked her to leave home; she saw herself forced to independence. We could surmise that both, when they met, manifested apparent autonomy. But his was a sort of exaggerated performance, defending against the wish for dependency lest he be sucked into a total helplessness, and her seeming self-sufficiency masked profound yearnings to be cared for so as to make up for earlier deficits.

In psychoanalytic treatment, the most important clues to the patient's psychomythology in its conscious and unconscious aspects emerged in the transference. In his hours with me, Mr. B tended to conduct a monologue. When I would venture a comment, his response would be, "I know," and then he would talk on as though I had not spoken. Although in the context of our relationship he did come to recognize a longing to enjoy some experiences of leaning on another, he found it difficult to feel safe with that. He wanted to be able to experience love, for he never had, although he had married twice before. He imagined, however, that a prerequisite to that would be going through some "ordeal." Trying to fathom what he could mean by that, he observed that we speak of "falling in love," and for a time that phrase seemed to symbolize for him the dangers. He produced dreams of tumbling into an abyss. He called up "memories" of having been retarded in walking (which in Mahler's schema might hint at complications in separation-individuation) and of father's scorn that he was a "mama's boy," destined to become homosexual.

Gradually he began to examine the probable overcompensation in his attempting always to have the answers, both to his own problems and to those of others. Indeed, his wife complained that he attended to everyone but her. He acknowledged some validity to that accusation, as he hungered for the praise his attention sometimes awarded him from others. With no direct confrontation from me he tentatively questioned whether the negative transformation in his wife was, in part, due to his maintaining the dominant role and not really sharing with her.

One dream afforded us important clues. He is in an auditorium, and Bob Hope is entertaining. The patient goes up to the stage and tells some jokes that top Hope's. The audience applauds in appreciation. The scene is repeated; he "brings down the house." But when the show is over, he meets with disapproval backstage, "perhaps from the family." It was not too hard to transmute that dream narrative into fairy tale, even to legend. Mr. B, compensating for felt inadequacies in many areas, including sexual, had, indeed, liked to hold court, to have center stage, and, as evidenced with me, to beat the "experts" at their own game. Socially he had experienced some success with this behavior and was famed as a raconteur, the "life of the party," although privately he felt his real friends to be few. My interpretations included not only the reparative wish in such demonstrations of wit and humor but also the disappointment that when "backstage" there was frustration of the wish for good connectedness. I noted, empathically, that hope could easily be defeated when one must constantly perform, since the accolades are not felt to be for the authentic self.

Another dream was offered in the context of further "working through" or "working over" these salient themes. As he told it: "It is my wedding day, and I am being conducted to the ceremony in a Rolls Royce, but my bride is nowhere in sight. I see other Rolls going by and chuckle to myself that [and here he names a big movie tycoon] is really going all out for this affair. But then I find myself confused and uncertain whether it is I who am going to be married." The "historical truth" here is that there was, indeed, a big show with celebrities present at the patient's wedding. As we elaborated the dream into story, he pondered why the bride was not there. Taking his reflection as a moment of rare permission to comment, I noted, "How could you see her without hearing her?" I was reminding him of what we had discussed a session before, that he had poured out his story to her but had not invited her to tell her own, even as he rarely invited response from me. Monologists find obstacles to knowing another, and of course the risks in relationships with one who is not "seen" (or heard) are immeasurably increased.

Like Narcissus, my patient seemed to relegate the other to an echo and to be fixated on a certain image and sound of himself. The "self" he put forth to elicit approval from others was, in Winnicott's (1960a) terms, a "false self," that is, already distorted by what the person imagines will win acclaim from the world. Thus, in his dream he is uncertain "whether it is I who am going to be married." Even if his big show is spectacular, he is left feeling unfulfilled, for the true self, including the still repressed longings for passivity, remains ungratified. He represents his bride as the presence of an absence and himself as the absence of a presence (Fayek, 1981). The dream catapulted him into an effort to rework and eventually to replay those aspects of his life narrative that had made the tale somewhat dull and repetitive.

At last the story became unstuck. He took his wife away for a weekend, and, in a quiet spot in the woods, they sat and talked. He told her he had been self-preoccupied when courting her and had not really listened to her, and now there were things he wanted to know about. Mr. B chose the scene well and took some responsibility for his own behaviors. To his pleasurable surprise, she opened up and poured out her story; sometimes she wept; sometimes he wept with her. Following that exchange, he reported, "For the first time in months we made love and did not just fuck."

I was not necessarily predicting a fairy tale ending but observed the revival of hope, now that communications were freer, mutual pleasures in bed resumed, and some mutual identifications began.

A dream narrated on the eve of a two-month vacation from treatment seemed to approach the mythic in form. He is in a temple or synagogue and is ridiculing the service that is being conducted. One of the elders chastises him, "You are a lazy, no-good one!" Mr. B then somehow goes away, and there are other scenes involving "ordeals" that he cannot recollect now. Then he is back with the elder, asks for work, and tells him that he will put forth more effort than anyone and that it will be an opportunity for each to demonstrate something to the other.

The patient's roots were in orthodox Judaism, and there was much in that heritage that he overtly ridiculed. He saw himself as having departed from what the temple symbolizes, as he had undergone trials, with some victories, some defeats. In a selective way he returned to certain aspects of his cultural beginnings. But, like all dreams, this one was rich in potential meanings, and many narratives might be derived from it. I was also that elder, into whom he projected his conscience; hence he imagined my scolding him, specifically for not working on his marriage. To ward off my scolding, his attitude sometimes was one of subtle ridicule, which also served to keep a certain distance between us. Now he was experimenting with going away from me. Unlike his mother, I did not disapprove but tried to help him know what he wanted to gain from this intermission. I thought he wanted to know that it was possible to have a relationship that did not constrict, that permitted one to take one's own measure of when to reach for closeness and when to opt for periods of separateness.

The adventure on which he embarked was the adventure of his marriage. He allowed his wife to share the agent role in planning the trip, and she shared in the driving and navigating so that he could experience some caretaking from her. In this context of conjoint participation in the odyssey, he hoped that they might enjoy a new beginning through furthering the dialogue that they had started and through reviving the identifications with each other that are essential to mutual empathies. He thus set forth, in touch with the wish to change old patterns that have been self-defeating, in his quest for an intimacy that would not preclude autonomy. The image of the return was of a self equipped with a fresh intent to work together, with me and with his wife, so that each could be seen and heard in ways that promoted their own best images of self.

RETROSPECT AND PROSPECT

In the past we projected onto the institution of marriage all our dreams of self-repair. We had imperfect parents who imperfectly reared us. They left us with mistrusts, doubts, shames, guilts, feelings of inferiority, inadequacy. Marriage was to be our salvation; the spouse was to be all that the former caretakers were not and was to heal, cure, perfect us, so that happiness should at last be ours. With such high hopes and elaborate expectations, there was an inevitable fall, with ensuing disappointment and despair. We turned on marriage as once we had turned on our parents, with outrage. What should have been the source of restoration left us still bad, still flawed. So we sometimes seemed to repudiate marriage itself, except for short-term commitments.

Secretly hope survived, especially in the private dream, with its wish for new versions of the primary illusion, for the recurrence of a state in which autonomy and intimacy could coexist nonconflictually. It may be that in an era in which many new social options are available to the individual, there may be room for the wish to erupt in new myths. These may manifest themselves through fairy-talelike ceremonials such as the royal wedding but are gestated in the psychomythology of everyday life. We might even surmise that ordinary people have more individual options than do princes and princesses. Infinitely less bound by prescribed roles, they may be freer to invent new story lines for their life narratives.

CHAPTER 11

Playing and Interpretation

I was recently consulted by a candidate in an analytic institute regarding possible supervision. In the course of telling me something of who she was and her relationship to psychoanalysis, she described her first analysis, with a candidate, as having left her in rather bad psychological shape. He had, she said, recurrently confronted her with aspects of herself of which she had no previous inklings and had, after several years of this analysis, pronounced her ready for termination, although she herself felt not better but worse. After suffering for a while a sense of not-good self, she sought another type of psychotherapy, which she found more congenial and in which some healing took place. Of course, the question in my mind as I heard this story was, Why, then, had she undertaken training in psychoanalysis? In spite of disappointment in her own experience, she had held to the belief that psychoanalysis did not have to be as hers had been. She had from many sources, including having heard me speak at a Winnicott conference, a glimmering of other possible models. She was currently in analysis with someone who did not leave her feeling that the analyst knew her better than she could know herself.

It would be comforting to say to ourselves, well, that first analysis was by a candidate who, after all, was not yet as skilled as he eventually would be; anyway, we do not know from the patient's story what actually happened. I tend to feel, however, that the customer is always right. Such tales do not come only from persons analyzed by candidates. A fellow professional recently consulted with me about his conflicts in reaching out for a second analysis because of residual problems after eight years of treatment with a training analyst. He was aware – and demonstrated to me – that he could talk "psychoanalese"; his intellectual grasp was impressive! This physician did believe that there had been benefits, which he sketched, but he continued to feel, both in work and in love life, that something was missing, that in spite of obvious capacities and ambitions, he had just not "got it together." He mentioned, with attempted humor that ill-concealed a sadness, having run into his analyst at a recent event, and the latter did not recognize him. "After all," he jested, "he could see only the top of my head!"

That such persons continue to seek analysis is testimony to the ubiquity of the self-righting tendency in the human psyche. We do not have to see their inclination to return to what disappointed them as necessarily a manifestation of the repetition compulsion; rather, they believe that, imperfect as it may be, psychoanalysis yet holds the greatest promise. In these two instances, I would posit that there is an intent not only to continue to repair the self but even to repair the source, psychoanalysis itself.

As I write about interpreting reparative intents with patients, I simultaneously observe the reparative intents that motivate changes and improvements in our theories and our practices.

The notion of a basically reparative intent in the human psyche is not new in psychoanalysis. In his article on the mechanism of paranoia as observed in the Schreber case, Freud (1911b) wrote, "The delusional formation, which we take to be the pathological product, is in reality an attempt at recovery, a process of reconstruction." He adds, "What forces itself so noisily upon our attention is the process of recovery, which undoes the work of repression and brings back the libido again on to the people it had abandoned" (p. 71). Freud hypothesized that it was not only in paranoia that "detachment of libido" occurs but in other clinical syndromes and in "normal mental life," and this detachment is followed by "looking about for a substitute for the lost attachment" (p. 72).

Freud (1933) likened this reparative intent to what, on the physiological level, seems to motivate bodily repair: "A power of regenerating lost organs extends far up into the animal kingdom, and the instinct for recovery to which, alongside of therapeutic assistance, our cures are due must be in the residue of this capacity which is so enormously developed in lower animals" (p. 106). He was offering us a way of looking at the "compulsion to repeat," which he was then attributing to the "conservative nature of the instincts." He went on to question, "What earlier state of things does an instinct such as this want to restore?" (p. 107). What he came up with was an instinct to do away with life and reestablish an inorganic state.

If that instinct is so, some of us have reasoned that it can only be in the context of the fantasy of a new beginning. Shor and I (1978) posited a model of the "earlier state of things" toward which the intent to repair will aim: a primary illusion (from *in ludere,* in play), consisting of a comfortable sense of self gently oscillating with an easy sense of the other, with no conflict as yet. Analogous to the sense of intact bodily self, this model represents an ideal psychic state, new versions of which will be sought throughout life. We suggested a clinical approach that emphasizes the reparative intent in every symptom and complaint (p. 119).

Freud (1933) wrote that "from the moment at which a state of things that has once been attained is upset, an instinct arises to create it afresh and brings about phenomena which we can describe as a 'compulsion to repeat' " (p. 106). Shor and I (1978) instead posited that the motive would not be precisely to repeat moments of primary illusion but to create new versions of the original model. If the mani-festations were in the nature of seeming "compulsions," then attempts to restore the qualities of prior satisfactions had somehow misfired. It would be important, we affirmed, that, in the psychoanalytic context, the search be not only for the "fragment of lost experience" (Freud, 1937) that was felt to be malignant but for the equally crucial fragment of lost benign experience. For this was the source of the model toward which the hoped-for repair would move. We reasoned that if the person were in touch with the quality of experience yearned for, that person would be in a better position to evaluate the measures tried and to discover wherein they had fallen short and to institute more effective ways to achieve the wanted ends.

It is my thesis here that when these are our premises as analysts, we begin to think differently about interpretation, what it is at its best, who does it, in what context, in what way, and toward what purpose.

We have historically tended to think of interpreting as a kind of translation done by the analyst, who, after listening to the patient's talking and being quite sure of the truth, offers to the analysand a statement of the hidden reality behind what is manifest, of the unconscious meanings of what the patient is reporting. In recent years a number of writers have questioned that view. Some point out that there may not be an ultimate "truth" or "facts of the case" (Schafer, 1982). The philosopher Langer (1942) affirms that "a fact is an intellectually formulated event" (p. 269), and she agrees with Freud (1886) that our memories are "subjected from time to time to a *rearrangement* in accordance with fresh circumstances – to a *retranscription*" and that "the successive registrations represent the psychic achievement of successive epochs of life" (p. 233). Clinicians know that patients' stories change over time, that meanings are capable of infinite growth. In our heart of hearts, we also know that the meanings we might attribute to our patients' "data" change as we absorb new theories by which we "interpret" both their stories and the stories of their psychoanalyses with us.

To what we hear we apply the story line dictated by our theoretical predilections. Schafer (1982b) declares that he uses "specifically psychoanalytic abstracting and organizing concepts (i.e., sadism, regression, orality, danger situations)" (p. 78). Although Kohut (1984) admonishes us to "resist temptation to squeeze our understanding of the patient into the rigid mold of whatever theoretical perceptions" (p. 67), he is well aware that his stories of analysis would be different from those of clinicians who put drives into the center. His point of view, for example, about the once-thought-to-be ubiquitous Oedipus complex is that it would not even come into being in the oedipal phase had the child been adequately mirrored. So, clearly his interpretive comments would be different, based more on "empathic immersion," which was what was missing in the patient's childhood. He can be seen as the "spiritual descendent" of Ferenczi, who once attempted to give to patients the love of which they had felt deprived, and of Alexander, with his "corrective emotional experience" (Stone, 1981). But he is quite clear that "objective reality always includes the subject" (p. 55).

The burgeoning of self psychology, simultaneous with new discoveries about infancy and with the infusion of ideas from the British Independent Tradition, has served to move us toward a different view of psychoanalysis, which sees this enterprise more in terms of meaning reorganization than in terms of unearthing motivations of which the patient has no inkling. The goal becomes not to arrive at "truth" but to hone abilities to engage in a process of ever fresh "retranscribings."

What babies are teaching us, now that we consult them directly rather than reading backward from experiences with our adult analysands, is that they are born interpreters. Far from being satisfied with their organization of information gleaned from the events of their daily lives, they show great impatience with sameness. They seek fresh stimuli and keep reaching out for novelty (Berlyne, 1966), and – as Freud intuitively guessed – this tendency seems to have a biological basis in the central nervous system itself (Sokolov, 1960).

Some of us tend to think that the built-in tendency to order the data of experience is what we must mean when we speak of the unconscious. Certainly the infant is not yet ready to comprehend the principles by which she constructs schemas of self and social world. Perhaps, as Lacan (1966) suggested, the unconscious is structured like a language.

In any event, the very first sense of self is, Stern (1985) says, a sense of self in emergence, that is, a sense of organization in the processes of formation. The form of that organizing will be influenced by the idiosyncratic features of this baby – or what Winnicott (1960a) thinks of as the "true self" – and by the interactions with persons in the immediate environment, the "transformational objects" (Bollas, 1987). If these latter are attuned to the infant, she can "start by existing and not by reacting" (p. 148). If not, however, she must begin by sacrificing some of her spontaneous "sensori-motor aliveness" to preserve the attachment between herself and mother. So there is set up a preoedipal conflict between the sense of self and the sense of connection with a needed other. These become incorporated into those early maps of the world, long before they can be consciously evaluated.

By the time in which we assume a sense of core self to be forming, babies are busy making what Stern (1985) calls RIGs, or representations of interactions generalized out of these experiences of self with other. The intent in creating RIGs is to have schemas to evaluate experiences and guide reactions. To the extent that they are "hung onto," the purpose must be to safeguard one's sense of self and of outer world. RIGs are basic units for the representation of the core self, the one who acts, feels, has unique perceptions, feels unified. They are memories of lived episodes that thus become represented preverbally and that serve to create a sense of continuity, or what Winnicott calls "going-on-being."

As the baby has more and more experience with life, the RIGs are constantly updated. One of the advantages of the episodic memory system is that it permits indexing and reindexing of self and other invariants (Shank, 1982). So we could note this innate "reparative intent," a biological tendency not only to generalize but to keep one's schema current, since only by taking into consideration the variations from former expectations could one keep one's map reliable. Whether the regulating role of the other is obvious or unobtrusive, "the alteration of self-experience always belongs to the self" (Stern, 1985, p. 109). But the self-experiences and the regulating role of the other are both accommodated in the RIG.

When, therefore, one attribute is present, say the self-experience one had when with another, it calls to mind the other, the "evoked companion." When another engages the baby in ways reminiscent of the original transformational other, the associated qualities of self-experiencing are evoked. This retrievable memory permits comparison of a current interactive experience with the simultaneously occurring one of that "evoked companion." We could imagine that the infant has a multitude of experiences in which the "new" other does not behave exactly as others in the past, and so she begins to create RIGs that have to do with experiences with those who are different from the familiar ones—perhaps persons with whom one might have either a better or a not-so-good self-experience, and so there could be RIGs that represent the average expectable contacts with other-than-family or with total strangers. I make this point because these RIGs will be activated in the transference, too. We have had some trouble thinking about where to place the "search for new experience" as we recognize it in our analysands, and I am hypothesizing that the concept of RIGs lets us look at this element as it is evident from the beginning with many persons. It could also let us speculate that the more limited kind of transference, that is, an expectation that we will be like the original figures, is much more probable in persons who have lived their lives with minimal contacts with the broader social world. Their RIGs would not have been so thoroughly updated.

It could be fun to try out the idea that in analysis the unit that we address is likely to be the RIG, although the attachment theorists are calling our attention to the notion of "working models." The RIG is a basic component of the working model, which – as it is now being defined – concerns the regulation of attachment states, while RIGs are about mutually created alterations in self-experience, "such as arousal, affect, mastery, physiological state, state of consciousness, curiosity" (Stern, 1985, p. 115) and not just about attachment, although clearly attachment might contain any or all of the above. The working model is conceived in highly cognitive terms; it detects deviations from average expectations, while the "evoked companion," as an activated RIG, is close to the affective component of being with other, to the vividness of subjective experience, and is not just a guiding model (although it serves that function, too). Development, says Stern (1985, p. 118), is "a constant, usually silent, dialogue" between the actual external partner and the evoked companion (p. 118). The evoked companion is more subjective and more experience near than is the working model, and so, in the context of analysis, the "dialogue" may become conscious.

Of course, the working model will change as the RIGs that compose it are altered, subtracted, or added to. Analysis, by definition, according to the *American Heritage Dictionary,* is "the separation of an intellectual or substantial whole into constituents for individual study" (from *analuein,* Latin for "to undo"; from *ana,* back, and *luein,* to loosen). A wide array of "constituents" in the form both of "evoked companions" and of "evoked self-states" will ordinarily become available for "study" in the course of analysis. These are what we have called transference reactions, the past and present intermingling, the here and now with the there and then. Perhaps we should be speaking not of the transference but rather of an array of possible transferences, affected by qualities and quantities of past experiences and also by qualities and quantities of what is available in this psychoanalytic relationship.

When we begin to think in this way, we may see that interpretation is likely to be most mutative when attention is paid to the eternal self-righting tendency in the human psyche.

ON REPARATIVE INTERPRETING

The scene must be one in which, as Freud (1914b) wrote long ago, transference can be used as a playground. In recent years other analysts also echoed that idea. Levinson (1988) is impressed, as many of us are, with the "powerful internal, out-of-awareness ordering of experience," the patterning of which leaves him with the "uncanny sense that someone inside the patient's head knows what the patient doesn't know, and is slipping out hints" (p. 136). He describes the therapist-patient field as one "used as a *playground* for the reenactment and reexperiencing of the cardinal issues, which, although historical, have their current manifestations in the patient's present life and in the therapy" (p. 142, italics added). For Levinson, it is the "isomorphism" between insight and relationship that distinguishes psychoanalysis from other therapies, its "recursive patterning," like a "hall of mirrors" (p. 137). I like his metaphor there, reminiscent as it is of a "fun fair," and it invites us to see the listener-analyst as a mirror, without which there would be no narrative. As one writer in the literary world has pointed out, Narcissus needed a second mirror; it was not enough that he could see himself; he had to see himself seeing himself (Bronnimann, 1987) if he were to learn to engage in the discourse without which he could not grow and change.

When one speaks of scene, one must also include time. It has often been affirmed that to be mutative, interpretation must be in the context of a conflict alive at the moment (Strachey, 1934). But some writers currently, such as Bollas (1987), see insights arriving when the patient is in private experiences within analysis, and is using the analyst as transformational object to facilitate a state of being open to "news from deep within" (p. 248). These are not conflictual moments but moments of being "alone together," experiences that Winnicott (1971a) posits as a stage in the development of the ability to play or – we would add – to engage in the dialogue of psychotherapy, which for him is essentially two people playing together in potential space.

In this therapeutic space each of the two participants is interpreting the other, albeit not always in words. Therapists, too, come with working models, the components of which are RIGs, and theirs, too, will have been formed not only out of the earliest life episodes but out of numerous later ones, including some amount of previous experiences with patients, both similar to and different from this one. So each member of this dyad will size up the other according to his theories at the time. The treatment relationship will be created by the two of them (Saari, 1986), and each will be looking for what is reliable about his own schemas and for what may be new variables in this situation. Ideally, the therapist holds his theories lightly and knows the importance of being open to surprise (Reik, 1937), but to some extent the patient is hoping for surprise, too, of a pleasurable kind, although perhaps he is wary that it might be quite the opposite.

Until quite recently, most analysts seem to have arrogated to themselves the role of interpreter. Schafer (1982a) has said that via narrative search the *analyst* retells both present and past in ever more coordinated and condensed fashion, guided by his theory and by the analysand's *responsiveness,* but he does not include the latter's participation in making those interpretations. Even Green (1989), whom I see as much influenced by Winnicott, writes that *"we* present the analysand with another version of the personal myth to which he adheres" (p. 97, italics added).

Yet clearly, if a main goal is to facilitate healing of the "core" or "nuclear" self, the analysand's sense of self-as-agent must be restored. Even Kohut (1984), however, speaks of the interpretation as given by the analyst at the appropriate point, although, parenthetically, he does add, "if indeed the analysand has not come to this conclusion on his own" (p. 24). Some of his followers have more boldly affirmed, "Interpretation is a shared act" (Schwaber, 1990). We might all keep ourselves open to surprises, for even the often thought-to-be traditionalist Brenner (1976) has written that interpretation is a collaborative process.

What we are coming to is part of a new ethic: interpretations not made by the analyst for the patient but, rather, dialogically created. Meanings are not "owned" by one or the other of us, nor are they simply "truths" somehow "out there" (as in the culture); we own them (Holquist, 1982). As Shor (1990) puts it, they are "negotiated," and we should avoid imposing our meanings as superior to those of the person's own. Meanings are never final; they "grow, change, develop and are struggled over by two people and thus ultimately owned by *us*" (Stern, 1985, p. 170). In this sense, they are akin to transitional objects or phenomena, the words discovered or created by the analysand in interaction with the analyst, who, in her responses to an invitation to contribute, nevertheless stays in the "zone of proximal development" (Vygotsky, 1962) and never ventures far from "where the patient is," as social work analysts might put it.

Insofar as the analysand is open to hearing from the analyst, the latter's comments should ideally be, as Winnicott (1971a) prescribes, "as far as possible removed from authoritative interpretation that is next door to indoctrination" (p. 73) and, indeed, should be closer to playing. Winnicott tells us of his remorse that he has sometimes prevented or delayed deep change in patients by his "personal need to interpret" when, had he but waited, the analysand would have arrived "at understanding creatively and with immense joy" (p. 86).

Interpretation is, of course, creative, and the pleasure involved when one has deciphered a puzzle or answered a riddle is great, the narcissistic gain high. One analyst with whom Shor and I were discussing these ideas simply admitted, "But I like to be the wise man!" Not all analysts can come to Winnicott's achievement, to enjoy the patient's joy at arriving herself at insights more than his own sense of being clever (p. 86).

The analyst's role at its best is to sustain the illusion of potential space that permits a kind of play, characterized by "humor, surprise, discovery, originality" (Ogden, 1989).

What is it that is interpreted? The specific content, says Kohut (1984), may be less important than the meaning transmitted, interpretation being "a non-specific carrier of essential meaning" (p. 94). Indeed, empathic interpretations are as much to communicate understanding as to increase insight. He would include dynamic, genetic explanations as well as transference interpretations and thus, I conclude, would avoid the "ocnophilic" bias about which Balint (1959) worried. As for most psychoanalysts, the focus of interpretation is not the patient's behavior in the world but the nature of her inner experience (Schwaber, 1990).

For Kohut (1984), as for a number of the British Independents, analytic successes are due not necessarily to the ascendancy of secondary over primary processes but to the increased ability of the patient to be comforted, enjoy cultural events, be joyful (p. 76). "Man cannot live by reality alone," Klauber (1986) writes, "even less by psychic reality" (Kohon, 1986, p. 213). Green (1989) suggests that what we interpret is "tertiary processes," which are in the arena of Winnicott's "transitional phenomena"–in the realm of the symbolic, formed out of the interaction of the primary and the secondary (or the subjective and the objective). For him, as for a growing number of us, primary process has an implicit logic; in it repressed wishes find some satisfaction, so the logic is the logic of hope. I would add, that to make that concession is to recognize the reparative intent in preserving this area from possible censorship.

Green reminds us that the discourse of the analysand is not the analysand (p. 85). It is always an attempt to bring together what is separated—the analyst and the analysand, the conscious and the unconscious—so it is a "double compromise." Interpretation therefore is also a compromise between what the analyst can decipher with her conscious and what she may understand from her unconscious. In communicating this understanding to the analysand, she is mindful of paradoxical goals: contact and yet necessary distance. It is clear that Green has abandoned the model of the analyst's discovering the unconscious wish and then teaching the analysand's ego to recognize it. He is impressed, rather, by the capacity of the ego to distort so effectively that we reach not material but only historical truth, which Freud saw as what was considered true by the patient at a given time in his history (p. 96).

If we are interpreting wishes, we would be looking with the patient for the reasons he may have put things together in the way that he did or does. The primary motivating factors would be the wish for a favorable sense of self that would not threaten a sense of valued connection with others, a wish to balance autonomy and togetherness. The RIGs that we hope will become activated will be those that have to do with playful episodes, in which the person enjoys the illusion of no conflict between coveted senses of self and senses of self with other—akin to those in the play sequences when the core self was being formed and in which the dialogic mode was first learned (Stern, 1977). Whether or not they were actually experienced at three months when Stern described them—and with some of our patients they may not have been—or at later dates may not be relevant now.

What is relevant is whether the analyst is behaving in a way that respects the analysand's person and pace so that, as "recursive mirror," the "evoked companion" will evoke a sense of playful self, and the sense of playful self will evoke a sense of playful other—in the "then" and in the "now." As the mother's "interpretations" of her baby's state were not verbal, so the analyst's may be in other than the speech realm. Language is learned in contact with external "objects," and so for some persons, depending on the quality of their interaction with others both before and while words were being learned, there can be hatred and suspicion of words themselves. Rycroft (1958) reports on one patient who so hated them that their very existence showed the impossibility of real understanding. For my patient Elise, whose presenting complaint was that she could neither comprehend nor use language, I imagine that for some time my comments were "heard" not so much for their content but for their comforting "hum." In time, she reported to me, "It's not that I never used words; I just never felt they came from me" (Sanville, 1990a). Balint feels that at the level of the basic fault, words might be experienced either as tokens of affection or as cruelties (Kohon, 1986). Not all interpretations are verbal. Little (1986) suggests that for many patients a two-stage process is involved. The first is concerned with body happenings, which are themselves related to memories in earliest postnatal life. Because of discontinuities with later periods these memories of life's first events have not been assimilated, she says. If there are perhaps rudimentary RIGs, the other may find lesser representation there, and so they were not easily updated into language. In analysis they may be reactivated in ways that enable the patient to translate them into words, the second of Little's interpretive processes.

Closely related to "bodily events," are affects themselves. We know that since the baby cannot fully accomplish all his possible goals alone, he sends forth affective displays, or "other-directed regulatory behaviors" (Gianino and Tronick, 1988), and the caretaker's correct "interpretations" of these can enable her to transform her infant's failure into success (this transformation being one of the functions of the transformational other). In this case, the infant's general mood tends to be a positive one, and his interactions with mother reciprocal and coherent and synchronous. This description is partly what Emde (1983) means when he speaks of the "affective core" of the early self.

The mood generated in the infant, however, may not be a positive one if the mother, perhaps depressive or otherwise withdrawn, does not "get" the affective message and leaves the infant with his failure. Bollas (1987) tells us, "Moods typical of a person's character frequently conserve something that was but is no longer" (p. 110). The person may have a profound self-experience without being able to link the state with an "evoked companion," so negative mood states tend to be untranslatable into the symbolic order (p. 111). Bollas sees moods as often "the existential registers of the moment of a breakdown between a child and his parents" (p. 115) and does imagine that they can be addressed in analysis. The mood is linked with failed negotiation with parents, and its appearance in the present can be seen as an unconscious wish to repair, even though its manifestations may be such that we can feel the patient being in a state that is quite distant and off-putting (Sanville, 1990b). Our comprehension of the functions the mood serves enables us not to be "really" put off but to arrive with the patient at the reparative purpose in its presence now.

My inference from certain infant research is that the caretaker may not need to be always so well attuned for the person to emerge with a basically optimistic view of life. Tronick and Cohn (1988) have estimated that mothers and their infants achieve coordinated interactions only about 30% of the time. What then becomes important is the availability of measures for "repair" of the misattunements. If the other is not open to mending the breach, the baby may be forced to engage mainly in self-regulatory behaviors, such as rocking, self-clasping, dulling the expressiveness in his own eyes. Eventually if there is not opportunity for reparation, the child – and later the adult – may lose the capacity for concern, guilt lying dormant and only moodiness appearing. The importance of experiencing success in interpersonal repair confirms that the analyst is on the right track when he is open to reviewing with the analysand his responses that felt like empathic failures. His willingness to do so conveys his own "reparative intent" and invites that of the other; in their conjoint efforts to comprehend what went wrong, both may emend their interpretive capacities and may arrive at insights meaningful to the self as well as to the relationship. Self-esteem is established not only when one's attempts to signal the other are received and responded to but when one has confidence in one's ability to mend matters when things go wrong. If there is some success in repairing the disruption with the other, then the relatively "autistic" withdrawal of the bad mood does not have to be a central characteristic of the self.

Many persons who distrust words nevertheless are capable of representing material in vivid metaphor. I have found this capacity true of some of my most creative analysands. They present vivid dreams, sometimes spontaneously produce thoughts in the form of imagery. Some psychoanalysts seem to be leery of this type of symbolism. Schlesinger (1984), for example, concedes that in the early phases of treatment interpretation might be conducted in the patient's metaphor and that, during this time, the patient may even make interpretations for himself; however, he warns, as we move on from this stage, as "playtime" is over, we must expect a sudden rise in resistance. Why, I wonder, should we move away from the patient's own metaphor, which is, after all, close to play, an "as if" way of acting? (Aleksandrowicz, 1962).

The image is, as Piaget (1951) informs us, a "motivated sign," that is, closer to the sense of self than to the sense of need to be connected with the other. So it makes its appearance precisely in that "intermediate space" (Winnicott, 1971a) that is the psychoanalytic situation at its best. Indeed, the various transference manifestations can themselves be seen as metaphoric, as Freud (1914b) intuitively sees. I would agree with Siegelman (1990) that the resistance of some analysts to staying with the patient's metaphor signals the old fear and distrust of primary process and maybe of play itself. The metaphor does not immediately reveal its multiple meanings, so there seems a conviction the person should advance to language, with its presumably greater logic, to be able to "object relate" better. Perhaps, as Kohut (1984) suggests, the theory of drive primacy and drive taming and of the importance of movement from narcissism to object love leads to psychoanalysis, in some instances, becoming "part of a supraordinated moral system in scientific disguise," so practice can be "burdened by an admixture of hidden moral and educational goals" (p. 208). Maybe the urge to move the patient on to more purely verbal exchange is an aspect of that covert moralism.

After all, the analysand is already making a compromise with us when she puts her dream images into words for us to contemplate with her. If we value ambiguity, as Schlesinger (1984) does when he says that every interpretation should increase ambiguity, we could do no better than to play with the many possible interpretive schemas that can be applied to the patient's own images. As Langer (1967) declares, every really new idea tends to burst in on the human mind as metaphor.

We might also remember that among creative persons have been those who were perhaps not skilled at verbal dialogue with others but who have left us a heritage of poetry, a token of their reparative intent, which we ill-comprehended during their lifetimes (Grolnick, 1990) but which belatedly we deeply appreciate for the power of their images to repair our former deficits.

As Stern (1985) reminds us, language proper is a "double-edged sword," causing a split between interpersonal experience "as it is lived and as it is verbally represented" (p. 162). The self becomes a "categorical self" as against an "existential" or "subjective" self (Lewis and

Brooks-Gunn, 1979). When professionals are intent at finding diagnostic labels for their clientele or at imposing their interpretive schemas rather than accepting their roles as but facilitators of the patient's own aquisition of new meanings for both old and current events, they will not be fostering and equipping the person's intent to repair, particularly to reclaim the sense of self in emergence.

Our role is neither to label nor to be the interpreters. It is the patient who has the data about himself. We cannot know what the person does not share with us. He is the source of information about himself; only he can know his feelings, their intensities, and their shapes. His are the memories that over time were built into RIGs, and only he can know what qualities of "evoked companions" or senses of self are activated at different moments with us. We begin ideally with a state of "unknowing," not omniscience, as Winnicott (1971a) suggested, and when the patient manifests an openness to it, we participate with him in attempts to know, that is, to invent new schemas for explaining things. In the process there will be periods of form making alternating with periods of seeming chaos; both are important if interpretations are not to be taken as ultimate truths.

The "how" of interpreting on the part of the analyst is as important as the "what," for it is this "how" that the analysand, in some measure, adopts as his own, and it may determine whether he emerges from analysis with relatively rigid intellectualizations about himself and his situation or with flexibility to go on to devise new ways of thinking and feeling.

There is some sign that current analysts prefer to inject a tentative quality into their interpretations, not to offer opinions but rather to suggest what the person may be thinking (Etchegoyen, 1989), and not to regard the analysand's rejection of that as resistance. Instead, we are becoming aware of our own resistances to sharing the fun of interpreting with the patient and to the narcissistic blows we sometimes experience when our ideas are not immediately recognized for their cleverness and originality.

Many analysts write that confrontations should be used sparingly. Kohut (1984) admonished that they are often trite, superfluous, and in danger of eliciting repetitions of adverse childhood experiences. Although he declared himself very much influenced by Glover, he disagreed with him that interpretations must be exact. Were they exact, there would be no room for the patient's emendations and hence for his sense of agency in the process of self-healing. Winnicott (1969) has written, "I think I interpret mainly to let the patient know the limits of my understanding" (pp. 86–87). If the patient can sense the analyst's comfort with not being certain, he may come to tolerate that in himself and, relieved of the urgency to have all the answers, be open to the ongoing search that life usually demands of us and to ongoing modifications of ways of thinking and being.

Of course, not all analysts themselves think that way. Some believe that living systems tend toward a "steady state" and that the personality therefore resists change. For them, psychoanalysis must be a "tendentious process," their interpretations seen as necessary to disturb the patient's neurosis and to make for a period of instability. So they advocate "forceful and persistent" interpretation to prevent the patient's "sealing over" and returning to the status quo (Schlesinger, 1984). These analysts, too, see value in periods of instability, or the relative chaos of uncertainty, but would force the patient to stay with that rather than enable it by manifesting their own ability to endure genuine unknowing. We could fear that the quality of the unintegrated state in their patients would not be the same as that in Winnicott's. Winnicott must have been impressed, as current infant researchers are, with the advantages of the quiet alert state, in which the baby, with no urgent and pressing needs, is unusually open to taking in whatever from the surround. Analysts of the "old school" still seem to feel, as Strachey (1934) did, that to be mutative, the interpretation must be in the context of a felt conflict at the moment. In this model we are dealing not only with an inner conflict about whether it is safe to change one's way of conceptualizing but with a conflict with the analyst.

This "battleground model" is a far cry from the "playground model," originally adumbrated (but not developed) by Freud and now elaborated by Winnicott. In playfulness persons find their best fresh editions of the primary illusion toward which all reparative efforts aim. When RIGs associated with play are reelicited in analysis, together with evoked companions who are not powerful superiors but playmates, these RIGs will enter into the working models of the analysand so as to render the person ever more capable both of being alone and of engaging in the healing potential of dialogue.

According to this model psychoanalysis also becomes an aesthetic experience. Like art, it will have tapped into many sensory modalities and many levels of cognition from sensori-motor to concrete to abstract. Viderman (1979) has written that the analyst is more poet than historian. If this creating is the prerogative of the analyst, there is danger that we deprive the patient of the sense of primary creativity (Winnicott, 1971a), for which there is such abundant evidence in the human organism's ability to organize the data of experiences and to continue, if the environment is a facilitating one, to emend his schemas throughout life.

With each psychoanalysis, the analyst also continues to emend his own approaches and lets himself learn from the analysand and engage in that dialectic between theory and practice that is reparative for both.

CHAPTER 12

Endings and
New Beginnings

Much of the literature on termination of psychotherapy has been based on the traditional psychoanalytic model, which involves separation and loss, which lead to grief and mourning, those reactions themselves essential to "internalization." Yet over many years, distinctions were made between the briefer therapies and psychoanalysis. Patients not deemed suitable for analysis were not at the "oedipal level" and so were presumed incapable of mourning. Therefore, true terminations were not possible; there would likely be resumptions of therapy at later dates.

Gradually, however, psychoanalysts, too, have been taking on patients whose problems are seen as of "preoedipal" origin. Indeed, some of us are not sure that severe oedipal problems would even exist were they not based on still earlier developmental difficulties. So the old distinction between therapy and analysis – namely, that the latter achieves "total reorganization" of the psychic structure while therapy addresses only specific problems – has broken down. Indeed, "structural change" is to be seen in actions of the patient, in the way she relates to us and to others, in evidence of new understanding and of glimpsing new and better ways to live life (Schafer, 1982a, p. 66). We see these evidences of transforming features in persons who have been in psychotherapy as well as in those who have been in psychoanalysis. Just as there has come to be a doubt whether the superego is formed only on dissolution of the Oedipus complex, so there is coming to be some doubt about the resolution of the transference as characterizing the end of the treatment (Bergmann, 1988).

Perhaps it is not fully resolvable, as Reich (1958) suspected some decades ago, when the therapist is the first reliable figure in the patient's life. Object relations theory today supports this idea. Even psychoanalysis is no longer confined to the analysis of fantasy systems; when there have been gross failures in the original love objects, then "the analyst will replace the original objects as the major infantile prototype" and so will remain important (Bergmann, 1988, pp. 149–51).

The self psychologists have something of the same idea. With "transmuting internalization" having taken place, the person is now able to perform for self the former functions of the therapist/selfobject. Some of them are even writing that there may not necessarily be grief and mourning at termination but rather a sense of "relief and pride in the accomplishment of an important task" (Palombo, 1982, p. 26). In reading some of their case reports (Goldberg, 1978), however, I see evidence of patients' grief plus their pleasure in the many evidences of improved attitudes and functioning.

The ending of therapy with adults is coming more and more to approximate that with children. Child therapists, equipped with a developmental outlook, are content to be used for the child's immediate purposes, and few of us would judge our "success" by the somewhat perfectionistic standards by which therapies of adults have been evaluated. We aim mainly to remove obstacles to psychosocial growth and accept our probable inability to immunize the child against all further psychological difficulties. We know that much will depend, as, indeed, Freud himself said, on the vicissitudes of life and what stresses and strains will be entailed. In our attempts to achieve the best conditions for ego unfolding, we may be able to influence some of the environmental factors, in ways seldom attempted by therapists of adults, but we are always imperfectly accomplishing that instrumental goal. I suspect most of us have an "open door" policy and do not regard it as a necessary sign of the former shortcomings of our work if the child recurrently comes in for further therapy. Nor is the child likely to regard it in that way.

Of course, with children we have as allies the powerful developmental forces, and when we have freed those forces, we feel justified in ending treatment (A. Freud, 1970), although admittedly we cannot be sure we have really done so. Perhaps we worry less about the issue because, assuming we have been able to form a good working and playing relationship with this child, we tend to believe she will feel comfortable to return if problems feel too great to handle alone. If the child has had the pleasure of sensing her ability to create the analyst or therapist, then the return is in the expectation of re-creating one to meet the new age and circumstances. So, as I see it, it is a matter not just of internalization but of claiming one's own powers to design the relationship that will be healing, whether with the same or a different therapist.

In fact, I am in agreement with Pedder (1988) that termination is probably the wrong word to deal with the ending of treatment. The word connotes finality, and except for situations in which the ending is necessitated by the critical illness or death of one of the participants, there may not be this finality. Pedder concedes that termination is such a "received concept" that we may not abolish it, but he does feel that words such as "graduation," "rebirth," or "new beginning" may be more apt (p. 495). Whether or not we change our language, we are warranted in moving toward concepts that take into account the ongoing developmental processes in human life and in approaching endings as we approach both beginnings and what occurs between the two. Again, I feel we have something to learn from child therapy in this matter.

It has long been said that the working through of the transference neurosis was essential to successful terminations in analysis and often in any psychodynamic therapies. In treatment of children, it has been felt that since the real parents are still around, transference plays a somewhat different role (A. Freud, 1946). Transference manifestations do, of course, occur, since, as we have said, there is no way of understanding a current situation except by reference to past ones that manifested both similar and different features. But very clearly the child reaches out for "new objects" and quickly scans this scene and its occupant to ascertain what is similar and what is unlike that experienced in the past. Being very much in process, the child then proceeds to create of the new person what is felt to be needed in the service of her own self-repair, providing, of course, that the scrutinizing has resulted in finding a suitable object to be used.

Whether the child is transferring or is making a working alliance is not of much practical concern. Were there not some positive carryovers from former relationships, it is doubtful that a viable therapeutic relationship could develop. My little patient Rickie had received a lot of good-enough mothering, which enabled him rather promptly to trust me. But he also perceived something that let him play out the concerns that had previously led to psychosomatic symptoms. Probably this "something" was a comfortable emotional climate, which was even safer because mother was on the scene, too. Even with Katie, I assumed a basic or primary transference (Greenacre, 1954) in that new edition of the earliest wish for sensory contact. It was possible, beginning with this, to build a relationship that eventuated in our being able conjointly to work and to play.

The therapist for the child is not just real or just fantasied but someone in between. I think we rarely see a transference neurosis, if by that we mean the concentration of instinctual wishes onto the therapist. Of course, in therapy the child may play out conflicts, repressed wishes, and fantasies, sometimes by using the person of the therapist, but often by using an array of toys and equipment. This activity may make for a diminution of the manifestations of these conflicts elsewhere. Some of us are less convinced that we are dealing with instincts unless we speak of ego instincts (Stern, 1985). It is not just that the child can express drives that are not permissible elsewhere but that the way in which the therapist responds makes for a more positive view of self. Experienced child therapists follow the advice of Bornstein (1945) and attend first to the pain against which the child is defending before analyzing the defenses. When the child feels this understanding, defense analysis may even become unnecessary.

Today, both Kohutian and Winnicottian therapists of adults tend to follow similar approaches, are careful to offer interpretations in an empathic context, and are increasingly convinced that wounds to the sense of self are rarely therapeutic. In such a safe ambience, whatever transference neurosis develops would be likely to be of the playful sort that Freud (1914b) envisioned when he wrote that we admit the tendency to repeat "into the transference as a playground in which it is allowed to expand in almost complete freedom and in which it is expected to display to us everything in the way of pathogenic instincts that is hidden in the patient's mind" (p. 154). The "ordinary neurosis" was to be replaced by a "transference neurosis," of which the patient could be cured; the new condition would have all the features of the original but would be "artificial," which we could take to mean possessing a quality of make-believe, as in the play of our child patients. In terms close to Winnicott's own, Freud wrote here of "an intermediate region between illness and real life through which the transition from the one to the other is made" (p. 154).

Like the child who, in play therapy, converts the problems of real life into themes of "just pretend," most of our adult patients are capable of sensing that their feelings and responses to the analyst in this situation partake of this "intermediate quality" – being both real and artificial. It is just possible, however, that the term transference neurosis has not always connoted this quality to analysts. Greenacre (1959b) worried that this designation did not take into account that most patients maintain an observing ego; she suggested, instead, the term, "active transference-neurotic manifestations" (p. 653). Whatever we may decide about the language, when the analyst-analysand dyad can move the action closer to play than to repetition compulsion, fixations are more likely to be violated and healing to occur.

We can probably predict that psychodynamic therapists who permit their thinking to be enlightened by the new view of the basic human condition that infant researchers are revealing will continue to hone their approach in this direction. They will be influenced by the evidence for the presence of a sense of self and a sense of being with another from the start of life and of the conflict-free oscillation between the two under good-enough initial conditions. The concept of this primary illusion (Shor and Sanville, 1978) may even make for a somewhat different way of viewing what we have called transference. The model itself is, unlike either that of Freud's "primary narcissism" or that of Balint's "primary love," not a fixed one but includes the idea of movement and change. When we see the infant gazing into the eyes of the mother and then looking away for several minutes, we imagine that the sense of self is not quite the same as before the baby ever saw that other face. When he looks back again, neither the sense of his own being nor the sense of the other is as it was at the first seeing. The infant transfers to his sense of self his sense of being with the other and then transfers to the sense of being-with-other a fresh sense of self. So the dialectic begins, and from it comes what Stern (1985) calls the "sense of emergent self," as well as a sense of emergent other.

It is this sense that the patient seeks. In this writing I have tried to describe some of the intersubjectivities in the therapeutic dialogue that maximize the likelihood that the seeker will experience new editions of that primary illusion, with its easy oscillation between a sense of accepted and accepting self and a sense of accepting and accepted other, and the sense of fresh becoming that emerges from this spiraling movement.

I review this material here because the process that goes into ending the treatment will be inseparable from the processes that have characterized that treatment. Like Loewald (1988), I see termination as an exercise "at play from the beginning of treatment," sometimes "with a vengeance" (pp. 157–158), as he puts it, when the person is fearful of losing balance by dependent closeness. When the therapist is respectful of the patient's emphasis on self-sufficiency, the latter may come to realize the possibility of "intimacy in distance"–which is another way of describing what we have called the primary illusion. With growing confidence in this potential for relating, the patient experiments with carrying over what has been learned to the outside world and begins to think about termination. The process of parting then has a nonmourning dimension.

Like Pedder (1988), I would quote T. S. Eliot's, "Little Gidding" that "to make an end is to make a beginning. The end is where we start from" (Eliot, 1962, p. 144). When patients are able, over the course of treatment, to move toward a confidence that they can generate relationships that are not threatening to their valued senses of self, they often design endings that are quite creative.

One such patient, Sara, entered analysis with a history of relationships in which she was the "strong" one, one on whom others always depended. She defended against the longing to be taken care of by noisy protestations of self-sufficiency, but the rejected longings would break through regularly in furies against those who took but did not give to her. Slowly, over several years with me, she discovered that one could, as she said, "depend without losing independence."

Sara planned the ending of her treatment over a period of several months. On the occasion of the next-to-the-last hour, she commented that she had arrived at a state of thinking and feeling that I was not, in fact, indispensable. But, she said, she was going to miss my house (in which, as I have described, my office is located). She spoke affectionately of the little lizards that greeted her on the steps of the entrance, of how she watched the many plants in the waiting room as they moved through their life stages in the different seasons, of her appreciation of the art she saw here and of her fantasies of me in relation to various items of it, of her special attraction to certain primitive pieces, of her awareness that things moved around somehow and her surprise at that fact. From her position on the couch, she told me, a certain book appeared and disappeared from her line of vision, *Not by Words Alone,* and she was always glad when it came once more into view. She entertained wishes that she could leave something of herself here. It was not only that she did not want me to forget her but that a bit of her might inhabit this place.

When she appeared for the last session and was carrying a bonsai, the metaphor was immediately apparent to us both, but she wanted to put it into words. She preferred to sit up for this hour, so she seated herself on the couch, and we talked of the plant. When she found it, she had a sense that it was exactly what she wanted to leave here with me. Although a "growing" thing, it was, like her, petite, "well formed," pleasing aesthetically. She was pleased with the "shape" she was now in. Once somewhat bothered by her small stature, she had come to see it as no handicap to "bigness" inside. Laughing, she explained to me that this tree would require some regular attention from me. It had to remain outside but could be brought in from time to time for enjoyment in this room. She pictured it on the coffee table next to the couch. She observed that she took me "inside" and that several people whom she supervised had commented on their taking her inside them.

She reviewed briefly some memories of treatment, including how there were many hours in which she was "not exactly working" and would not be able to say just what was happening. Yet things had seemed to come together. (I was hearing what she said as testimony to the inherent organizing capacity of the unconscious and was thinking of Freud's [1915] reiteration that "the repressed does not cover everything that is unconscious" [p. 166] and his assertion that mental processes are in themselves unconscious and that we could "liken the perception of them by means of consciousness to the perception of the external world by means of the sense organs" [p. 171]. When Sara had been open to news from within, she had discovered a lot about her internal world.) She contrasted what she was trying to describe with the approach of a therapist whom she knew who made complex interpretations and then wondered why patients could not take them in. Sara had felt at times almost as if "on vacation" and seemingly not talking of anything urgently important; yet she had had a sense of "shaping things up."

She reflected on how it felt to be sitting up, looking this much at me. Observing that I was at that moment "backlighted," with the window behind me, she declared I looked like an angel. But, she laughed, she had never really thought of me that way! She imagined that she would see me sometimes in the professional world. She had told one of her own departing patients that they would probably encounter each other from time to time at meetings or conventions. Like the plant, however, she would be mostly in my "outside world." It would not be like being on the couch, where she had felt "held" in those years. Even sitting up was not the same. It was, we decided, a "transitional position," not quite like the one in which she had begun, on a chair and facing me.

She again mused how much had seemed to transpire not just by words and how she had a growing sense of her own ability to put things together. Now she called attention again to the bonsai and to the copper wires that held the tree's limbs in place and to the set of instructions that these should not be removed until they began to bind on the bark. She had not, she said, felt that I had a "design" for her. We both laughed, observing the imperfection of metaphors. I wondered if we could imagine that she, like the bonsai, had come with some bindings, ideas about forms she might want to assume, but that now was the time to remove those, to determine whether they were or were not the directions in which she may want to grow. Sara declared she was not sure she even had a design for herself; that had just seemed to unfold. It was not perfect, she admitted; she still had some resistance to time and its constraints and was still sometimes late. But, unlike the attitude she once took that she could not help it, she could very well be on time when she elected to do so, as with the patients in her developing private practice.

She reviewed some past relationships and contrasted their qualities with the new one she had now attained. She always used to find people for whom she had to be caretaker; with her present man, there was mutual concern, and they were joyous and playful together. She thanked me "for everything" and warmly shook hands as she left.

As Milner (1950) notes, when we in the therapeutic professions leave our analysts or therapists, we may bypass the experience of persons not in the mental health field. We do not part in the expectation that we may never see each other again; quite to the contrary, we are almost certain to meet in our institutes or at meetings or conferences. Indeed, we might add, that likelihood may modulate the pain for each participant. For some pangs of parting are inevitable.

Although there are differences between terminations and endings in so-called reality, there are equations made between the two in the human psyche.

A patient grieving the recent death of her mother reported "the first dream of mother since then." Mother is in the dream, and they find some bracelets, the kind that children make of woven strands. Mother calls her attention to the fact that they are somewhat imperfectly constructed.

The immediate context for the dream was that she and her new husband were rearranging her apartment to accommodate his possessions. In the course of this activity, Anna found herself sorting through things, deciding what to discard and what to keep, and making boxes of the things about which she cannot yet decide one way or the other. It occurred to her that, had she been more like mother, she would never have accumulated so many unused things; mother would have disposed of unnecessary stuff all along the way. Also, when the day's work was over, Anna looked at the apartment and could see so much that was as yet unfinished, needing more attention. From our past knowledge of mother, we both clearly recognized the voice of mother within her, ever perfectionistic, ever chiding that tasks were not quite well enough done.

I commented that perhaps among the aspects of mother that she might wish not to have to take on was that of the critical mother, never exactly pleased with what her daughter had accomplished. Anna weepingly described her feelings of guilt at several favors mother had wanted of her, things she had never got around to doing, and her voice took on the complaining tone that she so often heard in her mother's. As friends called, she had to go over the whole story again and again, and she could not keep from crying. I wondered whether there was something wrong with crying at this time. She said that she felt "not in control." The problem was not that the other persons were not understanding; some cried themselves. They all told her what a good daughter she was and how her mother appreciated her. But she knew of the ways she could have been better.

A coming task was the dismantling of her mother's apartment. To determine what to do with her possessions made the mother's death "more real." In the past, when she helped mother move, mother was there, directing what to do with everything; now she may not do it "right."

The bereaved go through some grieving about the loss of the scene as well as the person and the action that took place there, and it seems frequently that undoing the physical space makes more real the loss of the person and the relationship.

Anna associated in this session to a dream that she had as she ended her analysis: I am going through a house and examining a vast array of things and trying to determine what to leave and what to take with me. We both recognized that she wished it were a matter of choice now, that, if she could, she would like to leave the supercritical aspects of mother. We reflected on the scene at mother's death, when mother herself tried to depart without leaving her daughter feeling guilty about some decisions of which mother had earlier disapproved. She had made it clear that she loved her child deeply, and the critical stance that had so often marred their relating was absent.

As it happens, this patient will be ending her therapy with me shortly, and because of the vacations of the two of us before her ending date, there are not many sessions left. This therapy has been relatively short-term, and the reasons for our ceasing to meet are that she has resolved the problems for which she came and will be departing from the community for an extended time. She came to me originally because the critical illness of a former therapist necessitated closure, and during the time I have seen her she has been preoccupied with a seriously sick mother and her ultimate dying. So the doors were not open for return to these other relationships, as we hope they will be for this one with me. Sometimes there are actual and final terminations (Alexander et al., 1989).

For many patients whose past experiences included the loss of a loved one at a special milestone of life, the ending process may include the reworking of this theme, since achievement has become linked with doubts about whether one "deserves" to move ahead when the other is left in a precarious condition and with guilts about surviving and even thriving when the other may not. When the analysis, however, has enabled the person to reclaim essential aspects of the core self, especially the sense of agency, this work may also include a growing playfulness, manifested in dreams and in metaphors; in a fresh perspective on self, other, and the potentials for easier relating; and in daring once more to aspire.

Some vignettes from the last six months of analysis with Clare may illustrate these developments. I tend to respect the patient's own ideas about timing the ending. I simply listen to the person's reasons for feeling ready and to whatever apprehensions are manifest. We reflect together on both (Sanville, 1982). Clare pondered her own sense about what she had accomplished, together with worries about a significant new endeavor she would be undertaking in about six months and whether that would be in some jeopardy were I not available to her. She decided on a date, six weeks or so after my return from a vacation and shortly after her new project was to begin.

As though to confirm for herself that she was ready for this step, she reported a novel snake dream. Nightmarelike dreams of snakes had invaded her sleep time most of her life. We had worked and played with them and had come to understand them as representing the "demonic" qualities of self, poisoned and poisonous, especially her tongue, which could strike out in fury at unexpected moments (Eigen, 1984). But, Clare told me: "This snake is different from any other, not quite a real snake. It is domesticated, lives with us, and is very playful, tossing about the "blue mouse" that belongs to the cat, lying on its back like the cat. It's brown and white, like a pinto. I begin to worry about it; it looks deflated, hungry, comes to the refrigerator. It's sort of a cartoon snake, but I get a little afraid. So I call to my friend, who gives it cheese and tomato, and it goes to the back porch to eat. It's a vegetarian, playful snake!"

Asking, but only rhetorically, "What am I talking about here?" she went on to associate freely. The refrigerator and porch were like grandmother's (and I have, at times, been in the grandmother role in her transferences). She kept expressing amusement and surprise at the "endearing" quality of that snake and contrasted this dream with a dream she had at the ending of a previous therapy, when the snake was invasive, very frightening. This snake was a "character," a pleasure to watch. But, she sighed, "I wish I had symbols other than snakes."

Into this dream went a memory we shared, a "traumatic" situation for her and one of considerable amusement for me. One day, at the time she was due, I went out to the waiting room, although I had not heard the bell. She was outside the sliding glass doors on the lower level and was shouting at me, gesticulating with alarm, and admonishing me not to open my door. I went down to her, and she agitatedly told me there was a snake on my front door. Of course I went to investigate, and there was a magnificent king snake, with lovely patterns of brilliant colors, coiled around the protruding geometric wood designs of the door in vertical fashion. All that was lacking to make a caduceus, that ancient herald's wand that has come to symbolize the medical profession, was another snake in symmetrical position. For reasons not necessarily relevant here, I not only had no fear of that gorgeous reptile but was even secretly glad to have it, since it was a natural enemy of creatures I did not welcome in my domain. So, although I could utter intended empathic comments, perhaps she was essentially correct that I was something less than perfectly attuned to her terror.

Now, when Clare was dreaming of a benign snake, it was rather that the "twin" had been created, a pet reptile in her grandmother's house. She toyed with the idea that the frightening aspects of snakes for her had been "imaginary," connected with her own angers, which, indeed, could "suddenly strike." Now, she wondered, were they somewhat tamed, even sources of amusement? She expressed a wish, "If only I could turn my anger into a character!" I thought there was indication she was doing so, not only recognizing her furies but seeing herself seeing them, as from the outside, a recognition that may have been close to converting them to a "character." She hoped, she said, in her attempted writings not to be like one author whom she saw as having a "forked tongue," attacking those whose opinions he did not like.

That she was continuing to make friends of her aggressions was evident in the next session, when she reported that at a conference she had let herself ask a question of a speaker. She even went up and talked with him afterward and was very '"turned on" by this exchange. But the old depressive reaction set in after she also permitted herself some correspondence with writers she had been reading. She reflected that nobody in her family had "gone out into the world," so it had been important that she felt my encouraging her corresponding. Had the conference speaker not put his hand on her arm when someone interrupted them, as a signal she should not leave, she might have felt that she should not have approached him and that he must have been angry that she had been daring to speak.

In subsequent sessions she renewed worries whether, once she had ceased analysis, she could ever come back. "Technically" the door might be open, but she might not be able to turn the knob. Perhaps I would disappear. "Or die as your analyst?" I asked. "You might change from being my analyst," she said. She revived memories of her anguished decision to go on to graduate school, although her mother was dying, and of dancing with grandfather while grandmother was confined to a wheelchair. These old scripts alternated with new ones. She dreamed of our talking, face-to-face, "and not in the office. It was a real back and forth!" She took that one as a "promising sign" and had felt calm that weekend.

She found it odd, however, that memories of mother kept returning. She had been angry that mother had not seemed interested in what Clare was learning at college. She had seemed unable, she thought, to verbalize her experience in ways that mother could share; that inability made the felt separation acute. The old experience was organizing this one. I observed her apprehension that there would be this gap in our sharing, as she would be experiencing things outside my ken. She took some comfort when she saw me at a meeting, and saw that we "moved in the same world." Laughing, she said she did not see me as suffering social anxiety as did mother. "At the meeting, you were not different, just elaborated. You could interpret that I want to make you more real, but I also want a mother who has a better life than mine had!"

In a situation in which she felt blocked in something she wanted and urged by others to partake in a protest she preferred to avoid, she had another snake dream. With amusement, she told it, "Snakes were coming out of a building. One had legs, long, slow-moving. Maybe they were evolving into dinosaurs. The head snake had a brightly colored comforter wrapped around it – was it a snake, a dinosaur, a stuffed animal? They were moving away, not at me. They were not real, more like comets, or moving exclamation points, friendly." Clare saw the dream as having been set off by an art exhibit in which some "comic" snakes were climbing up one artist's construction and, of course, by the provocations to anger that nearly caused her "to run out of maturity." It was a great dream, with a "comforter" present and hints that the "snakes" could become transitional objects, a la Winnicott, and be connected to the "cultural" and even the cosmic.

Occasionally she would "play out" some angers at me. One day she noted that the office was brighter than usual, since the trees outside had been trimmed. It felt less private to her. Should she get used to it or ask me to pull the drapes? I got up and closed them, and her tears welled. It had reminded her of not having a private room as a child. "I was angry that you hadn't closed the gates," she said and was astonished at her slip of the tongue. The only gate she could think of was at a child-care center that she attended before first grade and maybe after school while mother was working. So gates were connected with early separations. Now there was going to be a gate between us. She comforted herself by thinking that "a gate is not a wall."

Knowing that a presentation I had been going to make had been postponed, she asked whether she might read the paper. She would prefer reading it to hearing me give it, she said, since it was still "too stimulating" to have to take me in visually, too. My "facial movement" both fascinated and made her get "lost," unable to think. "You talk in my fantasy, but you don't move or smile," she told me. (An artifact of the analytic couch, I thought.) Originally Clare adroitly avoided looking at me when she entered and at some point accused me of never looking at her. This eluding eye contact had changed, but, she said, "Here when we look at each other, I can control and mute reactions. . . . It's warded off love that is overwhelming." She feared she might "lose boundaries." I commented that she might partly want to do so, provided she could be sure she could reestablish them. She returned to her fears in asking to read my paper; I might say "no" and then she would have to be angry. I told her she might then have to be angry, since I had only notes, not a whole paper.

In the following session, Clare reported a "beautiful dream, like a vision. I am in a place like Hawaii, where one can walk way out to a sandbar, with incredible plants, palms, where waves wash up gently and one can be in them. You can be playful there, because everything is benign, warm, lovely. It has an eternal quality. I wanted to get back there, but my friend drove the car in the wrong direction, and we were bogged down in the sand. But I lifted the car out and we kept going, although it had turned cold and gloomy." It surprised her to have such a benign dream when she had had a series of contentious encounters. I heard it as a dream of something close to primary illusion, at first in the absence of conflict. Then conflict entered in, and paradise was momentarily lost. It was not disaster, though, for her reparative abilities allowed movement to occur.

Thoughts of death, the ultimate stasis, alternated with evidences of her own movement. She began to imagine that she could return if she ever felt "stuck." Subtle differences in her relationship to me were manifest. She looked directly at me on entering and even freely made little comments, such as, "Well, I see you got your fountain going again." She could let herself observe that things could become stalled for me, too, at times.

I found myself reflecting on her "use of the object" in Winnicott's (1969) sense. As she could increasingly place me "outside the area of subjective phenomena" and diminish her projections and identifications, she could render me even more real. Winnicott put it that "the subject destroys the object" (p. 89), that is, does away with the projective identification. Those projected images were of a somewhat rigid hierarchical order, higher and lower, with Clare on the lower. Indeed, in those sessions, she was reflecting on "vertical" versus "horizontal" gaps; to break through to the "vertical" would require, she said, "breaking the frame" and owning some relative autonomy to pursue her own ambitions.

I was aware of changes in my own countertransference reactions; for example, I was admiring of her project and experienced a growing collegial sense and occasionally let myself make suggestions as to writings that might be of interest to her pursuits. No doubt she experienced this change, for she talked of her dislike of the word "exhibitionism," since it makes "bad" what she suspected to be a "need to have a good thing seen in the eyes of others." She reported on seeing a little girl jumping rope and wanting to hear from her admiring father once more, "Very good!" A friend chided her, "Why can't you just enjoy your triumphs!" Doing so was, she avowed, just what she aimed to be able to do.

There were, of course, the inevitable moments of disappointment in analysis, as when she overidentified with a neighbor who developed cancer, and Clare imagined that she could suffer the same fate as had mother and would be unable to bear it, with all the medical interventions. She had "little moments" of panic about stopping analysis. "I'll have the mental Jean but not you!" she decried. "I do often know what you will say, but not all that you say." "And," I added, "I won't know the new dimensions you may attain." She nodded, tears welling. "In a sense I'll be deprived, too," I told her. She acknowledged that she felt that sense of deprivation about people with whom she had worked. She went on to tell of a stimulating relationship with a responsive friend and of how her own ideas were "taking off."

At times she catapulted herself into "playing out" themes of emotional import and made clear that there was an element of conscious pretense. On an occasion when she was enjoying dressing in a way that was newly pleasurable, she declared that the room was too bright and I might see her too well. "Some figure here hates me, and it's not you! But I feel like leaving the room." She had intended to talk of envy this hour, though she was not sure she was envious of me. We both recalled with humor the time she had told me, "I envy you everything but your age." By now she had absorbed something of my philosophy about envy, that it is malignant only when one feels some block to moving to attain the wanted qualities for oneself. Now, she announced, she felt no such obstacles. She used to envy her mother her beautiful clothes and lovely hands, but by her early 20s she could see that her own hands were in better shape and that her mother's body had aged harshly. Yesterday, she told me, she had thought I seemed sad; later she saw an image of me bent over in sorrow. (Her perception was not altogether wrong, although her elaboration of it was a bit extreme.) Both of us could see that she did not want to find that I envied her youth, her sense that the world still lay ahead, since if I did, there was no way I could resolve it by "turning back the calendar."

This session had begun with Clare's reluctance to see so clearly the evidences for our existential circumstances, that I was ever closer to "real" ending and that her ending was but a "new beginning" (M. Balint, 1953). Careful not to imply that I "really" hate her, she conveyed at first an abstraction about what aging persons might feel toward youth, then gradually allowed her fantasies to come closer to us then and there. Once more there was working through or playing over the time of separation from home and mother in her sad condition. I saw her hope for repair as including the wish that I be in good shape, physically and spiritually, able, perhaps, as Erikson (1977) put it, to find "meaning to all births and deaths and the enigmas in between" (p. 124). In the best reedition of a primary illusion, this version would mean that in some measure there would be "shared visions," but with space for quantitative and qualitative differences that would not make for conflict between us but that could propel us both into further serious playfulness. Examining my countertransferences, I found I agreed with Pruyser (1987), who had described the eventual waning of oedipal tensions in advanced years, so that, not needing to experience rivalry, "aging parents can engage in peer relations or friendships with their progeny" and not mind at all to be bested by their offspring (p. 430).

More and more frequently there was a lighter note, as when she came in telling me teasingly that my reptiles were out that day, meaning the little lizards. Then, one day she announced, "I knew there was a snake around somewhere!" She had discovered that I had a new patient, someone she had never liked. Briefly she verged on bitterness about her "illusion of closeness that doesn't exist." But she moved shortly to a more "intermediate" space and said that she knew I had a place for her in my "mind" but that I might relate to someone else in the same way and be "distracted" from her. I might never go out to coffee with her. We played a bit with her fantasy of being so readily replaceable, and I said that the wonder of it all was that she would want coffee with one who was so fickle she could not hold an image of a departed one. This little teasing was not lost on Clare. Before she left on vacation, she said we had "'defused" the issue. "It was not just my recoverability," she insisted, "but that session." She thought to bring me an Auden poem, which speaks of how the human heart desires "to be loved for itself alone." She used to read it and feel sad; today she was thinking she might actually be thus loved.

When she returned, she rather wished she had said goodbye before she left. She kept reiterating that she couldn't "hold three things in her mind, maybe two but not three." So we played with what those three might be. Was I two: the old image of me and the new one she was beginning to form? Was she two: her old self and a new version? Clare was not sure she wanted to "stabilize" new versions, which all added up to "goodbye." Perhaps the three were she and I and her supervisor, whom she experienced as wanting her to practice in ways that were not like mine. I commented that she may not want to practice in either of our ways but that in time she may want to develop a style congenial to herself.

I returned from my vacation about six weeks before Clare had scheduled her ending of analysis. A recurrent topic in these weeks was the unhappy ending described to her by a dear friend, and it led to Clare's extended critique of that analyst compared to me. It was clear she saw gains in her friend as a result of the analytic experience, but it seemed to have closed on such an unhappy note, with actual friction.

One day Clare reported while walking in that she was startled to see that I had breasts. She found it funny that she had never noticed before. I offered, "While nursing, one may not be aware, but when weaning?" She laughed, "How did you think of that! It's nice." In the same hour, she teased herself while talking of Casement's (1985) "internal supervisor" and said that she had two – her analyst and her male supervisor. "If I move toward mother, father gets angry." The best supervisor may be the patient, she thought. One told her she was "stiff," and that comment amused her.

She arrived at many spontaneous insights, for example, about her propensity to become angry in behalf of others. In a dream, a friend was suing her for part of her house and said to Clare's attorney, "I want her temper!" We both laughed at her sense sometimes that her anger seemed to belong to others.

One day she wished I would give her a summary. She wondered what her diagnosis was. She knew, she said, that I did not "think in labels," but she was sure a recent lecturer would have labeled her. With such analysts, she would not have been trusting, she thought. "Especially in rocky times, I felt – not that you believed in me – it was something bigger, a drive toward something." She was quite right; what I believed in was the strength of the reparative wish – but it was *her* reparative drive in this case. In this context she told me of a breakthrough in some writing (symbol of the drive to express oneself and simultaneously to connect with others.)

Her own growing pleasure at feeling good about herself and about the coming end of her analysis was marred considerably by the depression of her friend. I thought that she was seeing that friend as the ailing mother and that to do so was to detract from her own joy. She agreed and contrasted the manifest strengths of her friend with her mother's frailties. One day I had to cancel an appointment, and this cancellation revived her fantasies that some health problem might beset me. When she was able to ask directly, "Where are you going tomorrow?" I answered directly, and she was much relieved I was not going to a doctor or hospital.

On the first day of our last week, Clare brought me a "plumed serpent," made from a sinuously curved stick, onto which she had affixed feathers at either end and some a bit down from the "head," rather like wings. With it came a poem about Quetzalcoatl and others of his ilk:

Serpents and Such

Maybe everyone has to deal with his snake.
In Mexico they call him Quetzalcoatl,
Lord of Life, Books, Writing.

Defeated by the War god, he moves on.
The Hopi knew him as Polokong,
who lived deep inside all Water.
If they misbehaved, he sent floods and earthquakes.
Unless he was fed, nature was disturbed.
No rains came, no corn grew.
Yet once they called him up, the Mudheads,
Never ones given to restraint or much wisdom,
Had to struggle hard to send him back.
Lawrence believed He lived in the Blood and that sex would
Save us from too much reason and
cold women. He should have learned
More from the Mudheads.
The priestess in Crete wound her snakes about her,
Doing god knows what.
Some folks like to tell how the Caduceus,
Twined serpents, stands for the healing arts.
But other folks point to the stick that, still,
In Africa, people use to twist out the guinea worms that
Fester inside and burst, like the Alien,
From sores in their crippled legs.
My snake burst inside me, in raging,
crippling nightmares.
Prayer, penance, and all manner of ceremony
Have not killed my snake. It seems I have
To learn to live with it, within my blood,
To learn what calls it up, what sends it back,
If anything living is going to grow in me.
This snake is for Jean
Who helped me deal with mine
When it entwined itself on the very door of my analysis.
When I called her in terror,
She came quietly to look at it,
declared it was not poisonous,
and
Called up Joel to bid it come down from the door.
She seemed almost sad that it never returned.

I was, of course, delighted with both gifts, symbolizing as they did not only the problems but the transcendings and even some of the further work and play she saw ahead to make peace with her "serpent." As though to continue that work, she reported on a situation that had "called up" her snake, and she recalled that I had once said, "Your snake needs issues." In this situation she saw herself using her anger against unreasonable authority. She mused that, although not unhappy with what we had been able to do, there remained "major mysteries," some to do with old family matters and some to do with how it might feel to her when she saw me away from here. "I'm afraid I'll cry," she told me.

In the next-to-last hour she brought me a "rain stick," used by the southwest Indians to bring on showers, and she showed me how to handle it to obtain the desired pattering sounds. She had, she said, bought this in case she could not write the poem she wanted. But she had produced another poem, which conveyed a playful sense of leaping and moving and was also delightful.

There were some tears in the last hour. "A dream is a wish your heart makes," she told me and explained that that line came from Cinderella, when a fairy godmother takes the young girl from her shabby tatters and gives her a sense of self. I commented on the power of the reparative wish that had made this possible. "My transformation has been more important to me than going to the ball and winning a prince. . . . My friend calls you the 'genie on the hill,' " she laughed. I protested that no genie could do other than enable Cinderella to manifest the "startling qualities" latent in her. Clare insisted, "But you survived my envy and my anger and made them both constructive. Here I had a mother I could envy. I had no wicked stepmother, just a mother too tattered by life." There was some talk of a party she was about to give. Her last comments were, "It's funny how attached I am to this place."

In communing with my plumed serpent, in rereading the poems, in shaking my water stick, and in remembering the line from the fairy tale, I have increasingly appreciated the symbolism in each individually and in combination. The Quetzalcoatl myth is "the complete fairy tale. All things change perpetually into something else, everything is elusive, intangible, yet permanent and true" (Nicholson, 1967, p. 78). The quetzal is a rare, green-feathered bird found in the highlands of Chiapas and Guatemala. "Coatl" is the Nahua word for snake. Interesting to play with here is that the word is made up of two words: "co," a serpent in Mayan, plus "atl," the Nahua word for water. So Quetzalcoatl was of "many orders of matter in creation: a kind of ladder with man at the centre, but extending downward into animal, water, and mineral, and upward to the planets, the life-giving sun, and the god-creators" (p. 82). Nicholson says that the word also has a secondary meaning: "precious twin." So my free association, that the caduceus had been completed, was not too way-out.

Quetzalcoatl is said to have had humble beginnings – in the god Nanautzin, with his crop of boils and scabs, whose courage in leaping into the fire, in a period of "spaceless time," created the era of the "sun of movement . . . when 'burning water' came to represent the living spirit of matter in constant activity" (p. 89). The serpent must learn to fly, to be transmuted into pure spirit, but the quetzal must also "descend into matter and join with the serpent to become part of the whole instinctive movement of organic life" (p. 89).

As though to emphasize a role for water in the transformations of living things, she had given me a water maker, a rain stick. My own early thoughts about this gift were that it represented the Indians of the southwest, which Clare knew better than did I. I imagined that she easily guessed from various figures around my house that I was familiar with Mexico and the pre-Columbian era. So in combination our two domains of interest found symbolization. I have come to add a special importance to the liquid that my rain maker promises, a bountiful supply of humor. Pruyser (1987) suggests that "a supreme point of maturity is the capacity to smile benignly at oneself, to accept one's inevitable foibles, and to accept realistically one's limitations in influencing the world without feeling lamed by such awareness," and he points out, "Etymologically, humor means liquid, and it is in liquids that substances can be resolved" (p. 433). Perhaps it is also that tears as well as laughter are essential to healing and even that one gains meaning against the other.

So, when I find myself "running short of maturity," I shall turn to Quetzalcoatl to remind me that any given state is but one order of creation and to my rain maker to help me dissolve that order so as to make room for a new era.

CHAPTER 13

The Play of Psychotherapy

Psychoanalysis and the psychoanalytically oriented psychotherapies have many of the characteristics of play as set forth by the historian of culture Huizinga (1944) in his seminal book *Homo Ludens: A Study of the Play Element in Culture*. The patient is offered a maximum of freedom to express thoughts, feelings, wishes, and dreads. A special time and place are set aside so as to constitute a sort of interlude from real life, and a sense of secrecy is fostered by the promise of confidentiality. Order is minimally imposed; ideally, the two participants design the arrangements that they feel will best serve their search. The accepting attitude of the analyst or therapist facilitates a feeling of relative safety to counterbalance the inevitable felt risks. For the therapist the most important rule is respect for the individuality and potential autonomy of the patient, the avoidance of an authoritarian stance and of any exploitation of the transference. The therapist is nonintrusive, so that the patient may enjoy moments of being "apart-together," and thus acquire the capacity for aloneness so necessary to satisfactory togetherness. Since the therapist has no need to win, the sense of contest is minimized or is more akin to that enjoyed in sports than in battle. Ideally, the patient is enabled to use this relationship to represent other relationships, real and fantasied, and hence to learn about them and about the self. With the patient, a ritual is created that furthers this insight, and a ritualism that can stultify imagination and creativity is avoided.

However conscientiously the psychoanalytic therapist may attempt to provide an environment for playfulness, the best violator of old fixities, a crucial variable will be the inner experience of the patient. As Escalona (1968) so well described for the infant, so it is for the adult: the sensations, body feelings, and affective states linked to perceptions will be important determinants in the person's reactions and responses. And, we would add, the reactions and responses of the therapist to those of the patient will influence the story of their therapeutic work and play together.

Attempting to talk of playing as it may enter into the processes of psychotherapy, I sought for terms that might allow a fresh look at that drama in which patient and therapist are at times constrained and again relatively free to improvise their interactions. Medical language seemed singularly inappropriate. Diagnosis too often designates a label affixed by the professional. A prescription is a treatment plan that is written at the beginning by the therapist. Prognosis is a prediction based on the therapist's knowing ahead of time the course and outcome of this disease. More promising are the five key terms of dramatism offered by the literary critic Burke (1945): *act, scene, agent, agency,* and *purpose.* This pentad offers speakers a "synoptic way" to "talk about their talk about."

Wanting not to report further case material but rather to attempt some abstraction of a type of psychotherapy intended to maximize the play element, I thought it might be useful to invoke terms not quite those of our usual lexicon.

Act, of course, refers to what is done. Burke tells us that "a thing's *essence* or *quiddity* can become identical with its principle of *action,*" so we would seek for the essence of any psychotherapy in the way that is peculiar to it. Actions need not always be overt; attitudes can be thought of as incipient acts. What I do from within as an act, you may see from without as an event or scene. I can consider my act in your terms and thus see it from without, and you can respond to my behavior from within, that is, you can vicariously participate in my act. Particularly when we are dealing with transformations, as we are in psychotherapy, act can become scene, and scene, act.

The *scene,* the when and where, must constitute a fit container for the act. Burke tells us that scene is to act as implicit is to explicit, and for our considerations here we can include in the scene the relationships prevailing between the two dramatis personae. Therapist and patient thus constitute the "environment" of one another, and the acts of each will be part of the context that motivates subsequent acts.

The *agent*, the who, is the one who acts. Psychoanalytic psychotherapies tend to be idealistic philosophies that start and end by featuring the agent. We practitioners speak of ego, self, superego, consciousness, will, and the like. Our ideals tend to serve as standards, guides, incentives and, as such, may lead to new, real conditions. Thus, we believe that, equipped with knowledge of self as agent and of situation as scene, a person can exercise creativity in solving life problems.

Agency, the how, refers to the instrumentalities used. There are debates on what our major means and methods are, debates often centering around whether it is insight or empathy that is the most mutative. Always, on the symbolic level, we recognize that persons can be used as instrumentalities for carrying out the primary intentions of others. The infant formatively experiences a realm of personal utility in the mother, and the patient can experience a realm of personal utility in the therapist if the therapist has developed self as a suitable tool for being so used. Certainly the theories held by the latter are agencies, ideally to be held lightly as provisional rather than ultimate and final.

Purpose, the why, has to do with intentions. Implicit in the concepts of act, of agent, and of agency is the concept of purpose. Clinically we think of purpose in terms of needs, wishes, and motivational patterns, conscious and unconscious, the overall intent of which is always repair and re-creation, moving toward greater "happiness," which, says Burke, is a realistic synonym for purpose. One of the purposes of psychodynamic therapies is to enable the patient to be aware of his own purposes and to acquire the tools and methods to move toward them.

As Burke forewarns, we shall not, by using these terms, avoid ambiguity but, rather, will observe where ambiguities arise and will exploit those areas to achieve transformations. Burke's principles are dialectic ones. Distinctions arise out of a "great central moltenness," and substances, if they are to be remade, must return to this "alchemic center" to enter into new combinations. Although this grammarian's language is different from that of clinical usage, his principle is one articulated in different ways by different analytic theorists, both of human development and of therapy: the inevitability that phases of progression will be followed by phases of regression, for only thus can psychic structures be undone and reformed. In their turn, these new configurations will be dissolved to give way to still others. Without this flexibility there could be no education, no psychotherapy, no creation of culture.

As we apply these five terms to psychoanalytic psychotherapies, the margins of overlap will be quickly apparent. The words are both deceptively simple and impossibly complex.

The story line that we might try to outline could take the form of a three-act play. It is a story about "the overlap of two areas of playing, that of the patient and that of the therapist" and about how, when playing is not possible, "then the work done by the therapist is directed toward bringing the patient from a state of not being able to play into a state of being able to play" (Winnicott, 1971a, p. 38).

ACT ONE

The curtain rises on an act in which it could appear that the patient is intent on replaying old themes. In fact, his seeming compulsion to repeat familiar patterns of seeing, thinking, and doing could make for dull drama were it not for the transformations to occur in the interactions with the therapist. The plot has to do with how patient and therapist play out together the former's tendency to cast the therapist in agent roles inappropriate to the purpose of their meetings and how the therapist therefore uses her skills, her agencies, to create a scene in which the transference can be admitted "as a playground in which it is allowed to expand in almost complete freedom," thus serving as "an intermediate region between illness and real life through which the transition from the one to the other is made" (Freud, 1914b, p. 154). The new situation that will arise will be both "artificial" and a "piece of real experience," as is all playing.

The playbill will announce the time and place, the external scene, and we may anticipate some of the action from that. It is the 90s, a period of rapid change and uncertainty; there is an emphasis in this culture on transcendence, immanence being played down. There are new roles to be rapidly learned, even fundamental ones such as how one is to act as man or as woman. Men formerly had a wider arena for actualization, while women preserved potentiality; there are radical shifts in those arenas, with drastic effects on the family, once the basic agency for socialization. There are new opportunities for experimentation but also newly experienced angers and uncertainties.

The scene in hard-pressed, underfunded clinics and agencies is not likely to permit maximum freedom of interaction between our characters. There are both time and procedural limitations, trends toward conformity, imposition of procedures that, although intended to be efficient, necessarily constrict potential playfulness. Therefore we shall make the place for the meeting the office of a private practitioner, at home in her own surroundings, autonomous, able to negotiate independently with the patient the terms of their working and playing together and of the rules of the game in which they will engage.

The patient, having arranged the appointment, enters the office for the first time and notes both consciously and unconsciously its atmosphere – furnishings, decor, seating or reclining equipment, lighting, temperature – and its occupant, the therapist – sex, age, appearance, manner, voice, and whatever other qualities feel relevant at this moment. The patient has surmounted his inevitable apprehensions enough to call for this interview but manifests in a number of ways, both bodily and in speech, that he still feels a sense of risk as he contemplates talking about self with this stranger. If the degree of initial anxiety is high, he may immediately reach out for some structure, as by requesting of the therapist what she wishes to know or what she wants the patient to do. If he is less fearful or perhaps more experienced in these matters, he may launch into telling the story in his own way and declare what he wants of therapy. It is already evident that we cannot talk much further about the act without talking about the players and their motivations.

This patient, although he may not yet realize it, is to be the main agent, the star, if you will, in this play. In some sense his complaint is fixity; something is not right, and he has been unable to remedy it. He has, to a certain extent, lost his sense of spontaneity and freedom; hence he has problems in reciprocity with others. He may see the world most subjectively, be "out of touch with the facts of life," or he may be too reality oriented, ill connected with the subjective, "estranged from the dream" (Winnicott, 1971a). But he has an implicit hope for a new quality of being and of relating; he brings a "reparative intent" (Shor and Sanville, 1978). He presents his complaints urgently and, implicitly or explicitly, invites the therapist to point toward solutions. There are signs of fears intermingled with the hopes, fears that he may be remolded and reformed by the therapist and therapy in ways that may not be his own or that he may be disappointed altogether.

Although attending carefully to the patient's complaint, both initially and throughout treatment, the therapist is also aware that intense purpose can be self-defeating, that urgent goal-directedness can preclude one's seeing and using untapped resources within and alternative pathways without. So she listens in a manner that does not make the achievement of some adaptive aim central but, rather, that makes the actions the patient is describing or manifesting in and of themselves of great interest.

In her response to the patient, the therapist sets about to create herself as part of the scene in which playfulness can occur, a safe outer-inner space, a playground in which the patient will not be so earnest but will relax and be able to communicate with himself and with her. She knows that such space will be created and changed by the acts that take place in it, so she assumes responsibility for playing her part in a nonauthoritarian way. This means, of course, that the therapist, to whom the patient would, consciously or unconsciously, assign the role of agent, is intent on not playing that part; rather, she covets the role of agency and wants the patient to use her for his own objectives. To bring that goal about, she may first have to play agent and bring to bear all the agencies in her professional repertoire to enable this person to deal with this relationship unconventionally and to convert what feels too real into partial make-believe.

She begins with a sort of creative curiosity. She does not ask the patient to fill out a form with questions that would immediately reveal what she thinks important, nor does she take a social history, which again would direct the patient's offerings along preset channels. Instead, she invites the patient to share what he has thought or done about the problems that beset him and about himself generally.

Now there occurs a play within a play as the patient's story unfolds. The act of the therapist becomes that of listening, of being audience to the patient's relating whatever it is that he feels inclined to tell at the moment. This listening is, at first, somewhat passive, the therapist lending herself to the productions of the patient in much the same manner as playgoers approach the theater, with a willingness to suspend disbelief, to maintain an openness to the plot and the actions of the players. In her attentive listening, she communicates via body posture, facial expressions, and nod that she finds interesting and important what she is hearing. The patient, like all actors playing to an appreciative audience, finds himself also feeling that what he has to say – his act – holds her attention and is worthwhile. So he is less afraid than he anticipated. The act of the therapist is thus the scene for the patient, the container for the patient's act. She does not need to intervene, but in her mind she begins an oscillation between this passive listening and a more active sort and brings to bear an agency called empathy, a source of knowing that is less useful for matters of the inanimate world.

Its use depends on a comfort with some "regressive" aspects of self, for it is based on the capacity for identification, a sense of oneness with the other, of identicality, which can be frightening if one is not sure of the capacity to return to one's own psychic skin. A flexibility is required, the ability to disengage, to become oneself once more, to gain perspective. In these imaginative dippings into the being and plight of the other, the therapist may well meet with something of herself, for there are universals in the human condition. Therefore she knows empathy to be fallible as well as valuable, requiring to be checked by recourse to "objective" knowledge, in this case the patient's reported subjectivity. Particularly does she alert herself to this need when there are many commonalities in the histories of the patient and of herself, similar ethnic, racial, sexual identities or similar events and traumas, for she is aware that "overidentification" can distort perception. The same events do not predicate the same experiences in different individuals.

The patient may well request some feedback from the therapist. In the early stages of therapy, the therapist may confine her responses to reflecting back, "mirroring" what the patient has been saying or the feelings that have been in evidence, perhaps the hopes and fears that have been expressed. What is important is that the patient sense that the therapist wants to understand, not that she already does. The therapist, not needing to be omnipotent or omniscient or even particularly clever, rarely interprets in those first hours. She is developing some hunches, but she is not yet sure of their reliability and validity. Most important, however, is that she is aware that premature interpretations can be experienced as indoctrination and can produce a compliance in the patient, both reactions antithetical to the play spirit.

The sensitive therapist often has ways of knowing, seemingly without the use of rational processes, via what we call intuition. This capacity for accurate guessing is born of a kind of acting with the patient in imagination, combined with memories of other patients and with the theories from which the therapist operates. These systems of organized knowledge are not the enemies of intuition, although they have sometimes been so accused; they can sharpen intuitive skills when they are well mastered, constantly tested, flexibly used. Good theories, in interplay with empathy and self-awareness, enable the experienced clinician to sense what is not immediately evident, to fill out the picture from a few relevant details. Intuition is thus a way of seeing holistically, globally (as does the infant), a right-hemisphere function. But, like empathy, it is subject to error; its data must be processed also by the left side of the brain. Thus our model therapist is initially reticent about her intuitive hunches; she wants to be neither presumptive nor premature, but–most of all–wants to avoid seeming omniscient.

She uses the agency called theory as a provisional convenience, always imperfect, necessary, and–like all her other tools–not totally trustworthy. She does not regard it as a religion, an embodiment of absolute truths. Unlike the more "orthodox" ones, this therapist does not condemn as heretics those who would differ. She is aware that without theory she would be blind and senseless; theory enables her to see and to organize what she sees. She knows, too, that her system of assumptions can limit her perceptions, that there is a tendency to see what one looks for and to fit the facts into the existing schema. The therapist strives, therefore, to endure the tension between the abstract and the concrete, to play with her theory without being dominated by it, and to play from time to time with erasing accustomed formulations and attending to original data that may or may not fit easily: what the patient says and does about what he thinks and feels.

Although theory acts as a partial guide, the psychodynamic therapist does not have any systematic procedures by which to accomplish the task; she has no techniques like those of the physical scientist. Unlike the pragmatic therapist, she may even eschew techniques that "work" and choose seemingly less efficient means that are more in keeping with a core conviction: the belief in the individual's capacity for self-initiated change. To release that capacity is her purpose, to restore to the patient the sense of agency that he sometimes seems inclined to relinquish. To that end she uses her skills in establishing and maintaining for a time a special kind and quality of relationship, one aimed at its own ultimate dissolution.

Ideally, this therapist does not need the patient, either financially or emotionally. She feels good in her own center, abundant, autonomous, and capable of satisfying exchange with significant others. She has suffered problems of her own, and – as part of her efforts at solution – she has in the past played the role of analysand. Having lived a creative experience in her own therapy renders her now more likely to recognize and respect the imaginative powers of the patient and less likely to impose. She has claimed her own inner resources and her capacities to visualize and to choose between alternative pathways. She has made her peace with the once-painful realization that human problems have no set answers. She affirms the capacity of the individual to move toward more gratifying solutions, although the course of that movement is not ever upward and onward but entails recurrent regressions. She has learned to endure, even to enjoy, periods of relative chaos in her life, for she has discovered that a too-soon structuring can foreclose on exciting potentialities; she has progressed enough to afford regressions. She knows herself quite well and knows the routes by which she has traveled to reach her present place: the alternating of phases of involvement in relationships and then of withdrawal to digest those experiences in the service of self-development. She values both, as they have contributed to her unfolding, to her reaching for experiences in which there are minimal conflicts between togetherness and selfishness, in other words, experiences of benign regression in which playfulness predominates.

This actor, the therapist, is aware that she plays a role, that the inequality between her and the patient is, in many respects, a fictional inequality. Her actual superiority lies largely in her being conscious that this unfolding drama is a kind of play and that her education, therapy, practice, and habitual introspection have prepared her to enact her part: enabling the patient to engage with her in a kind of imaginative playing together, halfway between fantasy and reality, so that he may elude old fixities and initiate action toward an equality that will also be, in part, fictional.

The patient comes equipped with agencies of his own, some very like those of the therapist. He, too, is capable of empathy. Indeed, the creation of that safe scene that both want depends on his capacity to feel the therapist's nonjudgmental attitude. He, too, potentially has at his disposal intuition, ways of feeling and knowing what is not apparent. Behind his hunches, too, are "theories," for he has also organized the knowledge that experience has taught him; he approaches this encounter with a system of assumptions by which he analyzes, explains, predicts. While the therapist, at her best, is keenly aware of the errors into which her empathy, intuition, and theory can lead her, the patient is generally less aware, even that he uses such tools, let alone that they are so fallible. To move more fully into the agent role both in analysis and in his own life, he will need to develop and cultivate consciousness of self, without which he will lack the freedom both to believe and not to believe what these instruments of appraisal reveal to him. Since the insight that is required is not only cognitive but emotional, he reaches for both dimensions.

Assuming that the patient in our play is not so "out of touch with reality" that he is unable to feel the therapist's interested responsiveness and that he has therefore been able to experience the latter's attentiveness and tentative feedback as positive, he decides to try a period of treatment. The two discuss arrangements. If the patient attempts to defer to the therapist on the question of how often interviews should be scheduled, the therapist, instead, explores the person's feelings and preferences. She indicates the limits and the possible flexibilities of her time and suggests that they might experiment with the usefulness of different pacings at different phases. She thus indicates a confidence in the patient's capacity to measure the when and how much of their work together and, by implication, his measure of the value of times of retreating to work by himself. It is implicit, too, that they will discuss these shifts in schedule as one of their many ways of understanding and of furthering insight.

The matter of lying on the couch or sitting up is left to the patient. He is free to experiment with either position in different hours or within the same hour and to discover for himself the advantages of one or the other as each might suit his shifting purposes.

The therapist discusses with the person her considerations about cancellations and usually specifies the number of hours of advance notice required if an appointment is not to be billed. Providing her schedule permits, she may indicate her willingness occasionally to change an appointment time if something makes that change necessary for the patient. She promises to let the person know well in advance when she herself will be away and indicates that she expects the patient likewise to inform her of vacations or other commitments that might entail absences.

Fees are, of course, discussed, including any problems the patient may have with them or with the preferred manner of payment. Depending on her own circumstances, she may or may not be willing or able to make adjustments to accommodate to the patient's situation or his measure of what he feels able to spend.

A certain ritual is thus negotiated, born of considerations important to both participants. It is definite but not necessarily fixed for all time. It is designed to allow the patient maximum leeway and scope but without leaving the therapist with any feeling of being exploited.

A relationship is being established in which it would appear that there is a minimum of conventional interaction. One person does most of the talking; the other listens. They meet only during the scheduled hours, for outside contact would tend to diminish the necessary ambiguity out of which their creativity is to come. The therapist, although sometimes questioned about herself, does not share facts and feelings about her own life; she has no need to use this patient as a confidante. Her act consists in staying in a role that enables the patient to experience some playfulness as nonthreatening and to enlarge his capacity to take felt risks safely.

ACT TWO

The patient now begins to risk acting on some of his own theories in a way that could look as though he were acting up. He does not adhere so much as he did in the beginning to the usual rules of polite behavior. He ventures a slight, treats the therapist callously, contemptuously; he is arrogant, disdainful. Paradoxically, he seems both angry and not "really" angry; in fact, he is rather enjoying himself. He does not appear to be "reacting," for we see little provocation from the therapist, but he may find some in what she says or sometimes in what she does not say or do. Often, in the midst of these seemingly provocative behaviors of his own, he may ask reassurance that the therapist will not dismiss him, or he may voice apprehension that he has "hurt" the other.

The therapist does not respond in any of the ways that the patient fears. She does not reject or abandon him, nor does she in any way appear to take offense or to be destroyed by the patient's attack. Instead, her act is to "stay herself" and survive the patient's projections. She does not change in her attitude toward him; she does not retaliate; she is not hurt. At this juncture, she may not even interpret, for she knows that the patient could experience interpretation as counterattack or as the therapist's self-defense. She sees these acts of the patient's as destructive only in the original sense of the word, that is, as attempts to undo some structures that must be dismantled if new ones are to replace them.

She sees these acts as attempts of the patient to place her outside of his area of omnipotent control. He must destroy the "subjective object" to perceive self and other more objectively. The therapist in this play thinks of this destructiveness as an agency used by the patient, a projection onto the other of inner images and ideas, a testing out of them against what he finds there. If it has to do with a "drive," it is of an epistemological nature, exploratory and in the service of "research."

Because the therapist sees the patient's destructiveness as reparative in intent and because she is secure in her own inner space, she is able to elude incitement to anger or a feeling of loss of self-esteem. She even rejoices inwardly that the patient has dared to carry on these experimental maneuvers, for she sees them as necessary preliminaries to the patient's use of her and of his use of transference as a playground.

Indeed, the patient rejoices, too, for he has attained a diminished fear of his own aggression and a diminished fear of punishment from this authority. He even feels a new liking for this therapist. In their playacting, they have begun to create a scene in which the delicate balance between risk and safety has been tipped toward the latter. In this context, the patient can proceed to play out themes of his particular life drama and "transfer" attitudes from the past to the present so as to comprehend how they have been impairing his understanding of self and of togetherness.

So long as the patient firmly believes what his old schemas reveal, the transference is not analyzable; it must have a quality of make-believe if it is to be an instrument of change, an agency for him. He can use it with greater freedom when it has acquired an element of pretend that will permit him "really" to experience it from a new perspective. This playfulness will be invaluable as he works to undo the repressions and constrictions that have limited his spontaneity.

The therapist is on the way to accomplishing an instrumental goal, namely, that the patient be able to use her either as part of the scene, when it is simply a facilitating environment that he wants and needs, or as coagent, when he wants and invites feedback or input. This goal, as we shall see, is not attained once and for all; there will be times when the patient will have to retest the acceptability of certain newly emerging themes. Both patient and therapist are now more confident that they can render the potentially malignant relatively benign.

The patient begins to allow himself to trust the therapist and hence to depend on her. This felt dependence, however, stirs up feelings of vulnerability again, and the scene can, for a time, become highly charged emotionally. The patient's act feels to him passive, like a relinquishing of adult ways of speaking and doing; indeed, he may find himself at a loss for adequate words to describe what he is experiencing, and he does not know what to do about this recognition of needy feelings. If he has been trying the couch, it may be feeling problematic, since this position is more the position of the baby vis-à-vis the mother than the position of an adult in conversation with another adult. He may therefore elect to sit up and face the therapist for a while and scan the latter's reactions for cues. This position, too, may render him uneasy, and he may even want to stand or to walk around. The therapist accepts this restlessness, and her act is mainly to help the patient become agent through putting into words what he might be experiencing in these different positions—what he hoped for, what fears and obstacles arose, and how he is attempting to solve his dilemma.

The patient would seem to be seeking optimal distance between self and therapist and to be measuring the degree to which regressions could feel safe. His conflict has been intensified; he both wants and does not want to relinquish autonomy to this other person. Although he fears that his dependence will entail such abandonment of his adult ways, it does not feel altogether dangerous. He has at his disposal the agency of his own movement and of his capacity to give voice to his feelings and the agency of the therapist's words to enable him to understand, to work through, and to play through what he is experiencing. If the two of them are successful in this interchange, the patient will begin to recognize and be able to monitor his own swings between the intense need for closeness and the equally intense need for independence.

Throughout the rest of the treatment there will be evident such swings between times when the patient reaches out for connectedness with the therapist and times when he seems to want to "do his own thing." Although some professionals would say that these times are phases of "object relatedness" and "narcissism," this therapist prefers the somewhat playful terms of Balint (1959), "ocnophilia" and "philobatism." The first one he coined from the Greek word meaning "to cling to, to shrink, to hesitate, or to hang back," and the second, from the Greek "acrobat," "one who walks on his toes, away from the safe earth"; both contain philo, love. Balint's idea that all thrills entail the leaving and rejoining of security is relevant for this patient, who wants to restore a measure of fun and zest to his life. His experiences with the therapist should, therefore, afford him opportunities both to leave and to rejoin. The sensitive therapist will stay attuned to the patient's wishes and capacities to oscillate toward and away from her, and she will adapt her act accordingly.

In the phases of ocnophilia, the patient reaches for some gratifications by the therapist. He experiences the sessions themselves as rewarding, a time and place apart from life's obligations, with the full attention of a valued and interested listener all to himself. There are frustrations, too, for, as his felt "love" for the therapist emerges, he has to come to terms with the limits, especially limits to gratification of his wishes for affection and sex. So there are "hate" feelings emerging, too.

When the positive feelings predominate, he opens up, talks at some length, is receptive to the responses offered. When negative feelings enter in, he may sometimes find himself in uncomfortable silences.

In such phases, the act of the therapist can be that of attempting to formulate the meanings of the patient's productions and behaviors beyond those that are quite obvious. She uses the agency of interpretation, the content of which will be determined by an internal act that has been transpiring in her mind as she has listened actively and passively and has observed both patient and self and the interplay. Her interpretation usually contains evidence garnered from transferences, verbal and nonverbal indications of the attitudes of the patient toward her. This interpretation accomplishes ties between past and present, data from proffered history combined with consideration of the current complaints about work, about love, and often about the limits of fun and pleasure. The therapist also draws on her empathic responses, her self-awareness, her intuition, her theoretical orientation. Her formulation always alludes to the specific reparative intent she imagines to be a prime motivational force, even in defenses that on the surface could appear as "resistances." Such interpretation joins the patient's and the therapist's modes of problem solving.

The timing of the act of interpretation is of utmost importance. As a rule, the therapist avoids offering any reconstructions she is making in her mind until she feels "right" about them and senses they will feel so to the person. Until then she may remain quiet, perhaps confirming her attentive interest by emitting an occasional "uh" or "mmm" or nodding or at times by acknowledging the message by responding to it at face value or by inviting further information. The ideal is that the patient be able to interpret for himself, so the therapist who does not need to show off her cleverness will wait when it seems likely that the patient is about to be able to make his own interpretation. Articulating her own wondering, she might even invite the patient to tie together some of his own experiences. Or she might musingly play back some of what she has been hearing, piecing together parts that seem to fit. When she is ready to make an interpretation, she does so in a tentative way, allowing the patient the freedom to accept or to reject or to modify it. She has no need to push her formulations if the patient is disinclined toward them.

The style of the therapist's act of interpretation will be a combination of her available emotion, of her imaginative and creative capacity, and of her skill in the use of language. Ideally, the language employed will be that of the person's own metaphor (which word comes from the Greek work for transference, *metapherein*). The therapist's words are most likely to inaugurate change when they stay close to symbols that have particular meaning for the patient and, at the same time, open up the possibility of new meaning schemes. Thus, they offer a fresh way of reorganizing experience and increase the leeway and scope of the patient's responsiveness to stimuli inner and outer. A new game may be played.

The insight, actually a creation of this therapeutic dyad but articulated by the therapist, who is finely attuned both to the productions of the patient and to her own responsiveness, and emanating from emotional as well as cognitive processes, evokes a response in the patient that may foretell whether it is likely to have a mutative effect.

The reaction of the patient is often surprise, amusement, and delight; he may even laugh. It may be a playful moment, with tensions released. The patient is encouraged, more confident of self, and more trusting in the therapist. Both participants experience pleasure, for what has seemed puzzling and difficult suddenly begins to make sense, and their joint adventure seems to be paying off. Each has a feeling that the insight belongs to both and belongs to each. Their play has opened up a new scene in which new actions are possible. Now communication between them flows more freely, and new insights spontaneously follow.

The patient sets out to play with his new schema, the new vision he has attained. He tries it on retrospectively to organize data he has already presented and to discover and order fresh facts. He may elaborate on it or even change it. There are times when he seems to be communicating with himself more than with the therapist. He may shut his eyes, muse quietly. If the therapist desires to speak, she may be told, either in so many words or by the patient's ignoring her, that now is a time to hold her tongue.

Indeed, the patient may lapse into silences, different from earlier ones that may have felt frightening. The therapist does not regard these withdrawals from her now as evidence of resistance but rather as evidence of an achievement on the part of the patient. It may well be the first time that the patient has been able to be comfortably alone in the presence of someone. This "act of acts," as Burke calls it, the act of being, is made possible because the patient is full of the good experiences he has enjoyed together with the therapist.

This act changes the scene and dictates a different act on the part of the therapist, who, free of ocnophilic bias, does not need to keep the patient in constant contact with her. Now she uses interpretations sparingly, if at all, mainly to ensure that the patient may continue to feel his regression as benign. She just remains there and available.

It may be that the patient now begins to speak of taking time off from therapy, of a possible intermission. The therapist responds by acknowledging the patient's wish to experiment with his felt independence and by noting, too, any apprehension or doubts the patient may signal or express. She does not interpret the wish to leave therapy as resistance but indicates her continuing availability whenever the patient might wish to return.

Thus, Act Two may have a number of intermissions. The patient, not guilty, as he might feel had he left "against advice," and not ashamed, as he might feel had both he and the therapist pronounced him "cured," feels free to oscillate more widely between phases of connectedness and phases of apartness. He has claimed for himself a new sense of freedom, as defined by Balint (1959): "the rediscovery of the friendly expanses of the philobatic world demanding the possession of adult skills, and behind it the world of primary love which holds one safely without making any further demands" (p. 103). If and when he finds that his adult skills are insufficient for his own purposes, the patient returns for a period of further therapy.

ACT THREE

Sometimes in this play there may be no third act. Or perhaps it takes place away from the therapeutic scene, in the outside world, and we may never know what has occurred.

Whether or not the patient has taken intermissions, there comes a time when he wants to try himself out in actuality and verify the world via immediate immersion in action (Erikson, 1963). He must take his act away from this felt-to-be secure scene, must test the potentials of his newly developed capacities in the world of participation where he will discover the extent to which he can minimize his old unsuitable defensive maneuvers and maximize the processes of mutual activation that he has been learning.

He may report that he finds himself engaging in some of his former behaviors as he tries out his new courage for risk taking, behaviors somewhat akin to those agencies he originally used for ascertaining "facts" about therapist and therapy in the first stages of treatment. He sometimes deliberately "acts out," testing self and other in a kind of self-provocation that has as its purpose getting rid of the remnants of "bad introjects," or he may, in a kind of self-traumatization, assign himself the role of the "bad one" so that those to whom he is relating may seem "good" (Shor, 1972). But now he is likely to be more conscious, if not in the moment of doing, then shortly thereafter, and he is not fixated in these ways of repairing either self or other. They have become somewhat playful regressions, to which he can resort voluntarily without becoming stuck in them. His attitudes toward self and others have been reshaped by those of the therapist reflected in him, and his changed attitudes are modifying his actions.

It is not only the patient who has been transformed by his acts. In the therapist, too, implicit possibilities have been actualized, in proportion as she has been open to this patient and to herself in the course of their therapeutic interaction. Sometimes the treatment will have progressed smoothly, and neither patient nor therapist can say just why the former feels better. The therapist perhaps does not learn as much from such cases; in the more difficult ones, in which obstacle after obstacle has arisen, she is forced to think more, be more scrutinizing of self in process, perhaps sacrifice some of her cherished assumptions. It may be that for the patient, too, the sense of having richly learned may be greater in proportion to the obstacles confronted and surmounted.

Although the therapist does not instigate a review, the patient contemplating termination may do some summing up of the story of this therapy and compare the beginnings with the self he feels himself to be now. He recalls the complaints: his dissatisfactions with the former sense of self and with relationships with others, his inability to bear anxieties about choice, his sense of catastrophic risk in all alternatives. By contrast he feels he has a better understanding of his own nature and also of the long processes, both joyful and painful, through which he was formed.

His sense of "new beginning" leads him at times to act almost manic in his happiness. It is a state not unlike what we see in the infant who has just claimed his capacity for independent mobility, "a love affair with the world," and a pleasure in being his own cause. Of course, like the infant, he still suffers inevitable bumps and falls and so must become aware of still existing vulnerabilities vis-à-vis the outer world. These now serve to tone down his excessive exuberance and make him conscious of the work he has yet to do with himself.

He has seen the therapist as a source of care, safety, and protection and as someone with whom he could participate in arriving at insights and understanding. There is a limit, however, to the fullness of this relationship, for it is not one of balanced exchange. The therapist has her own life and does not need the patient in it. She therefore does not gratify the patient's growing wish for equal and mutual interrelating. Although the inequality that characterized the two at the beginning has diminished, the patient now looks elsewhere to actualize his felt potential for mutuality.

He is powerfully motivated for the search, for he has experienced moments of closeness between his self-interests and connectedness with another, between his "narcissism" and his "object-relatedness." He is equipped with knowledge of the probable obstacles and with a wide repertoire of ways in which he might work through – or play out – those impediments. He no longer needs to cling desperately; he also has the ability to stand alone, to trust his own perspective. He has no need for pseudo-self-sufficiency; he can turn to others when he wants comfort or support.

The patient exercises his newfound freedom of choice by deciding when the termination shall be. As before the intermissions, the therapist reflects back to him his wishes and hopes about independence and speaks matter-of-factly about any residual doubts and anxieties that the person seems to be experiencing. The door is left open to return. This "leaving without parting" is itself an antidote to the hostile or painful partings that have often been significant events in the person's past.

Ideally, the patient will have progressed enough to afford those regressions that are essential aspects of love and of play – and of work, too, if it is not to be a stultifying experience. As the poet Ann Stanford (1970) wrote, "The sense of that height clings" (p. 63).

Both Huizinga and Winnicott believe that culture arises as a form of play. Huizinga (1944) winds up his treatise on this idea by affirming with Plato: "Life must be lived as play" (p. 212). Winnicott (1971a) contrasts living creatively with living uncreatively: "It is creative apperception more than anything else that makes the individual feel that life is worth living" (p. 65). To the degree that the patient has attained this sort of apperception from therapy, he will take back to "ordinary life" the capacity to generate ever fresh interpretations of self and social world.

References

Aleksandrowicz, D.R. (1962), The meaning of metaphor. *Bull. Menn. Clin.,* 26:92–101.

Alexander, F. (1958), A contribution to the theory of play. *Psychoanal. Quart.,* 27:175–193.

Alexander, J., Kolodziejski, K., Sanville, J. & Shaw, R. (1989), On final terminations: Consultations with a dying therapist. *Clin. Soc. Wk. J.,* 17:307–324.

Arlow, J. (1961), Unconscious fantasy and disturbances of conscious experience. *Psychoanal. Quart.,* 38:1–27.

_____ (1969), Fantasy, memory, and reality testing. *Psychoanal. Quart.,* 38:28–51.

Auerhahn, N.C. & Laub, D. (1987), Play and playfulness in holocaust survivors. *The Psychoanalytic Study of the Child,* 42:45–58. New Haven: Yale University Press.

Bachelard, G. (1958), *The Poetics of Space.* Boston: Beacon, 1969.

Bakan, P. (1978), Dreaming, REM sleep and the right hemisphere: A theoretical integration. *J. Altered States Consc.,* 3:295–307.

Balint, E. (1953), Distance in space and time. In: *Thrills and Regressions,* New York: International Universities Press, 1959, pp. 125–131.

Balint, M. (1932), Character analysis and new beginning. In: *Primary Love and Psychoanalytic Technique.* New York: Liveright, 1953, pp. 159–173.

_____ (1953), *Primary Love and Psychoanalytic Technique.* New York: Liveright.

263

_____ (1959), *Thrills and Regressions.* New York: International Universities Press.

_____ (1967), The unobtrusive analyst. In: *The British Independent Tradition,* ed. G. Kohon. London: Free Association Books, 1986, pp. 273–281.

_____ (1968), *The Basic Fault: Therapeutic Aspects of Regression.* London: Tavistock.

Bateson, G. (1953), Metalogue: About games and being serious. *ETC: Rev. Gen. Seman.,* 10:311–315.

_____ (1955), A theory of play and fantasy. *Psychia. Res. Rep.,* 2:39–51.

_____ Jackson, D., Haley, J. & Weakland, J. (1956), Toward a theory of schizophrenia. *Behav. Sci.* 1:251–264.

Beebe, B. & Sloate, P. (1982), Assessment and treatment of difficulties in mother-infant attunement in the first three years of life: A case history. *Psychoanal. Inq.,* 1:601–623.

_____ Stern, D.N. (1977), Engagement-disengagement and early object experiences. In: *Communicative Structures and Psychic Structures,* ed. M. Freedman & S. Grand. New York: Plenum Press. pp. 35–55.

Bentham, J. (1840), *The Theory of Legislation.* Boston: Weeks, Jordan.

Bergmann, M.J. (1988), On the fate of the intrapsychic image of the psychoanalyst. *The Psychoanalytic Study of the Child,* 43:137–153. New Haven: Yale University Press.

Berlyne, D.E. (1966), Curiosity and exploration. *Sci.,* 53:25–33.

Bettleheim, G. (1967), *The Empty Fortress.* New York: Free Press.

Bick, E. (1968), The experience of the skin in early object relations. *Internat. Rev. Psycho-Anal.,* 49:484–486.

Bion, W.R. (1962a), *Learning from Experience.* London: Heinemann. Reprinted in paperback, Maresfield Reprints. London: Karnac Books, 1984.

_____ (1962b), A theory of thinking. *Internat. J. Psycho-Anal.,* 43:4–5. Reprinted in *Second Thoughts.* New York: Aronson, 1967.

_____ (1963). *Elements of Psychoanalysis.* London: Heinemann.

Bleger, J. (1967), Psychoanalysis of the psychoanalytic frame. *Internat. J. Psycho-Anal.,* 48:511–519. Also in: *Classics in Psycho-Analytic Technique,* ed. R. Lang. New York: Aronson, 1981, pp. 459–467.

Bleuler, E. (1913), Autistic thinking. *Amer. J. Insan.,* 69:873–886.

Blum, H. (1976), Dreams and free association. *Internat. J. Psycho-Anal.,* 57:315–324.

Bollas, C. (1979), The transformational object. *Internat. J. Psycho-Anal.,* 60:97–107.

_____ (1987), *The Shadow of the Object.* New York: Columbia University Press.

Bornstein, B. (1945), Clinical notes on child analysis. In: *The Psychoanalytic Study of the Child,* 1:151–166. New York: International Universities Press.

Brazelton, T.B. (1989), Neonatal assessment. In: *The Course of Life, Vol. 1:*

Infancy, ed. S.I. Greenspan & G.H. Pollock. Madison, CT: International Universities Press, pp. 393–432.

_____ Yogman, M., Als, H. & Main, M. (1974), The origins of reciprocity: The early mother-infant interaction. In: *The Effects of the Infant on Its Caregiver,* ed. M. Lewis & L.A. Rosenblum. New York: Wiley.

Brenner, C. (1976), *Psychoanalytic Technique and Psychic Conflict.* New York: International Universities Press.

Bronnimann, W. (1987), Comments on R. Fischer, On fact and fiction – the structure of stories that the brain tells to itself about itself. *J. Soc. Bio. Struc.,* 10:343–351.

Bruner, J. (1977), Early social interaction and language acquisition. In: *Studies in Mother-Infant Interaction,* ed. H.R. Schaffer. London: Academic Press, pp. 271–289.

Buhler, C. (1927), *Kindheit und Jugend.* (Childhood and adolescence.) Leipzig, Germany: S. Hirzel, 1928.

Bullowa, M., ed. (1979), *Before Speech: The Beginning of Interpersonal Communication.* Cambridge: Cambridge University Press.

Burke, K. (1945), *A Grammar of Motives.* Berkeley: University of California Press, 1969.

Call, J. (1968), Lap and finger play in infancy: Implications for ego development. *Internat. J. Psycho-Anal.,* 49:375–378.

_____ (1980), Some prelinguistic aspects of language development. *J. Amer. Acad. Psycho-Anal.,* 28:259–289.

Campbell, J. (1949), *The Hero with a Thousand Faces.* Bollingen Series 17. Princeton, NJ: Princeton University Press, 1968.

Cardinal, M. (1983), *The Words to Say It.* Cambridge, MA: Van Vactor & Goodheart.

Carpy, D.V. (1989), Tolerating the countertransference: A mutative process. *Internat. J. Psycho-Anal.,* 70:278–294.

Casement, P. (1985), *Learning from the Patient.* London: Tavistock.

Chase, S. (1938), *The Tyranny of Words.* New York: Harcourt.

Chomsky, N. (1957), *Syntactic Structures.* The Hague: Mouton.

Cohen, J.F. & Tronick, E.Z. (1987), Mother-infant face-to-face interaction: The sequencing of dyadic states at 3, 6, and 9 months. *Devel. Psychol.* 23:68–77.

Darwin, C. (1872), *The Expression of Emotion in Animals and Man.* London: Methuen.

_____ (1877), A biographical sketch of an infant. *Mind,* 2:285–294.

Davoine, F. (1989), Potential space and the space in between two deaths. In: *The Facilitating Environment,* ed. M.G. Fromm & B.L. Smith. Madison, CT: International Universities Press, pp. 581–603.

Demos, V. (1982), Affect in early childhood. *Psychoanal. Inq.,* 1:533–574.

_____ (1980), Psychology of the self. Discussion of papers delivered by L. Sander & D.N. Stern. Presented at the Boston Symposium, Boston.

Diamond, M.C. (1978), Your brain: Use it or lose it. Lecture for California Institute for Clinical Social Work, Oakland, CA.

Doolittle, H. (1956), *Tribute to Freud by H.D.* New York: New Directions, 1974.

Dore, J. (1985), Holophrases revisited, dialogically. In: *Children's Single Word Speech*, ed. M. Barrett. London: Wiley, pp. 23–58.

Downey, T.W. (1987), Notes on play and guilt in child analysis. *The Psychoanalytic Study of the Child*, 42:105–125. New Haven: Yale University Press.

Ehrenreich, J.H. (1989). Transference: One concept or many? *Psychoanal. Rev.*, 76:37–66.

Eigen, M. (1984), *Evil: Self and Culture.* New York: Human Sciences Press.

_____ (1986), *The Psychotic Core.* New York: Aronson.

Einstein, A. (1955), A letter to Jacques Hadamard. In: *The Creative Process*, ed. B. Ghiselin. New York: Mentor Books, pp. 43–44.

Eissler, K.R. (1966), A note on trauma, dream, anxiety and schizophrenia. *The Psychoanalytic Study of the Child*, 21:17–50. New York: International Universities Press.

Ekman, P., ed. (1973), *Darwin and Facial Expression.* New York: Academic Press.

Eliot, T.S. (1962). Little Gidding. In *T.S. Eliot: The Complete Poems and Plays.* New York: Harcourt, Brace & World, pp. 138–145.

Emde, R.N. (1982), The prerepresentational self and its affective core. Presented at Conference on Early Life and the Roots of Identity, UCLA, March 6–7.

_____ (1983), The prerepresentational self and its affective core. *The Psychoanalytic Study of the Child*. 38:165–192. New Haven: Yale University Press.

_____ (1988), Development terminable and interminable. Innate and motivational factors from infancy. *Internat. J. Psycho-Anal.*, 69:23–42.

_____ (1989a), The infant's relationship experience: Developmental and affective aspects. In: *Relationship Disturbances in Early Childhood*, ed. A.J. Sameroff & R.N. Emde. New York: Basic Books, pp. 33–51.

_____ (1989b), Toward a psychoanalytic theory of affect: The organizational model and its propositions. In: *The Course of Life, Vol. 1, Infancy*, ed. S.I. Greenspan & G.H. Pollock. Madison, CT: International Universities Press, pp. 165–192.

_____ Buchsbaum, H.K. (1989), Toward a psychoanalytic theory of affect. *Emotional Development and Signaling in Infancy*. In: *The Course of Life, Vol. 1*, ed. S.I. Greenspan & G.H. Pollock. Madison, CT: International Universities Press, pp. 193–227.

_____ Klingman, D.H., Reich, J.H. & Wade, J.D. (1978), Emotional expression in infancy: A biobehavioral study. *Psychological Issues*, Monogr. 10. New York: Norton.

_____ Sorce, J.E. (1983), The rewards of infancy: Emotional availability and maternal referencing. In: *Frontiers of Infant Psychiatry, Vol. 1,* ed. J.D. Call, E. Galenson & R. Tyson. New York: Basic Books, pp. 17–30.

Erikson, E. (1950), *Childhood and Society.* New York: Norton, 1963.

_____ (1956), The problem of ego identity. *J. Amer. Acad. Psychoanal.,* 4:56–121.

_____ (1963), *Childhood and Society.* New York: Norton.

_____ (1977), *Toys and Reasons: Stages in the Ritualization of Experience.* New York: Norton.

Escalona, S. (1968), *The Roots of Individuality.* Chicago: Aldine.

Etchegoyen, R.R. (1989), On interpretation and its testing. In: *The Psychoanalytic Core: Essays in Honor of Leo Rangell,* ed. H.P. Blum & E.M. Weinshel. Madison, CT: International Universities Press, pp. 369–398.

Farb, P. (1973), *Word Play: What Happens When People Talk.* Kent, England: Hodder & Stoughton.

Fayek, A. (1981), Narcissism and death instinct. *Internat. J. Psycho-Anal.,* 62:309–322.

Ferenczi, S. (1931), Child analysis in the analysis of adults. In: *Final Contributions to the Problems and Methods of Psycho-Analysis.* London: Hogarth Press, 1955, pp. 126–142.

_____ (1955), *Final Contributions to the Problems and Methods of Psycho-Analysis.* London: Hogarth Press.

Fields, N. (1986), *The Well-Seasoned Marriage.* New York: Gardner Press.

Fischer, R. (1987), On fact and fiction: The structure of stories that the brain tells to itself about itself. *J. Soc. Bio. Struc.* 10:343–351.

Fliess, R. (1942), The metapsychology of the analyst. *Psychoanal. Quart.* 11:221–227.

Foulkes, D. (1978), *A Grammar of Dreams.* Hassocks: Harvester Press.

_____ (1985), *Dreaming: A Cognitive-Psychological Analysis.* Hillsdale, NJ: Lawrence Erlbaum Associates.

Fraiberg, S.H. (1980), *Clinical Studies in Infant Mental Health: The First Year of Life.* London: Tavistock.

_____ Adelson, E. & Shapiro, V. (1975), Ghosts in the nursery: A psychoanalytic approach to the problem of impaired infant-mother relationships. *J. Amer. Academy of Child Psychiatry,* 14:387–422.

Freud, A. (1946), *The Psychoanalytic Treatment of Children.* New York: Shadow Books, 3d ed., 1969, pp. 3–22.

_____ (1970), Problems of termination in child analysis. In: *The Writings of Anna Freud,* Vol. 3. New York: International Universities Press.

Freud, S. (1896), Letter 52 to Fleiss. *Standard Edition,* 1:233–239. London: Hogarth Press, 1966.

_____ (1900), The interpretation of dreams. *Standard Edition,* 4 & 5. London: Hogarth Press, 1953.

_____ (1905), Fragment of an analysis of a case of hysteria. *Standard Edition,*

7:3–122. London: Hogarth Press, 1966.

———— (1908), Creative writers and daydreaming. *Standard Edition,* 9:143–153. London: Hogarth Press, 1959.

———— (1909), Analysis of a phobia in a five-year-old boy. *Standard Edition,* 10:5–149. London: Hogarth Press, 1955.

———— (1910), The future prospects of psychoanalytic therapy. *Standard Edition,* 11:139–151. London: Hogarth Press, 1957.

———— (1911a), The handling of dream interpretation in psychoanalysis. *Standard Edition,* 12:89–96. London: Hogarth Press, 1958.

———— (1911b), Psychoanalytic notes on an autobiographical account of a case of paranoia. *Standard Edition,* 12:9–82. London: Hogarth Press, 1958.

———— (1912), Recommendations to physicians practising psychoanalysis. *Standard Edition* 12:111–120. London: Hogarth Press, 1958.

———— (1914a), On narcissism: An introduction. *Standard Edition,* 14:73–104. London: Hogarth Press, 1957.

———— (1914b), Remembering, repeating, and working through. *Standard Edition,* 12:143–153. London: Hogarth Press, 1958.

———— (1915), The unconscious. *Standard Edition,* 14:166–204. London: Hogarth Press, 1957.

———— (1917), A metapsychological supplement to the theory of dreams. *Standard Edition* 14:222–235. London: Hogarth Press, 1957.

———— (1923), The ego and the id. *Standard Edition,* 19:3–68. London: Hogarth Press, 1955.

———— (1925a), A note upon the mystic writing pad. *Standard Edition,* 19:222–232. London: Hogarth Press, 1961.

———— (1925b), Some additional notes on dream interpretation as a whole. *Standard Edition,* 19:127–138. London: Hogarth Press, 1961.

———— (1926), Inhibitions, symptoms and anxiety. *Standard Edition,* 23:75–175. London: Hogarth Press, 1959.

———— (1927), The future of an illusion. *Standard Edition,* 21:5–56. London: Hogarth Press, 1961.

———— (1933), Anxiety and instinctual life. In: New introductory lectures. *Standard Edition,* 22:81–111. London: Hogarth Press, 1964.

———— (1937), Constructions in analysis. *Standard Edition,* 23:257–269. London: Hogarth Press, 1964.

———— (1985), *A Phylogenetic Fantasy,* ed. I. Grubrich-Simitis. Cambridge, MA: Harvard University Press, 1987.

Fromm, E. (1941), *Escape from Freedom.* New York: Ferrar & Rinehart.

Fromm, M.G. (1980), Disturbances of the self in the analytic setting. In: *The Facilitating Environment,* ed. M.G. Fromm & B.L. Smith. Madison, CT: International Universities Press, pp. 489–515.

Galenson, E. (1969), The nature of thought in childhood play. In: *Separation-*

Individuation: Essays in Honor of Margaret S. Mahler, ed. J.B. McDevitt & C.F. Settlage. New York: International Universities Press, pp. 41–60.

Gavshon, A. (1987), Treatment of an atypical boy. *The Psychoanalytic Study of the Child,* 42:145–172. New Haven: Yale University Press.

Gianino, A. & Tronick, E.Z. (1988), The mutual regulation model: The infant's self and interactive regulation coping and defense. In: *Stress and Coping,* ed. T. Field, P. McCabe, & N. Schneiderman. Hillsdale, NJ: Lawrence Erlbaum Associates, pp. 47–68.

Gibson, J.J. (1979), *The Ecological Approach to Visual Perception.* Boston: Houghton Mifflin.

Gill, M.M. (1980), Psychoanalysis and psychotherapy, 1954–1979. Presented at Los Angeles Psychoanalytic Institute, December 12, 1980.

_____ (1982), *Analysis of Transference, Vol. 1: Theory and Technique.* New York: International Universities Press.

_____ & Hoffman, I.W. (1982), *Analysis of Transference, Vol. 2: Studies on Nine Audio-Recorded Sessions.* New York: International Universities Press.

Glauber, I.P. (1963), Federn's annotation of Freud's theory of anxiety. *J. Amer. Acad. Psychoanal.,* 11:84–96.

Goldberg, A. (1978), *The Psychology of the Self: A Case Book.* New York: International Universities Press.

Grayer, E.E. and Sax, P.R. (1986), A model for the diagnostic and therapeutic use of countertransference. *Clin. Soc. Work J.,* 14:295–309.

Green, A. (1989), Psychoanalysis and ordinary modes of thought. In: *Dimensions of Psychoanalysis,* ed. J. Sandler. Madison, CT: International Universities Press, pp. 83–98.

Greenacre, P. (1954), The role of transference: Practical considerations in relation to psychoanalytic therapy. In: *Emotional Growth, Vol. 2,* New York: International Universities Press, 1971, pp. 627–640.

_____ (1957), The childhood of the artist. *The Psychoanalytic Study of the Child,* 12:47–72. New York: International Universities Press.

_____ (1959a), Play in relation to creative imagination. *The Psychoanalytic Study of the Child,* 14:61–80. New York: International Universities Press. Also in: *Emotional Growth,* Vol. 2. New York: International Universities Press, 1971, pp. 555–574.

_____ (1959b), Certain technical problems in the transference relationship. *J. Amer. Acad. Psychoanal.,* 7:484–502. Also in: *Emotional Growth, Vol. 1.* New York: International Universities Press, 1971, pp. 651–669.

_____ (1967), The influence of infantile trauma on genetic patterns. In: *Emotional Growth, Vol. 1.* New York: International Universities Press, 1971, pp. 260–299.

_____ (1969), Discussion of Dr. Galenson's paper, The nature of thought in childhood play. In: *Emotional Growth, Vol. 1.* New York: International

Universities Press, 1971, pp. 353–364.

Greenson, R. (1970), The exceptional position of the dream in psychoanalytic practice. *Psychoanal. Quart.,* 39:519–549.

Grolnick, S.A. (1990), Emily Dickinson: The interweaving of poetry and personality. *Psychoanal. Rev.,* 77:111–132.

Grotstein, J.A. (1989), A revised conception of schizophrenia: An interdisciplinary update. *Psychoanal. Psychol.,* 6:253–275.

Grubrich-Simitis, I. (1988), Trauma or drive – drive and trauma: A reading of Sigmund Freud's phylogenetic fantasy of 1915. *The Psychoanalytic Study of the Child,* 43:3–33. New Haven, CT: Yale University Press.

Hack, M. (1975), *The amazing newborn.* Film made at Case Western Reserve.

Hartmann, E. (1976), Discussion of "The changing use of dreams in psychoanalytic practice": The dream as the royal road to the biology of the mental apparatus. *Internat. J. Psycho-Anal.,* 57:331–334.

Hartmann, H. (1958), *Ego Psychology and the Problem of Adaptation.* New York: International Universities Press.

_____ (1964), *Essays on Ego Psychology.* New York: International Universities Press.

Hartocollis, P. (1983), *Time and Timelessness.* New York: International Universities Press.

Haynal, A. (1989), The concept of trauma and its present meaning. *Internat. Rev. Psycho-Anal.,* 16:315–322.

Heimann, P. (1950), On countertransference. *Internat. J. Psycho-Anal.,* 31:81–84.

Hendrick, I. (1942), Instinct and ego during infancy. *Psychoanal. Quart.,* 11:33–58.

Hobson, J.A. (1988), *The Dreaming Brain.* New York: Basic Books.

Hoffman, M.L. (1978), Toward a theory of empathic arousal and development. In: *The Development of Affect,* ed. M. Lewis & L.A. Rosenblum. New York: Plenum Press, pp. 227–256.

Holquist, M. (1982), The politics of representation. In: *Allegory and Representation,* ed. S.J. Greenblatt. Baltimore: Johns Hopkins University Press.

Huizinga, J. (1944), *Homo Ludens: A Study of the Play Element in Culture.* Boston: Beacon Press, 1955.

Izard, C.E. (1978), Emotions as motivations: An Evolutionary developmental perspective. In: *Nebraska Symposium on Motivation,* ed. J.R. Cole, 25:163–200.

Jackson, P.W. & Messick, S. (1967), The person, the product, and the response. In: *Creativity and Learning,* ed. J. Kagan. Boston: Beacon Press, pp. 1–19.

James, W. (1890), *The Principles of Psychology, Vol. 1.* New York: Holt.

Jekels, L. (1932), The sense of guilt. In: *Selected Papers.* New York: International Universities Press, 1970, pp. 74–87.

Jekels, L. & Bergler, E. (1934), Transference and love. In: *Selected Papers*. New York: International Universities Press, 1970, pp. 178–201.

Jones, E. (1957), *The Life and Work of Sigmund Freud*. New York: Basic Books.

Kagan, J. (1970), Attention and psychological change in the young child. *Science*, 170:826–832.

Kahn, M. (1975), In search of the dreaming experience. *Internat. J. Psycho-Anal.*, 57:235–330.

Kahn, M.M.R. (1963), The concept of cumulative trauma. *The Psychoanalytic Study of the Child*, 18:286–306. New Haven, CT: Yale University Press.

Kanner, L. (1944), Early infantile autism. *J. Ped.*, 25:211–217.

Kegan, J., Kearsley, R.B. & Zelazo, P.P. (1978), *Infancy: Its Place in Human Development*. Cambridge, MA: Harvard University Press.

Kestenberg, J. (1975), *Children and Parents: Psychoanalytic Studies in Development*. New York: Aronson.

_____ (1978), Transsensus-outgoingness and Winnicott's intermediate zone. In: *Between Reality and Fantasy*, ed. S.A. Grolnick & L. Barkin. New York: Aronson, pp. 61–73.

Klauber, J. (1986), Elements of the psychoanalytic relationship and their therapeutic implications. In: *The British School of Psychoanalysis*, ed. G. Kohon. London: Free Association Press, pp. 200–213.

Klaus, M.H. & Kennell, J.H. (1970), Mothers separated from their newborn infants. *Ped. Clin. N. Amer.*, 17:1015–1025.

Klein, G. (1976), *Psychoanalytic Theory: An Exploration of Essentials*. New York: International Universities Press.

Klein, M. (1946), Notes on some schizoid mechanisms. In: *Envy and Gratitude and Other Works*. London: Hogarth Press, 1975, pp. 1946–1963.

_____ (1955), The psycho-analytic play technique: Its history and significance. In: *New Directions in Psycho-Analysis*, ed. M. Klein, P. Heimann & R. Money-Kyrle. New York: Basic Books, pp. 1–22.

_____ Stern, L. (1971), Low birthweight and the battered child syndrome. *Amer. J. Disabled Child.*, 22:15.

Kohon, G. (1986), *The British School of Psychoanalysis: The Independent Tradition*. London: Free Association Books.

Kohut, H. (1971), *The Analysis of the Self*. New York: International Universities Press.

_____ (1977), *The Restoration of Self*. New York: International Universities Press.

_____ (1984), *How Does Analysis Cure?* Chicago: University of Chicago Press.

Kris, E. (1952), *Psychoanalytic Explorations in Art*. New York: International Universities Press.

Labov, W. & Fanshel, D. (1977), *Therapeutic Discourse*. New York: Academic Press.

Lacan, J. (1966), *Ecrits: A Selection*, trans. A. Sheridan. New York: Norton, 1977.

Langer, S. (1942), *Philosophy in a New Key.* Cambridge, MA: Harvard University Press, 3d ed., 1976.

_____ (1967), *Mind: An Essay on Human Feeling, Vol. 1.* Baltimore: Johns Hopkins University Press.

Levine, P. (1979), Excerpt from "Lost and Found." In: *Ashes.* New York: Atheneum, pp. 65–66.

Levinson, S. (1988), Show and tell: The recursive order of transference. In: *How Does Treatment Help?,* ed. A. Rothstein. Madison, CT: International Universities Press, pp. 135–143.

Lewin, B. (1946), Sleep, the mouth and the dream screen. *Psychoanal. Quart.,* 15:419–434.

Lewis, M. & Brooks-Gunn, J. (1979), *Social Cognition and the Acquisition of Self.* New York: Plenum Press.

Lichtenberg, J.D. (1983), *Psychoanalysis and Infant Research.* Hillsdale, NJ: The Analytic Press.

Lifton, R.J. (1989), Suicide: The quest for a future. In: *Suicide: Understanding and Responding,* ed. D. Jacobs & H.N. Brown. Madison, CT: International Universities Press, pp. 459–469.

Little, M. (1986), On basic unity (primary total undifferentiatedness). In: *The British Independent Tradition,* ed. G. Kohon. London: Free Association Books, pp. 136–153.

Loewald, H.W. (1988), Termination analyzable and unanalyzable. *The Psychoanalytic Study of the Child,* 43:155–166. New Haven: Yale University Press.

Lorenz, K. (1971), *Studies in Animal and Human Behavior,* trans. R. Martin. Portsmouth, NH: Methuen.

MacFarlane, A. (1975), Olfaction in the development of social preferences in the human neonate. In: *Parent-Infant interaction.* Amsterdam: CIBA Foundation Symposium 33, new series.

MacMurray, L. (1961), *Persons in Relation.* London: Faber & Faber.

Mahler, M.S. (1952), On child psychosis and schizophrenia: Autistic and symbiotic infantile psychoses. *The Psychoanalytic Study of the Child,* 7:286–305. New York: International Universities Press.

_____ Furer, , M. (1968), *On Human Symbiosis and the Vicissitudes of Individuation.* New York: International Universities Press.

_____ Pine, F. & Bergman, A. (1975), *The Psychological Birth of the Human Infant.* New York: Basic Books.

Matte Blanco, I. (1975), *The Unconscious as Infinite Sets: An Essay in Bi-logic.* London: Duckworth.

McDougall, J. (1980), *Plea for a Measure of Abnormality.* New York: International Universities Press.

McGraw, M.B. (1945), *The Neuromusculature Maturation of the Human Infant.* New York: Hafner.

Mead, G.H. (1934), *Mind, Self and Society.* Chicago: University of Chicago Press.

Meissner, W.W. (1968), Notes on dreaming: Dreaming as cognitive process. *Internat. J. Psycho-Anal.,* 49:699–708.

Meltzer, D., Bremner, J., Hoxter, S., Weddell, D. & Wittenberg, I. (1975), *Explorations in Autism.* Strathtay, Perthshire: Clunie Press.

Menninger, K. (1967), The suicidal intention of nuclear armament. *Bull. Menn. Clin.,* 47:325–333.

Milner, M. (1950), A note on the ending of an analysis. *Internat. J. Psycho-Anal.,* 31:191–193.

_____ (1952), Aspects of symbolism in the comprehension of the not-self. *Internat. J. Psycho-Anal.,* 33.

_____ (1957), The ordering of chaos. In: *Suppressed Madness of Sane Men.* London: Tavistock, 1987, pp. 216–233.

_____ (1969), *The Hands of the Living God.* New York: International Universities Press.

Moran, G.S. (1987), Some functions of play and playfulness. A developmental perspective. *The Psychoanalytic Study of the Child,* 42:11–29. New Haven: Yale University Press.

Morson, G.S. & Emerson, C. (1989), *Rethinking Bakhtin: Extensions and Challenges.* Evanston, IL: Northwestern University Press.

Nelson, M.C. & Eigen, M. (1984), *Evil: Self and Culture.* New York: Human Sciences Press.

Nicholson, F. (1967), *Mexican and Central American Mythology.* London: Hamlyn.

Ogden, T. (1989), On the concept of the autistic-contiguous position. *Internat. J. Psycho-Anal.,* 70:127–140.

O'Shaughnessy, E. (1987), The invisible Oedipus complex. In: *Melanie Klein Today,* ed. E.B. Spillius. London: Routledge, pp. 191–205.

Palombo, J. (1982), The psychology of the self and the termination of treatment. *Clin. Soc. Work J.,* 10:1–26.

Palombo, S. (1978), *Dreaming and Memory.* New York: Basic Books.

Pedder, J. (1988), Termination reconsidered. *Internat. J. Psycho-Anal.,* 69:495–505.

Peterfreund, E. (1971), The phenomena of sleep and waking: A unified approach. In: *Information, Systems, and Psychoanalysis.* New York: International Universities Press, pp. 243–287.

Piaget, J. (1951), *Play, Dreams, and Imitation in Childhood.* New York: Norton, 1962.

_____ (1954), *The Construction of Reality in the Child.* New York: Basic Books.

Pine, F. (1982), In the beginning: Contributions to a psychoanalytic developmental psychology. *Internat. Rev. Psycho-Anal.,* 8:15–23.

Piontelli, A. (1987), Infant observation from before birth. *Internat. J. Psycho-Anal.,* 68:453–463.

_____ (1989), A study on twins before and after birth. *Internat. Rev. Psycho-Anal.*, 16:413–426.

Pontalis, J.B. (1981), *Frontiers in Psychoanalysis: Between the Dream and Psychic Pain.* New York: International Universities Press.

Prechtl, H.F.R. & Beintema, O. (1964), Prognostic value of neurological signs and the newborn infant. *Proceed. Res. Soc. Med.*, 58:35–48.

Pruyser, P. (1987), Creativity in aging persons. *Bull. Menn. Clin.*, 51:425–435.

Racker, H. (1968), *Transference and Countertransference.* New York: International Universities Press.

Rank, O. (1924), *Das Trauma ser Beburt and seine Bedeutung fur die Psychoanalyse.* Leipzig: International Psychoanalytischer Verlag.

Rapaport, D. (1951), *The Organization and Pathology of Thought.* New York: Columbia University Press.

Reich, A. (1958), A special variation on technique. *Internat. J. Psycho-Anal.*, 39:230–234.

Reik, T. (1937), *Surprise and the Psychoanalyst: On the Conjecture and Comprehension of Unconscious Processes.* New York: Dutton.

Roheim, G. (1943), *The Origins and Functions of Culture.* New York: Nervous and Mental Disease Monographs, 69.

Rosenfeld, H.A. (1971), Contribution to the psychopathology of psychotic states: The importance of projective identification in the ego structure and the object relations of the psychotic patient. In: *Problems of Psychosis,* ed. P. Coucet & C. Larin. Amsterdam: Excerpta Medica, pp. 115–128.

Rubinfine, D.L. (1962), Maternal stimulation, psychic structure, and early object relations. *The Psychoanalytic Study of the Child,* 17:265–282. New York: International Universities Press.

Runcie, R. (1981), Address at the Royal Wedding. *London Times,* July 30, 1981.

Rycroft, C. (1958), An enquiry into the function of words in the psychoanalytical situation. In: *The British School of Psychoanalysis: The Independent Tradition,* ed. G. Kohon. London: Free Association Books, 1986, pp. 237–252.

_____ (1979), *The Innocence of Dreams.* London: Hogarth Press.

_____ (1985), *Psychoanalysis and Beyond,* ed. Peter Fuller. London: Chatto & Windus.

Saari, C. (1986), *Clinical Social Work Treatment: How Does It Work?* New York: Gardner Press.

Sander, L. (1980), Reporter: New knowledge about the infant from current research: Implications for psychoanalysis. *J. Amer. Acad. Psychoanal.,* 28:181–198.

_____ (1983a), Polarity, paradox, and the organizing process. In: *Frontiers of Infant Psychiatry,* ed. J. Call, E. Galenson & R. Tyson. New York: Basic Books, pp. 333–346.

_____ (1983b), To begin with–reflections on ontogeny. In: *Reflections in Self Psychology,* ed. J. Lichtenberg & S. Kaplan. Hillsdale, NJ: The Analytic Press, pp. 85–104.

Sanville, J. (1976), On our clinical fantasy of reality. *Clin. Soc. Work J.,* 4:245–251.

_____ (1982), Partings and impartings. *Clin. Soc. Work J.,* 10:123–131.

_____ (1987a), Creativity and the constructing of the self. *Psychoanal. Rev.,* 74:263–279.

_____ (1987b), Theories, therapies, therapists: Their transformations. *Smith College Studies in Social Work,* March, pp. 75–92.

_____ (1990a), On primary trauma: The challenge to empathy and repair. *J. Smith Coll. School Social Work,* fall: 30–33.

_____ (1990b), Re-railing the dialogue. Presented at Conference on Treatment with the Severely Troubled Individual and Family, Duke University Medical Center, March 1990.

Sarnat, H.B. (1978), Olfactory reflexes in the newborn infant. *J. Ped.,* 92:624–626.

Schafer, R. (1980), *Narrative Actions in Psychoanalysis: Heinz Werner Lecture Series, 14.* Worcester, MA: Clark University Press, 1981.

_____ (1982a), *The Analytic Attitude.* New York: Basic Books.

_____ (1982b), The relevance of the "here and now" transference interpretation to the reconstruction of early development. *Internat. J. Psycho-Anal.,* 63:77–82.

Scharff, D.E. (1988), Epilogue: Countertransference as the interface between the intrapsychic and the interpersonal. *Psychoanal. Inq.,* 8:598–602.

Schiller, F. (1803), *Aesthetic and Philosophical Essays, Vol. 1.* London: Nimmo.

Schiller, J.C.F. von (1795), *On Aesthetic Education of Man in a Series of Letters.* New Haven: Yale University Press, 1954.

Schlesinger, H.J. (1984), Some ingredients of effective interpretation. Plenary address presented at fall meeting of the American Psychoanalytic Association, New York City.

Schwaber, E. (1990), Interpretation and the therapeutic action of psychoanalysis. *Internat. J. Psycho-Anal.,* 71:229–240.

Shank, R.C. (1982), *Dynamic Memory: A Theory of Reminding and Learning in Computers and People.* New York: Cambridge University Press.

Shor, J. (1954), Female sexuality: Aspects and prospects. *Psychoanal.,* 2:3–32.

_____ (1972), Two principles of reparative regression: Self provocation and self traumatization. *Psychoanal. Rev.,* 59:259–281.

_____ (1991), *Work, Love, Play: Self-Repair in the Psychoanalytic Dialogue.* New York: Brunner/Mazel.

_____ & Sanville, J. (1978), *Illusion in Loving: A Psychoanalytic View of the Evolution of Intimacy and Autonomy.* New York: International Universities Press. Penguin paperback, 1979.

Siegelman, E.V. (1990), *Metaphor and Meaning in Psychotherapy.* New York: Guilford Press.

Simon, B. (1988), The imaginary twins: The case of Beckett and Bion. *Internat. Rev. Psycho-Anal.,* 15:331–352.

Sokolov, E.N. (1960), Neurological models and the orienting reflex. In: *The Central Nervous System and Behavior,* ed. M.A.B. Brazier. New York: Josiah Macy, Jr. Foundation.

Solnit, A.J. (1987), A psychoanalytic view of play. *The Psychoanalytic Study of the Child,* 42:205–222. New Haven: Yale University Press.

Spence, D.P. (1982), *Narrative Truth and Historical Truth.* London: Norton.

Spitz, R.A. (1945), Diacritic and coenesthetic organization: The psychiatric significance of a functional division of the nervous system into a sensory and emotive part. *Psychoanal. Rev.,* 32:146–160.

_____ (1963a), *Dialogues from Infancy,* ed. R.N. Emde. New York: International Universities Press, 1983.

_____ (1963b), Life and the dialogue. In: *Counterpoint: Libidinal object and subject,* ed. H.S. Gaskill. New York: International Universities Press, pp. 154–176.

_____ (1964), The derailment of dialogue. *J. Amer. Acad. Psychoanal.,* 12:752–775.

_____ (1965a), The evolution of dialogue. In: *Drives, Affects, Behavior,* ed. M. Shur. New York: International Universities Press, pp. 170–190.

_____ (1965b), *The First Year of Life.* New York: International Universities Press.

_____ (1966), Metapsychology and infant observation. In: *Dialogues from Infancy,* ed. R.N. Emde, New York: International Universities Press, pp. 276–281.

_____ (1972), Bridges: On anticipation, duration and meaning. In: *Dialogues from Infancy,* ed. R.N. Emde. New York: International Universities Press, 1983, pp. 306–316.

Sroufe, L.A. (1982), The organization of emotional development. *Psychoanal. Inq.,* 9:575–599.

Stanford, A. (1970), *The Descent.* New York: Viking Press.

Stern, D. (1971), A micro-analysis of mother-infant interaction: Behaviors regulating social contact between a mother and her three-and-a-half-month-old-twins. *J. Acad. Child Psychiat.,* 10:501–517.

_____ (1974a), The goal and structure of mother-infant play. *J. Amer. Acad. Child Psychiat.,* 13:402–421.

_____ (1974b), Mother and infant at play: The dyadic interaction involving facial, vocal and gaze behaviors. In: *The Effect of the Infant on Its Caregiver,* ed. M. Lewis & L.A. Rosenblum. New York: Wiley, pp. 187–213.

_____ (1977), *The First Relationship: Infant and Mother.* Cambridge, MA: Harvard University Press.

_____ (1985), *The Interpersonal World of the Infant: A View from Psychoanalysis and Developmental Psychology*. New York: Basic Books.

Stokes, A. (1947), *Inside Out*. London: Faber & Faber.

Stone, L. (1981), Notes on the noninterpretive elements in the psychoanalytic situation. *Psychoanal. Assn.*, 29:89–118.

Strachey, J. (1934), The nature of the therapeutic action of psychoanalysis. *Internat. J. Psycho-Anal.*, 15:127–159, 1969.

Thomas, A. & Chess, S. (1980), *The Dynamics of Psychological Development*. New York: Brunner & Mazel.

Thompson, J.A. (1927), *The Minds of Animals*. London: Newness.

Todorov, T. (1984), *Mikhail Bakhtin: The Dialogical Principle*. Minneapolis: University of Minnesota Press.

Tomkins, S. (1980), Affect as amplification: Some modification in theory. In: *Emotion: Theory, Research and Experience. Vol. 1: Theories of Emotion*, ed. R. Plutchik & H. Kellerman. New York: Academic Press, pp. 141–161.

_____ (1981), The quest for primary motives: Biography and autobiography of an idea. *J. Pers. Soc. Psychol.*, 41:306–329.

Trevarthen, C. (1977), Descriptive analyses of infant communicative behavior. In: *Studies of Mother-Infant Interaction*, ed. H.R. Schaffer. London: Academic Press, pp. 270–277.

_____ (1979), Communication and cooperation in early infancy: A description of primary intersubjectivity. In: *Before Speech: The Beginnings of Human Communication*, ed. M. Bullowa. London: Cambridge University Press, pp. 321–347.

_____ (1982), Basic patterns of psychogenic change in infancy. In: *Regressions in Mental Development*, ed. T.G. Bever. Hillsdale, NJ: Lawrence Erlbaum Associates, pp. 7–46.

_____ (1984), Emotions in infancy: Regulations of contact and relationships with persons. In: *Approaches to Emotion*, ed. K.R. Scherer & P. Ekman. Hillsdale, NJ: Lawrence Erlbaum Associates, pp. 129–157.

Tronick, E., Als, H. & Adamson, L. (1979), Structure of early face-to-face communicative interactions. In: *Before Speech: The Beginning of Interpersonal Communication*, ed. M. Bullowa. New York: Cambridge University Press, pp. 349–370.

Tronick, E. & Cohn, J. (1988), Infant-mother face-to-face interaction: Age and gender differences in coordination and the occurrence of miscoordination. *Child Develop.*, 60:85–92.

Tuchmann-Duplessis, H., Auroux, M. & Haegel, P. (1975), *Illustrated Human Embryology*, Vol. 3: *Nervous System and Endocrine Glands*. New York: Springer-Verlag.

Tustin, F. (1981), *Autistic States in Children*. London: Routledge & Kegan Paul.

_____ (1984), Autistic shapes. *Internat. Rev. Psycho-Anal.*, 11:279–290.

———— (1986), *Autistic Barriers in Neurotic Patients*. New Haven, CT: Yale University Press, 1987.

Viderman, S. (1979), The analytic space: Meaning and problems. *Psychoanal. Quart.,* 5:45–62.

Vygotsky, L.S. (1962), *Thought and Language,* ed. & trans. E. Haufman & G. Vakar. Cambridge, MA: MIT Press.

———— (1978), *Mind in Society: The Development of Higher Psychological Processes.* Cambridge, MA: Harvard University Press, 1981.

Waelder, R. (1932), The psychoanalytic theory of play. *Psychoanal. Quart.,* 2:208–224.

Waldhorn, H. (1967), The place of the dream in clinical psychoanalysis. In: *Kris Study Group Monographs,* 2:52–106. New York: International Universities Press.

Watkins, M. (1986), *Invisible Guests: The Development of Imaginal Dialogues.* Hillsdale, NJ: The Analytic Press.

Werner, H. & Kaplan, B. (1963), *Symbol Formation: An Organismic-Developmental Approach to Language and the Expression of Thought.* New York: Wiley.

———— (1984), *Symbol Formation: An Organismic Developmental Approach to the Psychology of Language.* Hillsdale, NJ: Lawrence Erlbaum Associates.

Winnicott, D.W. (1947a), Aggression in relation to emotional development. In: *Collected Papers: Through Pediatrics to Psychoanalysis.* New York: Basic Books, 1958, pp. 204–218.

———— (1947b), Hate in the countertransference. In: *Collected Papers.* New York: Basic Books, 1958, pp. 194–203.

———— (1949), Mind in its relation to the psyche-soma. In: *Collected Papers.* New York: Basic Books, 1958, pp. 243–254.

———— (1950–1955), Aggression in relation to emotional development. In: *Collected Papers: Through Paediatrics to Psychoanalysis.* New York: Basic Books, 1958, pp. 204–218.

———— (1958). The capacity to be alone. In: *The Maturational Processes and the Facilitating Environment.* New York: International Universities Press, pp. 29–36.

———— (1959–1964), Classification: Is there a psychoanalytic contribution of psychiatric classification? In: *The Maturational Processes and the Facilitating Environment.* New York: International Universities Press, 1965, pp. 124–139.

———— (1960a), Ego distortion in terms of true and false self. In: *The Maturational Processes and the Facilitating Environment.* New York: International Universities Press, 1965, pp. 140–152.

———— (1960b), The theory of parent-infant relationship. In: *The Maturational Processes and the Facilitating Environment.* New York: International Universities Press, 1965, pp. 37–55.

_____ (1962), Ego integration in child development. *The Maturational Processes and the Facilitating Environment.* New York: International Universities Press, 1965, pp. 56–63.

_____ (1963a), Communicating and not communicating leading to a study of certain opposites. In: *The Maturational Processes and the Facilitating Environment.* New York: International Universities Press, 1965, pp. 179–192.

_____ (1963b), Dependence in infant-care, in child-care, and in various settings. In: *The Maturational Processes and the Facilitating Environment.* New York: International Universities Press, 1960, pp. 249–259.

_____ (1963c), The development of the capacity for concern. In: *The Maturational Processes and the Facilitating Environment.* New York: International Universities Press, 1965, pp. 73–82.

_____ (1963d), From dependence toward independence in the development of the individual. In: *The Maturational Processes and the Facilitating Environment.* New York: International Universities Press, 1965, pp. 53–92.

_____ (1963e), The mentally ill in your caseload. In: *The Maturational Processes and the Facilitating Environment.* New York: International Universities Press, 1965, pp. 217–229.

_____ (1963f), Psychotherapy of character disorder. In: *The Maturational Processes and the Facilitating Environment.* New York: International Universities Press, 1965, pp. 203–216.

_____ (1965), *The Maturational Processes and the Facilitating Environment.* New York: International Universities Press.

_____ (1967), The location of cultural experience. In: *Playing and Reality.* New York: Basic Books, 1971, pp. 95–103.

_____ (1969), The use of an object and relating through identification. In: *Playing and Reality.* New York: Basic Books, 1971, pp. 86–94.

_____ (1971a), *Playing and Reality.* New York: Basic Books.

_____ (1971b), *Therapeutic Consultations in Child Psychiatry.* New York: Basic Books.

_____ (1974), Fear of breakdown. *Internat. Rev. Psycho-Anal.,* 1:103–117.

_____ (1986), *Holding and Interpretation: Fragment of an Analysis.* New York: Grove Press.

Winston, J. (1985), *Brain and Psyche: The Biology of the Unconscious.* New York: Anchor Press.

Wolff, P. (1959), Observations on newborn infants. *Psychosom. Med.,* 21:110–118.

Index

A

Accommodation 3, 7, 18
Acting out 94, 99, 159, 224, 259
Adamson, L. 16
Adaptation xvi, 21, 93
Adelson, E. 8
Affect(s) 6, 8, 24, 71, 92, 120, 128, 130, 150, 174, 183
  attunement 17–18, 36, 44, 184, 215
  as signals 16, 23, 163–164, 214
  tolerance 98–99
  See also Emotion(s)
Aggression 65, 100, 232, 254
  hostile 122–123, 193
Aging 236
Aim *See* Purpose
Aleksandrowicz, D.R. 215–216
Alert, quiet xiii, 7, 37, 45, 75, 76, 135, 142, 218
Alexander, F. xvi, 21, 48
Alexander, J. 230
Als, H. 16
Alterity 126–127, 132
  See also Empathy; Exotopy
Ambivalence 133, 181
Analyzability 84, 221

Anger 98–100, 101, 122, 159, 254
Anxiety 45, 47, 48, 86–87, 101, 113, 122, 128, 132, 158–160, 165, 247, 260
Arlow, J. 89, 173, 181
Assimilation xvi, 3–4, 6
Auerhahn, N.C. xii
Auroux, M. 40
Autism 23–46, 49–51, 101, 122, 130
  normal 6, 24
Autonomy xiii, xviii, xx, 54, 119, 195, 200

B

Bachelard, G. 69–71, 74
Bakan, P. 171
Bakhtin, M. xviii, 125–128, 142–145, 147
Balint, F. xiii, 71
Balint, M. xiii–xiv, xviii, 2, 8–9, 71, 80, 93–96, 105, 131–132, 135, 154–155, 160, 186, 212, 214, 236, 256, 259
Basic trust 54, 72
Bateson, G. 19, 78–80
Bentham, J. 139
Bergler, E. 65
Bergman, A. 104
Bergmann, M.J. 222
Berlyne, D.E. 207

Bettelheim, G. 25, 122
Bick, E. 26
Bion, W.R. 49, 60–61, 98–100, 163
Blanco, M. 181
Bleger, J. 81
Bleuler, E. 23–24
Blum, H. 168
Body ego 61
Body image 10, 49, 99
Body language 55, 59, 62, 88, 92, 247, 257
Body sensation 6, 9, 19, 25, 145, 182, 183, 243
Bollas, C. 2, 3, 15, 62, 84, 105–106, 161, 207, 210, 214, 215
Bonding 7
Bornstein, B. 224
Brazelton, T. B. 103, 152–153
Brenner, C. 211
British Independent Tradition xvi, 2, 3, 25, 176, 206, 212
Brooks-Gunn, J. 6, 42, 216–217
Bruner, J. 5
Buhler, C. 4–7
Bullowa, M. 97
Burke, K. xix, 67–68, 244–246, 258

C

Call, J. 98
Campbell, J. xix, 189, 195
Cardinal, M. 20, 97
Carpy, D.V. 99
Casement, P. 2, 238
Chase, S. 181
Chomsky, N. 181
Clinging xiii, 53, 131, 256, 261
Cognition 6, 19, 34, 48–49, 128, 172, 183, 218, 257
    See also Dream(s); Fantasy; Illusion; Imagination; Insight; Intuition; Memory; Perception; RIGs; Symbolic functioning; Wish
Cohn, J.F. 215
Communication 9. 16, 19, 41, 109–110, 123, 132, 163, 172, 179, 183, 192, 258
    See also Dialogue; Emotion(s); Expression, facial; Feedback; Free association; Language; Metacommunication; Mother-infant interaction; Mutuality; Reciprocity

Companion
    evoked 15, 208–209, 213, 214, 217
    imaginary 43
Compliance 62, 90
Conflict 122, 129, 160, 176, 207, 218, 224, 255
Countertransference xv, xviii, 65, 91–96, 146–147, 235, 236
    "complementary" 27–28
Creativity 2, 4, 10, 22, 24, 48, 67, 216, 244
    primary 6
    See also Imagination
Cueing 103

D

Davoine, F. 165
Defense(s) xiii, 19, 62–63, 67, 76, 109, 122, 129, 153, 171, 185, 193, 194, 224, 257, 259
    character 131
    primitive 26
Demos, V. 104, 151–152
Dependency See sub Regression
Depression 14, 26, 152, 214
Deprivation xiii, 26, 27, 85, 118, 152
Developmental arrest 128
Developmental line xiii, 117, 153
Dialogue 125–128, 143–144
    as play 78–81, 129, 146–147
    between past and present 15, 90
    derailment of 129–132, 143, 147, 151, 164
    precursors of 8, 49, 129
    psychoanalytic xvi, xviii, 3, 95, 209, 213, 218, 225
Diamond, M.C. 27
Distance, optimal 131–132, 226, 255–256
Doolittle, H. 75
Dore, J. 18
Downey, T.W. 63
Dream(s) xii, xviii-xix, 24, 98–99, 101, 167–177, 179–187, 189–190, 215, 216
    censorship in 170, 174, 176
    condensation in 170, 172, 174, 179
    displacement in 170, 174
    material 73, 107, 112–113, 115–116, 121, 123, 136, 142, 156, 158–159, 161, 162, 177–179, 198–200, 229, 230, 231–234, 238
    secondary revision in 80, 172, 212

self-state 169
  See also REM state
Drive(s) 129
  See also sub Theory

E

Ego
  defect in 50
  infantile capacities of 5–6, 128, 150,
    164–165, 207
  mastery 21
  observing 225
  -relatedness 45, 120
  See also sub Theory
Ehrenreich, J.H. 85
Eigen, M. 231
Einstein, A. 182
Ekman, P. 93
Eliot, T.S. 226
Emde, R.N. 16, 60, 87, 141, 164
Emerson, C. 144, 145, 146
Emotion 8, 16, 18, 19, 29, 41, 104–105, 150,
    183
  See also Anger; Anxiety; Expression, facial;
    Empathy; Envy; Frustration; Gratifi-
    cation; Grief; Guilt; Hate; Love; Play-
    fulness; Rage; Safety
Empathy xii, 7, 17, 27, 41, 61, 64, 96, 120,
    123, 126, 132, 143–144, 200, 206,
    215
  analytic 106, 198, 224, 249–252, 256
  failure of 14, 26, 120, 215
Environment
  average expectable 55, 129
  facilitating xii, xvi, 25, 27, 67–68, 255
  holding 9, 80, 94, 102, 249
  See also Space; *sub* Therapy
Envy 192, 236
Erikson, E. xvi, 21, 49–50, 72, 89, 165, 190,
    192–193, 194–195, 236, 259
Escalona, S. 244
Etchegoyen, R.R. 217
Expression, facial 8, 39, 87, 92–93, 104, 128,
    249
Exotopy 126–127, 143

F

Fairy tales xix, 190–191, 198, 201, 240
Fanshel, D. 88

Fantasy 4, 20, 21, 47, 63, 90, 127, 149–150,
    222, 224
  of anal baby 54–59
  of killing father 136–137
  of omnipotence 11, 46, 119, 124, 129, 162,
    194, 254
  of parent about child 8, 93
  primal scene 123
  unconscious 48, 65, 80
  See also Illusion; Imagination; *sub* Play
Father, role of 26, 64
Fayek, A. 199
Feedback 120, 153, 170, 195, 249, 252, 255
Ferenczi, S. 152, 159, 206
Fields, N. 193
Fischer, R. xix, 189
Fleiss, R. 95
Foulkes, D. 171–173
Fraiberg, S.H. 8, 101
Free association 78, 143, 155, 168, 173, 179,
    241
Freud, A. 223
Freud, S. xiii, xiv, xviii, 1, 4, 5, 21, 47,
    51–52, 57–58, 61, 72, 83–84, 85–86,
    89, 91, 131, 135, 147, 149–150, 155,
    156–157, 159, 165, 167–171, 172,
    179–180, 183, 194, 204–206, 209,
    213, 218, 224–225, 227, 246
Fromm, E. 86
Fromm, M.G. 96
Frustration xiii, 71, 118
Furer, M. 6

G

Galenson, E. 48
Gavshon, A. 28
Gaze xiii, 11, 103, 226
Gianino, A. 214
Gibson, J.J. 5
Gill, M.M. 85, 194
"Going-on-being" 9, 56, 94, 125, 147, 154,
    158
Goldberg, A. 222–223
Gratification 3, 27, 117, 177, 179, 222, 256
Grayer, E.E. 91–92
Green, A. 211, 212
Greenacre, P. 9, 15, 20, 22, 47–49, 65, 76,
    164, 224, 225
Grief xix, 123, 230
  See also Mourning

Grolnick, S.A. 216
Grotstein, J.A. 130
Gubrich-Simitas, I. 150–151
Guilt 51, 65, 113, 122, 145, 200, 215, 226, 222, 230

H

Hack, M. xiii, 7–8, 129
Haegel, P. 40
Hartmann, E. 170, 173–174
Hartmann, H. xvi
Hate 50, 94, 122, 256
Heimann, P. 98
Hobson, J.A. 167, 174, 176
Hoffman, M.L. 17, 85
Holocaust xii, 149
Holquist, M. 211
Homeostasis 153
Huizinga, J. xix, 67–90, 243–244, 261

I

Id *See sub* Instinct
Identification 47, 55, 99, 117, 122, 123, 140, 143, 158, 235, 249
  primary 59, 64
Identity xvi, 192, 249
  See also sub Self
Illusion xvi, 7, 8, 18, 95, 143
  primary xiii, xiv, xviii, 8, 100, 117, 118, 123, 131, 185, 195–196, 201, 205, 218, 225–226, 236
Imagination xii, 4, 48, 89, 176, 179–182, 187, 244
  See also Creativity; Fantasy; Play
Imitation 18, 20, 55
  deferred 42
Incest 137
Infant observation xv, 2, 5, 49, 64, 84, 88, 92, 127–130, 135, 195
Insight 133, 144, 252, 257–258, 260
Instinct
  death 122, 205
  ego 2, 155, 224
  id 2, 45, 120
  of play xvi, 21, 86
Internalization 89, 221, 223
  transmuting 222

Interpretation xix, 13, 58, 60–63, 80, 91, 96–99, 121, 126, 155–156, 174, 175, 186, 193, 198, 205–219, 249, 254, 256–258
Intersubjectivity 15, 87–88, 117, 163, 225
  primary 64, 129
Introjection 70, 153
Intrusion 14, 97, 155–156, 164, 184, 243
Intuition 250, 252, 256
Izard, C.E. 93

J

Jackson, P.W. 179
Jekels, L. 65
Jones, E. 150
Jung, C.J. 175

K

Kagan, J. 72
Kahn, M. 164, 176–177, 186–187
Kanner, L. 24–25
Kaplan, B. 19, 183
Kearsley, R.B. 5
Kegan, J. 5
Kennell, J.H. 152
Kestenberg, J. 9–10, 40–41, 59
Klauber, J. 212
Klaus, M.H. 152
Klein, M. 16, 62–64, 152, 193
Kohon, G. 212, 214, 217
Kohut, H. xiii, xiv, 88, 89, 169, 206, 211, 212, 216

L

Labov, W. 88
Lacan, J. 164–165, 207
Langer, S. xix, 18, 182, 190, 206, 216
Language 18–20, 49, 117, 146, 163, 168, 179–184, 213, 216, 257
  See also Body language; Communication; Dialogue
Laub, D. xii
Legend xix, 190, 198
Levine, P. 165–166
Levinson, S. 209–210
Lewin, B. 187
Lewis, M. 6, 42, 216–217

Libidinal phase 48
Libido 122, 204
Lichtenberg, J.D. 43
Lifton, R.J. 165
Little Hans 51–52, 57–58, 61
Little, M. 214
Lorenz, K. 86
Loss 221, 230
Love 122, 256
   primary xiii, 8, 131, 225, 259

M

MacFarlane, A. 40
MacMurray, L. 18
Mahler, M.S. 6, 26, 27, 49, 68, 104, 197
Marriage 191–193, 195, 196–197, 200–201
Mastery, sense of 47
McDougall, J. 3
McGraw, M.B. 153
Meissner, W.W. 173
Meltzer, D. 26
Memory xii, 15, 27, 89, 127, 171, 173–174,
   207–208
   non-verbal xiii, 128
   See also RIGs
Menninger, K. 157–158
Messick, S. 179
Metacommunication 79–80, 93
Metapsychology 1, 20, 150
Milner, M. 2, 67–68, 122–124, 146, 184,
   186, 187, 228–229
Mirroring 9, 17, 77, 78, 206, 210, 249
Mood 214–215
Moran, G.S. xii
Morsong, S. 144, 145, 146
Mother
   "good enough" xiv, 8, 22, 25, 50–51,
      59, 64, 88, 102, 117, 129, 152,
      184, 224
   representation of 12, 15, 27
   schizophrenogenic 26, 130
Mother-infant interaction 8–9, 12, 18, 49,
   102, 213–214
   See also Primary paternal preoccupation
Mourning xix, 221, 222, 229–230
Muir, E. 19
Mutuality xii, 50, 260
Myth xix, 189–191, 210, 241
   personal 192, 194–196, 201

N

Narcissism, primary xiii, 6, 124, 128, 131,
   225, 260
Neurosis 149–150, 218
   See also sub Transference
Nicholson, F. 240–241
Nursing 10, 11

O

Object 128–129, 132
   autistic 26
   transformational 15, 41, 207, 210, 214
   transitional 10, 18, 34, 39, 41, 43, 59, 84,
      88, 186, 211, 233
Object constancy 43, 89
Object relations 3, 25, 64, 72, 169, 260
   See also sub Theory
Oedipal phase 60, 64, 221
Oedipus complex 59, 206, 222
Ogden, T. 25, 212
Olfaction 40
Oral phase 7

P

Palombo, J. 222
Palombo, S. 173–174, 181
Paranoia 204
Pathology xviii, 3, 24, 128, 130, 151
Patterning 12, 210
Pedder, J. 223, 226
Perception 6, 7, 18, 128, 183
Peterfreund, E. 170
Phobia 51
Piaget, J. 3, 20, 42, 61, 181, 216
Pine, F. 6, 104
Piontelli, A. 129
Play
   approach in analysis 4, 210–212, 243–261
   autoerotic 21
   doll 33–35, 38–39, 43, 57
   fantasy 28, 63
   forerunners of 9–12, 49
   meaning making and 1–22
   potential space for xii, 11, 17, 19, 88, 124,
      210, 212, 244

social xvi, xx, 49, 90, 98
symbolic 18, 20, 33, 43
See also Playfulness; *sub* Dialogue; Instinct;
    Transference
Playfulness xii, xvi-xviii, 2, 15, 20, 27, 28,,
    31, 65, 67, 89–91, 94–97, 118, 133,
    151, 173, 185, 194, 213, 218, 230,
    244, 247–248, 251
Pleasure principle 1, 3, 4
Pontalis, J.B. 176
Preoedipal phase 5, 84, 155, 207, 221
Primary maternal preoccupation xix, 8, 93
Primary process 80, 172, 182, 212, 216
Projection 70, 93, 98–99, 122–123, 153, 200,
    235, 254, 259
Projective identification 9, 92, 99, 193, 235
Pruyser, P. 236, 241
Psychoneirics 171, 172
Psychosis 3, 76, 130
Psychosomatic symptom 224
Purpose 245, 247

R

Racker, H. 27, 92
Rage 121, 123, 192
Rank, O. 150
Rapaport, D. 24
Reality principle 3
Reality testing 175
Reciprocity 21, 98, 128, 145, 247
Reflex 153
Regression xv, 44, 110, 143–144
    benign 5, 22, 75–76, 95, 100, 118, 184,
        246, 251, 259
    to dependence xviii, 94, 105, 118, 154–155
    developmental 48, 151, 153, 190
Reik, T. 211
REM state 167–168, 171, 173, 175, 183
Reparation *See sub* Self; Wish
Repetition-compulsion 47, 75, 88, 90, 158,
    204–205, 225, 246
Repression 254
Resistance 14, 78, 92, 155, 194, 215, 217,
    235, 254, 256–258
RIGs 15, 46, 207–210, 213–214, 217–218
Róheim, G., xvi
Rosenfeld, H.A. 98
Runcie, R. 191, 193–194
Rycroft, C. 1, 177, 213

S

Saari, C. 210
Safety, feeling of xii, 10, 13, 41, 67, 102,
    179, 243, 254, 260
Sandler, L. 88, 151
Sanville, J. 3, 7, 48, 92, 100, 127, 185, 192,
    194, 195, 214, 215, 225, 231
Sax, P.R. 91–92
Schafer, R. 42, 85, 90, 94–95, 125, 206, 211,
    221
Scharff, D.E. 144
Schiller, F. xv-xvi, 21
Schizophrenia 24, 130
Schlesinger, H.J. 215, 216, 218
Schwaber, E. 211, 212
Secondary process 172, 183, 186
Self
    affective 6, 10
    as agent 10, 39, 58, 145, 191, 194, 211,
        218, 230, 245, 250
    categorical 19, 216
    -coherence 10
    -concept 193
    -continuity 15, 125
    core xix, 10, 56, 117, 182, 159, 207, 211,
        230
    -cure xix, 5, 22, 131
    -esteem 78, 117, 129, 192, 218, 215, 218,
        254
    -experience 19, 184, 208–209
    false 14, 58, 119, 132, 199
    -history 11
    -in-relation xiii-xiv, xx, 6, 19, 48, 124, 184,
        216
    narrated 19, 125
    -regulation 13–15, 16, 163
    -representation 59, 194–185
    sense of xix, xx, 6, 16, 117, 192–193, 207,
        216, 225, 260
    sense of emergent 6, 48, 139, 161, 217, 225
    verbal 123, 165, 183
Separation 43, 154, 163, 221
Separation-individuation process 50, 56, 59,
    134, 197
Sexual orientation xviii, 103, 132
Shank, R.C. 208
Shapiro, V. 8
Shor, J. xii, 6, 7, 59, 72, 96–97, 100, 103,
    110, 117, 127, 131, 143–145, 160,

185, 192, 194, 195, 205, 211, 225, 259

Siegelman, E.V. 216

Simon, B. 163

Social referencing 16, 60, 87, 141

Sokolov, E.N. 207

Solnit, A.J. 23

Sorce, J.E. 60

Space
  intermediate 18, 20, 67, 84, 163, 216, 237
  interpersonal 13
  personal 62
  See also Environment; *sub* Play

Spence, D.P. 125, 168

Spitz, R.A. xviii, 6, 7, 14, 49, 55, 71, 127–129, 135, 151, 163, 164

Sroufe, L.A. 104

Stanford, A. 261

Stern, D. xv, xvi, xviii, 3, 5, 6, 7, 10–14, 15, 16–17, 19, 42, 49, 58, 87, 98, 103, 104, 117, 152, 161, 164, 165, 207–209, 211, 213, 216, 224, 225

Stimulation 5, 13, 14, 48, 103, 151–152, 170, 175, 207, 257
  See also Stimulus barrier

Stimulus barrier 6, 14, 128, 135, 163

Stokes, A. 186

Stone, L. 206

Strachey, J. 210, 218

Sublimation 48

Suicide 157–158, 160, 165

Superego 64, 65, 145, 222, 245

Supervision 203

Symbiosis 10, 195

Symbiotic phase 49

Symbolic functioning xii, 2, 17, 48, 49, 172, 241

T

Tension flow 40, 104

Theory
  attachment 208–209
  battleground vs. playground model 218
  drive 58, 150, 164, 165, 216
  ego 1, 61
  object relations 127, 169, 222
  seduction 149
  self psychology 206

Therapy
  child xi, xiv, 42, 46, 62–65, 222–225
  diagnosis in 20, 23, 102, 152, 173, 217, 244
  fees for 80, 253
  frame of 80–81, 96, 132, 235
  interruption of 43, 80, 258–259
  marital 193
  position in 76–78, 88, 93, 252, 255
  reconstruction in 64, 90, 145, 151, 204
  scheduling of 69, 71, 75–76, 80, 90–91, 243, 252–253
  setting of 67–71, 72, 74, 77, 84, 91, 216, 225, 237, 243, 246–247, 253 *See also sub* Play; Transference
  simultaneous 61
  termination of xix, 203, 221–223, 226–229, 258, 260–261

Thompson, J.A. 48

Todorov, T. 125–126

Toilet training 30, 41, 52

Tomkins, S. 120

Transference 119–120, 168, 193, 208, 209, 256
  basic 224
  mirroring/idealizing 84
  neurosis 75–76, 83, 84, 89, 94, 100, 223–225
  as playground xiv, xviii, 83–96, 98–99, 155, 157, 177, 185, 194, 209–210, 224, 246, 254

Trauma 149–153, 156, 164, 249
  birth 150
  primary xviii, 152, 154, 156, 162

Trevarthen, C. 40, 48, 64, 103, 129

Tronick, E. 16, 214, 215

Tuchmann-Duplessis, H. 40

Tustin, F. 25–26, 27, 40

U

Unconscious, the 1, 64, 207, 227

V

Viderman, S. 219

Vygotsky, L.S. 172, 183, 211

W

Waelder, R. vi, 47

Waldhorn, H. 168

Watkins, M. 127
Werner, H. 19, 183
Winnicott, D.W. iv-v, vi, viii, v, xii, 2, 3,
    6-7, 8, 9, 11, 14, 17, 19, 26, 39, 41,
    44, 45-46, 50, 54-56, 58, 61, 62, 64,
    67, 80, 84, 88-89, 90, 91, 93-94, 97,
    98, 99, 102, 105, 113, 118-120, 122,
    125, 126-127, 129, 154-156,
    158-159, 165, 207-208, 210,
    211-212, 216, 217-219, 235,
    247-248, 261
Winston. J. 171
Wish 18, 190, 224
  for baby 54

for reparation xii, xiv, xviii, xix, 60-61, 85,
    116, 118, 121, 124, 130-131, 145,
    147, 154, 164, 165, 185, 193, 196,
    198, 204-205, 208, 212, 214-215,
    217, 218, 238, 240, 247, 254, 257
fulfillment 24, 47
to grow up 21-22, 47
unconscious 83, 171, 213, 224, 227
Wolff, P. xiii, 7
Working alliance 223

Z

Zelazo, P.P. 5